CHINA IN FERMENT

CHINA IN FERMENT

Perspectives on the Cultural Revolution

Edited by
RICHARD BAUM,
with
LOUISE B. BENNETT

Prentice-Hall, Inc. *Englewood Cliffs, N. J.*

A SPECTRUM BOOK

Current printing (last number):
10 9 8 7 6 5 4 3 2 1

PRENTICE-HALL INTERNATIONAL, INC. (*London*)
PRENTICE-HALL OF AUSTRALIA, PTY. LTD. (*Sydney*)
PRENTICE-HALL OF CANADA, LTD. (*Toronto*)
PRENTICE-HALL OF INDIA PRIVATE LIMITED (*New Delhi*)
PRENTICE-HALL OF JAPAN, INC. (*Tokyo*)

To Carolyn

Contents

PART THREE—*The Cultural Revolution in Progress:
Trends and Developments*

PART FOUR—*The Cultural Revolution in Retrospect*

CHINA IN FERMENT

INTRODUCTION

Richard Baum

More than thirty years ago, on the eve of World War II, Winston Churchill was asked to comment on political and military trends in the Soviet Union. His reply was characteristically short and to the point: "I cannot forecast to you the action of Russia. It is a riddle wrapped in a mystery inside an enigma." Today, one is tempted to render a similar judgment about Russia's newly emergent neighbor to the south, the People's Republic of China. For over two decades since the founding of the PRC in 1949—but more dramatically since the onset of China's "Great Proletarian Cultural Revolution" in 1966—outside observers have generally found the Chinese Communists to be enigmatic indeed.

The popular notion of Chinese Communist "inscrutability" has been reinforced in the Western world by a number of widely shared myths and half-truths concerning Chinese society and its aging leader, Communist Party Chairman Mao Tse-tung. In the early 1950s most Americans came to learn of the Chinese Communists through grossly exaggerated and misleading stories about the diabolical "brainwashing" of American prisoners of war in China. Subsequently, in much of the popular literature of the late 1950s, the Chinese people were depicted as faceless "blue ants" laboring under the oppressive yoke of their sinister Communist overlords. And by the mid-1960s it had become commonplace to speak of Mao Tse-tung as a madman who had lost all touch with reality and was ready—nay eager—to plunge the entire world into nuclear holocaust.

The popular image of a China possessed by madness was further reinforced in 1966 with the open eruption of the Great Proletarian Cultural Revolution. Sensational stories about teen-age Red Guards rampaging through the streets of China, burning books, assaulting onlookers, and totally disregarding the authority of their elders, made front-page news throughout the Western world. By 1967 China was widely depicted as being in a state of total anarchy. Incomprehensible to most outsiders was the fact that the highly visible chaos of the Cultural Revolution had apparently been instigated not by Chairman Mao's enemies, but by the Chairman himself—further evidence, if such were needed, of the workings of a demented mind.

It is the purpose of this volume to cut through some of the many myths and half-truths that surround and becloud the popular understanding of China's Cultural Revolution and that, more generally, have served to inhibit enlightened thinking about China itself. The readings presented in Parts I through IV have been chosen from a wide variety of sources—some highly sympathetic to the aims and instrumentalities of the Cultural Revolution, some openly critical. Though the perspectives and points of view of the contributors vary considerably, there is an important common denominator—the search for understanding.

In talking to lay audiences about China's Cultural Revolution in recent years, we have found that certain questions concerning the nature and consequences of the Revolution are raised with great regularity. Before proceeding to the main body of this volume, we should like briefly to discuss some of these frequently asked questions.

Who were the Red Guards and what did they do? The Red Guards were groups of Chinese students of junior high school, high school, and college age who were recruited by Mao's supporters in the summer of 1966 to spearhead the Cultural Revolutionary attack against Mao's alleged opponents within the Chinese Communist Party (CCP). At the height of the Cultural Revolution some twenty million or more of these "revolutionary little generals," as they were called, participated in the movement to expose and criticize "bourgeois power holders" within the Party. Although the Red Guards have been likened to radical student groups of the New Left in the United States and elsewhere, there was one important difference: Unlike the New Left, the Red Guards were organized and instigated by establishment leaders.

How extensive was Mao's purge of the Party apparatus? Very extensive indeed. For example, over seventy per cent of the 172 members and alternate members of the CCP Central Committee were subjected to mass criticism and/or dismissal from their posts during the Cultural Revolution. In terms of the scope of the purge, the Cultural Revolution rivaled Stalin's "Great Purge" of the mid-1930s in the Soviet Union.

What became of the victims of the purge? Unlike Stalin's Great Purge, the victims of China's Cultural Revolution were not physically liquidated or even, in most cases, imprisoned. With a few notable exceptions, those Party officials who were purged as "anti-Maoist elements" during the Cultural Revolution were either (a) placed under house arrest for a certain period of time, during which they were made available to serve as "negative examples" to the Chinese people in mass demonstrations and public "struggle meetings"; (b) transferred to lower-level Party posts to pay penance for their errors; or (c) dismissed from the Party outright and sent to farms and factories to serve as ordinary laborers and be "reeducated" by the workers and peasants. The rationale for not liquidating or imprisoning the majority of purge victims lay in Mao Tse-tung's belief that the purpose of a purge is "like that of a doctor treating an illness . . . to cure the illness in order to save the patient." Thus Maoists typically stress the rehabilitative, rather than the purely punitive functions of a purge. This also helps to account for the otherwise curious fact that large numbers of Party officials who had been criticized and removed from office in the early stages of the Cultural Revolution were, at the end of the movement, "liberated" and restored to favor on a probationary basis.

Was China really in a state of total anarchy? Anarchy yes; total no. At the height of the Cultural Revolution in the spring and summer of 1967 and again in the spring of 1968, governing bodies in most of China's major cities and provincial capitals were paralyzed under the concerted onslaught of Red Guards and other "rebel" elements. In this situation, many of the normal services provided by such governing bodies—including law enforcement, fire protection, public transportation, and public safety—were temporarily disrupted. Moreover, at various times during the Cultural Revolution the Red Guards and "revolutionary rebels" did rampage through the streets of China, creating considerable chaos in their wake. And finally, there were a number of confirmed instances of armed conflict—what the Maoists called "unprincipled civil wars"—fought between the Red Guards and their opponents, with the opponents in many cases being rival groups of "revolutionary students." At least one city (Wuchow in the southern province of Kwangsi) was reliably reported to have been partially razed as a result of such a "civil war."

Nevertheless, and despite the prominent incidents of violence, to apply the term "total anarchy" to China's Cultural Revolution would be highly misleading. In the first place, outbreaks of physical violence were generally sporadic rather than sustained, with periods of relative order interspersed with periods of relative chaos. Secondly, organized violence was largely confined to China's major urban centers, which contain only about fifteen per cent of China's total population of 750 million people. Finally, when the situation in China's cities did threaten to get out of hand in the middle stages of the Cultural Revolution, the Maoists called upon the Chinese People's Liberation Army (PLA) to restore order and impose discipline upon the militant and fractious Red Guards. Moreover, in the face of incipient anarchy PLA units in many Chinese cities assumed direct responsibility for ensuring the continued functioning of vital government services such as law enforcement and public transportation. The record shows that in most cases the army performed creditably in these nonmilitary roles, thus limiting the potential scope and consequences of anarchy.

Has the army "taken over" in China? As indicated earlier, the PLA played an increasingly important role in civil affairs beginning in 1967. In addition to restoring "law and order" and performing certain vital administrative functions, military leaders were recruited to fill positions of political leadership in the newly formed "revolutionary committees" which were created in 1967 and 1968 in the wake of the paralysis of the existing Party apparatus. By the end of 1968, fully two-thirds of China's twenty-nine provincial-level revolutionary committees were headed by military figures. And of the 270 men and women elected to the CCP's revamped Central Committee in 1969, over forty per cent were ranking army leaders—in contrast to twenty-four per cent for the previous Central Committee. What these statistics indicate is that the power of the military in China indeed rose considerably during the Cultural Revolution. Moreover, this development ostensibly occurred in spite of Chairman Mao's long-standing maxim that "the Party commands the gun, and the gun must never be allowed to command the Party."

However, it should be noted that virtually all of the top military leaders who assumed positions of power in China's Party and governmental organs during the Cultural Revolution were veteran Communist Party members. And in many cases their Party credentials dated as far back as the legendary "long march" of 1934–35 and the subsequent anti-Japanese war, when civil and military roles were highly interchangeable and all ranking Party leaders held military command or commissariat posts. Thus, to view China's military elites as a group apart from—and with interests necessarily antithetical to—civilian officials would be to misperceive the historical relationship between Party and army in China. At a number of critical junctures during the Cultural Revolution, PLA commanders generally demonstrated their obedience to the authority of civilian leaders in Peking. And in all of China, during the entire three years of the Cultural Revolution, only one instance of outright mutiny by an army unit was recorded. For all these reasons it would be misleading to say that the army—despite its obvious political ascendency—has "taken over" in China.

What became of the Red Guards? Following the initial mobilization and "unleashing" of the Red Guards in 1966 and 1967, many of Mao's "little generals" apparently succumbed to the corrupting influence of power. In some cases they were overzealous and committed obvious excesses in their search for hidden "class enemies" within the Party, tending indiscriminately to "criticize everything, overthrow everything." In other cases they were plagued by internal dissension and conflict, leading to the splitting of many Red Guard organizations and the formation of rival "factions." As a result of the Red Guards' apparent inability to unite in common cause and maintain self-discipline, and as a result of their frequent resort to physical violence as a means of resolving factional differences, the Maoists were ultimately compelled to call upon the army to impose discipline upon the fractious youngsters. By the end of 1968, most Red Guard units had been disbanded and their members either sent back to school or, in the case of the most troublesome youths, sent out to the countryside to be "reformed and reeducated" through farm labor.

What is the extent of the damage to China's political system, economy, and foreign relations brought about by the Cultural Revolution? In the political sphere, Communist Party organs at the regional, provincial, and subprovincial (county, municipal, and local) levels throughout China were, as noted previously, completely paralyzed at the height of the Cultural Revolution. With large numbers of former Party officials having fallen into disgrace during the movement, there is now an apparent "crisis of authority" in China. Since 1969 a major drive has been underway to rebuild the shattered Party apparatus from the top down, beginning with the reconstitution of the Central Committee in April of that year. Yet it is not at all clear how quickly or effectively the Party's authority can be restored. For the residues of personal bitterness, confusion, and antiauthoritarianism left by three years of "uninterrupted revolution" are undoubtedly both widespread and deep. Nevertheless, at least some of the political damage seems to have been repaired. Government ministries now appear to be functioning at or near their previous levels of efficiency. Public services have been largely restored with military assistance. And life is once again approaching a condition of "normalcy" for the majority of the Chinese people.

Economically, the effects of the Cultural Revolution were not as disastrous for China as some outside observers had predicted. Although China's industrial production fell off by an estimated ten to fifteen per cent in 1967 and 1968, by 1970 it was apparent that the decline had ended. In the important agricultural sector, which includes almost eighty-five per cent of China's total population, the impact of the Cultural Revolution was limited by the fact that the manifestations of revolutionary turmoil—public attacks on Party officials, factional struggles, and work stoppages—seriously affected China's cities, but occurred in only a relatively small number of rural communes and villages. By and large, China's peasants were not involved in any large-scale political uprisings; and the negative consequences of the Cultural Revolution were thus minimal. Total agricultural production remained roughly at pre-Cultural Revolution levels throughout 1967 and 1968, and at no time were serious food shortages reported in China's major cities. In the area of foreign trade, China's total exports declined somewhat—perhaps on the order of ten per cent; and in 1967 this caused a certain aggravation of China's balance of payments problem. But by 1970 the pre-1966 trade balance had been restored, and the volume of Chinese exports was actually higher than before.

In foreign affairs, the overall impact of the Cultural Revolution is somewhat more difficult to measure. In the winter and spring of 1966–67 virtually all of China's diplomatic representatives abroad were recalled to Peking to "face the storm" of revolutionary ferment. In August of 1967 militant Red Guards invaded China's Foreign Ministry for a brief time, "taking over" the Ministry and conducting mass "struggles" against several leading ministry officials, including Foreign Minister Ch'en Yi. A number of foreign embassies in Peking—particularly those of the Western "imperialists" and the Soviet "revisionists"—were beseiged by Red Guards, and at least one, the British Chancery, was gutted. At the same time, Peking's relations with several of her Asian neighbors were strained near the breaking point when a short-lived drive to "export" the Cultural Revolution was launched among Chinese nationals living in Burma, Cambodia, and Hong Kong. In each of these places, pro-Maoist Chinese youths went on a brief rampage in the summer of 1967, waving copies of *Quotations from Chairman Mao*, chanting antiimperialist slogans, and committing acts of vandalism against preselected targets.

With the "recapture" of Peking's Foreign Ministry by diplomatic professionals in September, however, a semblance of order was restored to China's foreign relations. Acts of violence against the citizens and property of foreign countries were officially proscribed by Peking, and the Red Guards were sternly warned against "beating, smashing, burning, invading, and obstructing" in their demonstrations against foreign embassies in Peking. By the end of 1968, with the "radical" phase of the Cultural Revolution at an end, Peking's leaders had begun the difficult task of trying to restore China's badly tarnished image abroad. Beginning in 1969, Chinese diplomatic envoys returned to their posts in foreign capitals throughout the world; the militant, revolutionary ideologism of China's foreign propaganda was self-consciously toned down; new trade agreements were negotiated with several countries; and, in January, 1970, Peking agreed to resume bilateral Ambassadorial Talks with the United States—talks which had been suspended (at China's initiative) for over two years.

Perhaps the most serious effect of the Cultural Revolution on China's foreign affairs was the further straining of Sino-Soviet relations. Throughout 1967 and 1968 Chinese denunciations of Soviet "revisionism" and "social imperialism" became increasingly strident; and the Soviets, in turn, publicly reviled Mao Tse-tung as a "madman." Tensions between China and Russia reached a peak in the spring of 1969 with the eruption of armed conflict between the two sides along the Sino-Soviet border near the Amur River, in northeast Manchuria. Tottering on the brink of war throughout the summer, the two sides finally backed off and agreed to resume long-suspended border negotiations. But with a hot war thus narrowly averted, the cold war on the propaganda front remained as highly charged and bitter as ever.

Is it true that Mao Tse-tung is near death? What will happen to China when Mao dies? Now approaching eighty, Mao has been rumored to be in poor health for almost a decade. In numerous public appearances in recent years the Chairman has appeared tired, drawn, and unable to move about with facility. It is believed—though this is unconfirmed—that he suffers from Parkinson's disease, which manifests itself in the progressive deterioration of nerve cells and leads to the gradual loss of muscle control and the partial impairment of motor functions. Yet Mao is apparently healthy enough to have played an active role in launching and leading the Cultural Revolution. Moreover, he continues to receive foreign visitors in Peking, and is described by these visitors as being quite "alert" for a man in his late seventies. Hence the question of Mao's imminent death is a moot point. Actuarially speaking he is, so to speak, overdue. But actuarial tables can be misleading; and victims of Parkinson's disease have been known to survive until their late eighties or even longer.

Mao will, of course, die eventually—most likely within the next few years—but this has been provided for with the formal designation (contained in the revised Party Constitution of April, 1969) of China's Defense Minister, Lin Piao, as Mao's successor to the position of CCP Chairman. However, Lin Piao, who as commander-in-chief of the PLA was responsible for implementing many of Mao's policies during the Cultural Revolution, is himself physically infirm (he is known to have chronic tuberculosis). Moreover, Lin does not possess the kind of personal magnetism that has been one of Mao's greatest political assets.

For these reasons, it has been widely speculated that after Mao's death Lin will be unable singly to fill the Chairman's boots. If this is the case, then we might expect the transitional period following Mao's departure to be characterized either by (a) a form of collective leadership, with Lin Piao sharing power with top civilian leaders in the Party and government—leaders such as Premier Chou En-lai, who currently ranks third behind Mao and Lin in the post-Cultural Revolution Party hierarchy (other names frequently mentioned are Chiang Ch'ing, Mao's wife and patroness of the Red Guards, and Ch'en Po-ta, Mao's longtime confidante and political secretary); or (b) a struggle for power among the leaders of the three major organizational hierarchies in China—Party, army, and government. In either case, the period of transition will undoubtedly be a difficult one, for the extreme adulation and near-deification of Chairman Mao, which were hallmarks of the Cultural Revolution, have virtually insured that no one will fully inherit the Chairman's lofty mantle for a long time to come.

Recalling Winston Churchill's earlier-quoted remark, we cannot at this time forecast with any precision future developments in China. We do know a great deal about China's recent past, however. (A sharing of such knowledge is the *raison d'être* of this volume). To some extent, our knowledge of China's recent past does facilitate the task of making certain limited predictions about the future. But the element of uncertainty looms large; and in many crucial respects China's future behavior as a nation is likely to remain "a riddle wrapped in a mystery inside an enigma."

PART ONE

Background to the Cultural Revolution

On June 1, 1966, the *People's Daily* announced to the Chinese nation —and to the world at large—the beginning of the Great Proletarian Cultural Revolution. Thus began a three-year period of domestic political turmoil unprecedented in the history of the Chinese People's Republic.

The roots of the Cultural Revolution can be found in events and conflicts which occurred years before—in the aftermath of China's disastrous Great Leap Forward of 1957–1960. In Part I, we have chosen three selections which trace developments leading up to the outbreak of the Cultural Revolution. These selections have been drawn from both Western and Chinese sources in an attempt to present a balanced view of the varying interpretations of the key issues and events.

From these selections there emerges a basic chronology of the pre-Cultural Revolution period. By the end of 1958 China's massive experiment in human and social engineering, the Great Leap Forward, had begun to founder due to inadequate planning and widespread popular discontent. In mid-1959, at a plenary session of the Party Central Committee, Marshal P'eng Teh-huai, then China's Minister of National Defense, launched a thinly veiled attack on Mao Tse-tung's Great Leap programs and policies. This attack, which apparently received the tacit endorsement of a number of China's top economic and political leaders, coincided with the beginning of a three-year period of difficulty for China in which she faced severe economic dislocations and widespread food shortages.

Many components of the Great Leap, in particular the people's commune experiment, were either significantly modified or abandoned, and there was a severe loss of morale among both Party cadres and the general populace. Mao, either willingly or unwillingly, relinquished his chairmanship of the Chinese government and retreated to the "second line" of power within the Party. Capping off this decline, the Soviet Union withdrew the bulk of its technical assistance personnel from China in 1960.

In an attempt to recoup these losses, new liberalized economic policies were undertaken. With this change, a more technically and professionally oriented element rose to power in China's political bureaucracy. At the same time, previous restrictions on intellectual freedom were relaxed somewhat in an effort to enlist more fully the support of China's intellectual and technocratic elites in the cause of "socialist construction." In 1961 Wu Han, Vice-Mayor of Peking, wrote his controversial play *Hai Jui Dismissed from Office*—a play which, some four years later, in November, 1965, would be attacked as "anti-Maoist" in the opening salvo of the Cultural Revolution.

In September, 1962, at the Tenth Plenum of the Party Central Committee, Mao, distressed by the loss of ideological fervor among Party members and by the consequent spread of "bourgeois revisionist thought" in China, launched a comeback by calling for intensified "class struggle" on all fronts in Chinese society. The first step in the new Maoist campaign was the initiation of a nationwide ideological rectification drive—the Socialist Education Movement—designed to awaken the Chinese people to the danger of a "capitalist restoration." In addition, based on the success of P'eng Teh-huai's successor, Marshal Lin Piao, in his political indoctrination drive within the People's Liberation Army (PLA) during 1960–61, a number of emulation campaigns were inaugurated that called upon the Chinese people to "learn from the PLA." In 1964 these campaigns were intensified, and the attack on "revisionist" thinking—both within and without China—was heightened.

Looking at the period 1958–65 with the benefit of hindsight, it appears that in the aftermath of the Great Leap Forward a struggle gradually developed between two competing "lines" within the Chinese Communist Party. Broadly speaking, it was a conflict between "experts" and "reds." The former comprised technicians and professionals within the bureaucracy who favored more liberal and pragmatic economic and administrative policies and advocated closer ties with the Soviet Union. The latter, more ideological and idealistic, favored a return to the radical developmental programs of the Great Leap and placed greater emphasis upon the need for "self-reliance" in China's socialist construction. The two sides differed on a wide range of policy issues in literature, economics, education, foreign policy, and military affairs.

Beyond this basic account of trends and developments leading up to the Cultural Revolution, there is some disagreement in interpretation. Maoists, such as China's Defense Minister and heir-apparent to Party Chairman Mao Tse-tung, Lin Piao (pp. 12–16), see these developments as the reflection of a profound "class struggle" in China between the proletariat and the bourgeoisie. Lin argues that the post-Great Leap period of economic difficulties, 1959–61, was seized upon by "bourgeois power holders" within China as the occasion for launching vicious attacks on Mao's "proletarian headquarters." While feigning support for Mao, these "revisionists," led by China's "traitorous" Chief of State Liu Shao-ch'i, deliberately attempted to undermine public confidence in Mao's policies and push through their own program for the "restoration of capitalism" in China.

Other observers view this struggle differently. Philip Bridgham (pp. 17–30) dismisses the idea of an organized anti-Maoist opposition. Instead, he sees the charge of "bourgeois revisionist sabotage" as a blind thrown up by the Maoists in an attempt to explain the failures of the Great Leap and the resulting crisis of confidence in Mao's leadership. Seeking to restore his tarnished image, it is argued, Mao blamed "revisionists" in the Party organization for blocking the implementation of his policies; and bypassing the regular Party organization (which he regarded as unreliable), he used Lin Piao's PLA to initiate a series of political indoctrination campaigns. When these measures met resistance within the Party bureaucracy, Mao resorted to Stalinist tactics of terror and the "cult of personality" to carry out his will.

A third interpretation of the pre-Cultural Revolution period by Charles Neuhauser (pp. 31–48) stresses the organizational aspects of the conflict between Mao and his opponents within the CCP. While concurring with Bridgham that no concerted anti-Maoist opposition existed that was deliberately sabotaging Maoist programs, Neuhauser nevertheless argues that these programs were effectively, if implicitly, undermined through being "scaled down" within the Party bureaucracy. The result, he argues, was the creation of an organizational crisis in the CCP. The Party's revolutionary élan was fading, and new value was being placed on expertise, economic rationality, and bureaucratic efficiency. The ensuing conflict between old revolutionaries and younger bureaucrats—and the subtle "scaling down" of Maoist policies effected by the latter—are what Mao ostensibly recognized and reacted to when he warned of the imminent danger of a "capitalist restoration" in China.

Given the emergence of a clear and open struggle for power among competing groups and factions in the Cultural Revolution, the key questions which divide and distinguish the three interpretations of the pre-Cultural Revolution period presented in this section are: To what extent was opposition to Maoist policies within the CCP in the early 1960s self-conscious and deliberate? To what extent was it organized and cohesive? And to what extent was it directed at Mao personally? There are no definitive answers to these fundamental questions, and the reader is forewarned that more exhaustive research will have to be done before these questions can be finally and satisfactorily resolved.

REPORT TO THE NINTH NATIONAL CONGRESS OF THE COMMUNIST PARTY OF CHINA, Part 1

Lin Piao

. . . The Great Proletarian Cultural Revolution in our country is a genuine proletarian revolution on an immense scale.

Chairman Mao has explained the necessity of the current revolution in concise terms:

> The current Great Proletarian Cultural Revolution is absolutely necessary and most timely for consolidating the dictatorship of the proletariat, preventing capitalist restoration, and building socialism.

In order to comprehend this scientific thesis of Chairman Mao's fully, we should have a deep understanding of his theory of continuing the revolution under the dictatorship of the proletariat.

In 1957, shortly after the conclusion of the Party's Eighth National Congress, Chairman Mao published his great work *On the Correct Handling of Contradictions Among the People,* in which . . . he comprehensively set forth the existence of contradictions, classes and class struggle under the conditions of the dictatorship of the proletariat, set forth the thesis of the existence of two different types of contradictions in socialist society, those between ourselves and the enemy and those among the people, and set forth the great theory of continuing the revolution under the dictatorship of the proletariat. Like a radiant beacon, this great work illuminates the course of China's socialist revolution and socialist construction and has laid the theoretical foundation for the current Great Proletarian Cultural Revolution. . . .

As early as March 1949, on the eve of the transition of the Chinese revolution from the new-democratic revolution to the socialist revolution, Chairman Mao explicitly pointed out: . . . After the nationwide seizure of power by the proletariat, the principal internal contradiction is "the contradiction between the working class and the bourgeoisie." The heart of the struggle is still the question of state power. Chairman Mao especially reminded us:

From Lin Piao, "Report to the Ninth National Congress of the Communist Party of China," *Peking Review*, no. 18 (April 30, 1969), pp. 16–35. The second part of Lin Piao's report is reproduced on pp. 178–90, below.

After the enemies with guns have been wiped out, there will still be enemies without guns; they are bound to struggle desperately against us, and we must never regard these enemies lightly. If we do not now raise and understand the problem in this way, we shall commit the gravest mistakes.

Having foreseen the protracted and complex nature of the class struggle between the proletariat and the bourgeoisie after the establishment of the dictatorship of the proletariat, Chairman Mao set the whole Party the militant task of fighting imperialism, the Kuomintang and the bourgeoisie in the political, ideological, economic, cultural and diplomatic spheres.

Our Party waged intense battles in accordance with the . . . general line for the transition period formulated by Chairman Mao. In 1956, the socialist transformation of the ownership of the means of production in agriculture, handicrafts and capitalist industry and commerce was in the main completed. That was the crucial moment for the question of whether the socialist revolution could continue to advance. In view of the rampancy of revisionism in the international communist movement and the new trends of class struggle in our country, Chairman Mao, in his great work *On the Correct Handling of Contradictions Among the People,* called the attention of the whole Party to the following fact:

In China, although in the main socialist transformation has been completed with respect to the system of ownership . . . there are still remnants of the overthrown landlord and comprador classes, there is still a bourgeoisie, and the remolding of the petit bourgeoisie has only just started.

Countering the fallacy put forward by Liu Shao-ch'i in 1956 that "in China, the question of which wins out, socialism or capitalism, is already solved," Chairman Mao specifically pointed out:

The question of which will win out, socialism or capitalism, is still not really settled.

The class struggle between the proletariat and the bourgeoisie, the class struggle between the different political forces, and the class struggle in the ideological field between the proletariat and the bourgeoisie will continue to be long and tortuous and at times will even become very acute.

Thus, for the first time in the theory and practice of the international communist movement, it was pointed out explicitly that classes and class struggle still exist after the socialist transformation of the ownership of the means of production has been in the main completed, and that the proletariat must continue the revolution.

The proletarian headquarters headed by Chairman Mao led the broad masses in carrying on the great struggle in the direction he indicated. From the struggle against the bourgeois rightists in 1957 to the struggle to uncover P'eng Teh-huai's anti-Party clique at the Lushan Meeting in 1959, from the great debate on the general line of the Party in building socialism to the struggle between the two lines in the Socialist Education Movement—the focus of the struggle was the question of whether to take the socialist road or to take the capitalist road, whether to uphold the dictatorship of the proletariat or to restore the dictatorship of the bourgeoisie.

Every single victory of Chairman Mao's proletarian revolutionary line, every victory in every major campaign launched by the Party against the bourgeoisie, was gained only after smashing the revisionist line represented by Liu Shao-ch'i. . . .

Now it has been proved through investigation that as far back as the First Revolutionary Civil War period [1921–23] Liu Shao-ch'i betrayed the Party, capitulated to the enemy and became a hidden traitor and scab, that he was a crime-steeped lackey of the imperialists, modern revisionists and Kuomintang reactionaries and that he was the arch representative of the persons in power taking the capitalist road. He had a political line by which he vainly attempted to restore capitalism in China and turn her into an imperialist and revisionist colony. In addition, he had an organizational line to serve his counter-revolutionary political line. For many years, recruiting deserters and turncoats, Liu Shao-ch'i gathered together a gang of renegades, enemy agents, and capitalist-roaders in power. They covered up their counter-revolutionary political records, shielded each other, colluded in doing evil, usurped important Party and government posts and controlled the leadership in many central and local units, thus forming an underground bourgeois headquarters in opposition to the proletarian headquarters headed by Chairman Mao. They collaborated with the imperialists, modern revisionists, and Kuomintang reactionaries and played the kind of disruptive role that the U.S. imperialists, the Soviet revisionists, and the reactionaries of various countries were not in a position to do. . . .

At the many important historical junctures of the new-democratic revolution and the socialist revolution, Liu Shao-ch'i and his gang always wantonly opposed Chairman Mao's proletarian revolutionary line and engaged in counter-revolutionary conspiratorial and disruptive activities. However, since they were counter-revolutionaries, their plots were bound to come to light. When Khrushchev came to power . . . Liu Shao-ch'i and his gang became all the more rabid.

Chairman Mao was the first to perceive the danger of the counter-revolutionary plots of Liu Shao-ch'i and his gang. At the working conference of the Central Committee in January 1962, Chairman Mao pointed out the necessity of guarding against the emergence of revisionism. At the . . . Tenth Plenary Session of the Eighth Central Committee of the Party in September of the same year, Chairman Mao put forward more comprehensively the basic line of our Party for the whole historical period of socialism. Chairman Mao pointed out:

> Socialist society covers a fairly long historical period. In the historical period of socialism, there are still classes, class contradictions and class struggle, there is the struggle between the socialist road and the capitalist road, and there is the danger of capitalist restoration. We must recognize the protracted and complex nature of this struggle. We must heighten our vigilance. . . . Otherwise a socialist country like ours will turn into its opposite and degenerate, and a capitalist restoration will take place. . . .

This Marxist-Leninist line advanced by Chairman Mao is the lifeline of our Party.

Following this, in May 1963, . . . Chairman Mao again warned the whole Party: If classes and class struggle were forgotten and if the dictatorship of the proletariat were forgotten,

> then it would not be long, perhaps only several years or a decade, or several decades at most, before a counter-revolutionary restoration on a national scale would inevitably occur, the Marxist-Leninist party would undoubtedly become a revisionist party or a fascist party, and the whole of China would change its color. Comrades, please think it over. What a dangerous situation this would be!

Thus Chairman Mao still more sharply showed the whole Party and the whole nation the danger of the restoration of capitalism.

All these warnings and struggles did not and could not in the least change the reactionary class nature of Liu Shao-ch'i and his gang. In 1964, in the great Socialist Education Movement, Liu Shao-ch'i came out to repress the masses and shield the capitalist roaders in power. . . . He raved that whoever refused to carry out his line was "not qualified to hold a leading post." He and his gang were working against time to restore capitalism. At the end of 1964, Chairman Mao convened a working conference of the Central Committee and . . . denounced Liu Shao-ch'i's bourgeois reactionary line. . . . For the first time Chairman Mao specifically indicated: "The main target of the present movement is those Party persons in power taking the capitalist road." This new conclusion drawn by Chairman Mao after summing up the historical experience of the dictatorship of the proletariat, domestic and international, set right the course of the Socialist Education Movement and clearly showed the orientation for the approaching Great Proletarian Cultural Revolution.

Reviewing the history of this period, we can see that the current Great Proletarian Cultural Revolution with the participation of hundreds of millions of revolutionary people has by no means occurred accidentally. It is the inevitable result of the protracted and sharp struggle between the two classes, the two roads and the two lines in socialist society. The Great Proletarian Cultural Revolution is

> a great political revolution carried out by the proletariat against the bourgeoisie and all other exploiting classes; it is a continuation of the prolonged struggle waged by the Chinese Communist Party and the masses of revolutionary people under its leadership against the Kuomintang reactionaries, a continuation of the class struggle between the proletariat and the bourgeoisie.

The heroic Chinese proletariat, poor and lower-middle peasants, People's Liberation Army, revolutionary cadres and revolutionary intellectuals, who were all determined to follow the great leader Chairman Mao closely in taking the socialist road, could no longer tolerate the restoration activities of Liu Shao-ch'i and his gang, and so a great class battle was unavoidable.

As Chairman Mao pointed out in his talk in February 1967:

> In the past we waged struggles in rural areas, in factories, in the cultural field, and we carried out the Socialist Education Movement. But all this failed to solve the problem because we did not find a form, a method, to arouse the broad masses to expose our dark aspect openly, in an all-round way and from below.

Now we have found this form—it is the Great Proletarian Cultural Revolution. It is only by arousing the masses in their hundreds of millions to air their views freely, write big-character posters and hold great debates that the renegades, enemy agents, and capitalist-roaders in power who have wormed their way into the Party can be exposed and their plots to restore capitalism smashed. It is precisely with the participation of the broad masses in the examination of Liu Shao-ch'i's case that his true features as an old-line counter-revolutionary, renegade, hidden traitor and scab were brought to light. . . . This was a great victory for the hundreds of millions of the people. On the basis of the theory of continuing the revolution under the dictatorship of the proletariat, our great teacher Chairman Mao has personally initiated and led the Great Proletarian Cultural Revolution. This is indeed . . . a new and great contribution to the theory and practice of Marxism-Leninism. . . .

MAO'S 'CULTURAL REVOLUTION': ORIGIN AND DEVELOPMENT, Part 1

Philip Bridgham

. . . In the fall of 1965, Mao Tse-tung initiated the Great Proletarian Cultural Revolution featuring Stalinist techniques of violence and the public purge.[1] What has produced this sharp reversal of Maoist strategy in dealing with such long-time "comrades-in-arms" as Liu Shao-ch'i (Mao's heir-apparent for 20 years)? Why is it necessary to organize Red Guards to terrorize and maltreat all segments of Chinese society, including the once sacrosanct Chinese Communist Party?

These are large questions to which, lacking many of the relevant facts, one can only provide partial and tentative answers. Some must await the further unfolding of the Cultural Revolution which will undoubtedly shed more light on its purposes and objectives. Some are to be found in a close scrutiny of the events of the past 15 months which, according to the official Chinese Communist version, comprise the history of the Great Proletarian Cultural Revolution proper. Other and equally important answers, however, can only be found by tracing Mao's Cultural Revolution back to its point of origin.

The main conclusions of this attempt to reconstruct the history of the Cultural Revolution are: (1) that its point of origin was the Lushan Central Committee Plenum in mid-1959 when the whole range of Mao's radical domestic and foreign policies was subjected to attack by the then Minister of National Defense, P'eng Teh-huai; (2) that the events of the ensuing three year period (featuring the Soviet withdrawal of technicians and the collapse of the Great Leap Forward and commune programs) largely demonstrated that in this great debate P'eng had been right and Mao had been wrong; (3) that the resulting crisis of confidence in Mao's leadership, first reflected by China's intellectuals, permeated the ranks of the Chinese Communist Party up to and including the Politburo; (4) that the Socialist Education Campaign initiated at the Tenth Plenum (September 1962) for the purposes of ferreting out opposition to and arousing mass support for Mao's policies and programs was adjudged a failure by Mao in the fall of 1965;

Philip Bridgham, "Mao's 'Cultural Revolution': Origin and Development," *The China Quarterly*, no. 29 (January–March 1967), pp. 1–35. Reprinted by permission of the publisher. The second part of Mr. Bridgham's article is reproduced on pp. 107–20, below.

and (5) that the Cultural Revolution is essentially a continuation of the Socialist Education Campaign in pursuit of the same goals, but under new management (Lin Piao and the others on Mao's new team) and employing new methods (systematic terror and violence).

Mao Is Attacked

The Chinese Communist regime has confirmed what had already been credibly reported in the West—that P'eng Teh-huai mounted an across-the-board attack on Mao's radical domestic and foreign policies at the Lushan Plenum in mid-1959, advancing instead programs featuring Soviet military, economic and technical assistance.[2] The great significance of the P'eng Teh-huai affair for the Cultural Revolution lies in the fact that for the first time in the history of the Chinese Communist movement since 1935, Mao's personal leadership and programs had come under attack by a long-time, trusted "comrade-in-arms" who, moreover, had managed to muster support within the top leadership.[3]

The origin of the Cultural Revolution must be traced to the shock and sense of betrayal experienced by Mao Tse-tung at Lushan. It is here that seeds of doubt concerning other "close comrades-in-arms" must have been planted, producing an incipient distrust which in time would become the "sickly suspicion"—as Khrushchev said of Stalin—which recently has characterized Mao's attitude and behavior toward his long-time comrades. As is now well documented, it was Mao's conviction that Wu Han's play *Hai Jui Dismissed from Office* constituted a defense of P'eng Teh-huai and therefore an attack on him personally which prompted the launching of the Cultural Revolution in November 1965.

Other elements of what would come to be known as the Great Proletarian Cultural Revolution also originated at this time, at least in rudimentary form. First, it is significant that Mao, at a time when he felt personally threatened, should have turned to Lin Piao for support and protection. In his first published article as the newly appointed Minister of National Defense, Lin Piao responded with a declaration of personal allegiance pledging "the unconditional loyalty of the People's Liberation Army to the Party and Comrade Mao."[4]

Of equal importance was the appearance in the fall of 1959 of a nationwide "cult of Mao Tse-tung." For the first time Mao was acclaimed publicly by a high-level Party spokesman as "the most outstanding contemporary revolutionary, statesman and theoretician of Marxism-Leninism."[5] Also of interest was the appearance at this time of a tactic which would be central to the carrying out of the Great Proletarian Cultural Revolution—testing the loyalty of Party leaders on the basis of their devotion to, and understanding of, Mao's thought. This tactic was implicit in the formulation: "The yardstick to judge whether any individual is a genuine Marxist is his comprehension of Mao Tse-tung's ideology."

The purposes of this nationwide glorification of Mao Tse-tung in 1959–60 appear to have been threefold: (1) to repair Mao's self-esteem, which must have been badly scarred in the confrontation with P'eng Teh-huai at Lushan; (2) to restore confidence, badly shaken by the failure of the Great Leap Forward program, in Mao's leadership; and (3) perhaps most important, to substitute "the ideology of Mao Tse-tung" for the false "revisionism" of Khrushchev as the true expression of contemporary Marxism-Leninism. These objectives remain important motivating factors in the Cultural Revolution today.

Mao Retreats

Developments in the three year period following the Lushan Plenum (1959–62) demonstrated in important respects that, in the great debate over domestic and foreign policy staged at this historic meeting, P'eng Teh-huai had been right and Mao Tse-tung had been wrong. The combined effect of irrational economic policy, successive bad harvests and the Soviet withdrawal of technicians in the summer of 1960 dealt Mao's Great Leap Forward program of economic development a shattering blow. Confronted with the threat of economic and political collapse, the Chinese Communist regime responded with a series of urgent corrective measures in the winter of 1960–61, and then, reluctantly and painfully, with even more drastic remedies in a period of further retreat from mid-1961 to mid-1962. The record of this period of protracted retreat is also of fundamental importance in assessing the origin and motivation of the current Cultural Revolution.

Although the immediate Chinese response to Soviet withdrawal of technicians was one of defiant optimism, Peking's view of its domestic problems in the winter of 1960 suddenly changed to one of alarm. The basic cause of this alarm was, of course, the severe shortage of food, reaching famine proportions in the disaster areas of East and North China. There is abundant evidence of widespread outbreaks of malnutrition diseases and of a sharp jump in the mortality rate at this time. To cite but one graphic example from the *Bulletin of Activities,* the results of an investigation showed that ten percent of China's First Army had experienced "unnatural deaths" in their families during the winter of 1960–61.[6] There was ample cause for Lin Piao's warning in January to expect "political troubles" and his call for extraordinary measures "to ensure that the armed forces do not get out of hand."

The successful execution of this mission—ensuring the loyalty of the People's Liberation Army during a time of national emergency—goes far to explain why five years later Mao Tse-tung would select Lin Piao as his deputy to head up the Great Proletarian Cultural Revolution. In part, Lin's success was due to initiating such corrective measures as increasing army rations, giving preferential treatment to the families of servicemen and halting all nonessential work programs. But of greater significance in tracing the rise of Lin Piao to his present position of eminence in the Chinese leadership was the successful campaign of intensive political indoctrination carried out in the PLA at this critical period.

A major objective of this political indoctrination campaign was to extricate Mao Tse-tung from responsibility for the Great Leap Forward debacle. According to the propaganda strategy, Communist China's domestic crisis had been caused by the deliberate "sabotage" of "class enemies" and by unwitting distortion of "correct" Party policies. Stated more bluntly, it was designed to show that "the Party Central Committee and Comrade Mao Tse-tung had all along made clear and correct directives" and that "the Party Central Committee is not wrong, but rather the thinking of rural cadres is confused." [7] Above and beyond this strategy, however, it was the tactics devised by Lin Piao in successfully implementing this campaign which would make a lasting impression on Mao and provide important guide lines for the Cultural Revolution five years hence.

In the charter of the military rectification campaign of 1960–61 ("The Resolution of the Enlarged Session of the Military Affairs Committee Concerning the Strengthening of Indoctrination Work in Troop Units," October 20, 1960),[8] Lin Piao set forth and expounded his famous concept of the "four firsts." Hailed as a "creative application of the thinking of Mao Tse-tung," these provided clear-cut directives in handling the relations between man and weapons (man comes first); between political work and other work (politics come first); between ideological and routine work (ideological work comes first); and between ideas in books and living ideas currently in people's minds (living ideology comes first). Although each of these reflected long-standing Maoist maxims, it was the fourth (the need to get hold of living ideology) which most nearly qualified as a "creative contribution" and which has figured prominently in the unfolding of the Cultural Revolution.

This was a restatement of Mao's famous "mass line," but with the responsibility for the success or failure of this mass line clearly assigned to Party cadres in the middle. Under the slogan "grasp both ends," these cadres in the middle were directed, at one end, to transmit and properly implement the "instructions of the Central Committee, of Chairman Mao and of the Military Affairs Commission" and at the other end, to grasp and properly interpret the "ideological condition" of the masses to the leadership at the center. Failure of Party policies, then, was the fault of Party cadres who had "created a communication block by failing to relay in time instructions to the Party and their superiors on the one hand and failing to submit reports to their superiors on the other." [9] The utility of this formulation at a time of national disaster was obvious—it exculpated the Party leadership from responsibility and provided a foolproof formula in defense of Mao Tse-tung's infallibility. At the time of the launching of the Cultural Revolution, it would provide the rationale for a similar purge of defective Party cadres, but with an important difference. At that time, Mao would hold the entire Party apparatus as defective and therefore responsible for the failure of his policies. . . .

Intellectual dissidence, as the voluminous record of the Cultural Revolution has made clear, was rife in China during this time of troubles in 1961–62. It is important to recognize, however, that many of the ideas and suggestions now attacked as dissident were not so considered at the time of their utterance. Along with such other urgent and distasteful measures as the dismantling of the communes in 1961, the Chinese Communist regime felt impelled to inaugurate a policy of "liberalization" (a kind of "second Hundred Flowers campaign") toward China's intellectuals, especially its scientists and technicians. With this caveat firmly in mind, the fact remains that a number of China's leading intellectuals (both inside and outside the Party) utilized this new freedom to go well beyond the limits of permissible criticism of Party policies. Disaffected by the widespread suffering caused by the disastrous Great Leap Forward program, they committed the most unforgivable act of all—criticizing Mao Tse-tung.

Well aware of the outcome of the earlier experiment with "liberalization," Mao's critics in 1959–62 were careful to cloak their criticism by the use of historical allegory, of pseudonyms and of Aesopian language. Wu Han's play, *Hai Jui Dismissed from Office*, the debate over which precipitated the Cultural Revolution, has been adjudged (and, it is believed, rightly so) as an example of "using ancient things to satirize the present"—in this instance, likening the case P'eng Teh-huai to that of a Ming Dynasty official who had been unjustly dismissed by the Emperor.

The criticism of Mao by Teng T'o, a secretary of the Peking municipal committee who was charged with overseeing the cultural life of the capital city, was much more comprehensive and damning. Writing under cover of a pseudonym in two literary columns in the Peking press, Teng T'o, together with Wu Han, . . . "In the guise of recounting historical anecdotes, imparting knowledge, telling stories and cracking jokes . . . launched an all-out and venomous attack on our great Party, using ancient things to satirize the present, reviling one thing while pointing at another, and making insinuations and oblique thrusts." [10] An examination of the contents of these literary columns, of which sizeable excerpts were reproduced in May 1966, leads to the conclusion that this charge is substantially correct.

In foreign policy, Teng ridiculed Mao's famous dictum "The East Wind Prevails over the West Wind," as "great empty talk" and advocated reconciliation with the Soviet Union—"learning from" and "uniting with countries stronger than our own." In domestic policy, Teng directed a number of jibes at the follies of the Great Leap Forward, characterizing it at various times (indirectly, of course) as "boasting," "indulging in fantasy" and "substituting illusion for reality." Most incriminating of all, Teng insinuated that Mao himself was responsible for the tragic failures of China's domestic and foreign policies, alluding to him as "boastful and conceited" and as suffering from a type of "amnesia" which could be cured by "hitting the patient on the head with a specially made club." [11] What made these charges all the more self-incriminating was the fact, stressed subsequently by the protagonists of the Cultural Revolution, that they echoed charges being made at the same time by Khrushchev against Mao and the Chinese Party.

As Mao surveyed the ideological scene in Communist China in mid-1962, there was, on the one hand, order and discipline within the ranks of the military and, on the other hand, unrest and dissidence in much of the rest of Chinese society. The conclusion which Mao would derive from this state of affairs is, in retrospect, clear. It would be desirable to extend application of the more extreme methods and techniques of political indoctrination perfected within the People's Liberation Army to encompass all of Chinese society. The story of the development and ultimate surfacing of the Cultural Revolution in the ensuing four year period would be one of the progressive application of these military thought-control techniques to all sectors of Chinese society.

Mao Counter-attacks

At the time of the Tenth Plenum of the Central Committee in September 1962, three years of privation and ignominious retreat from the original goals of the Great Leap Forward and commune programs had bred apathy, disillusionment and dissatisfaction among large segments of Chinese society. Even more alarming, a large proportion of Party cadres extending into the upper echelons had begun to display the same symptoms of cynicism toward Mao's programs. It was in response to this crisis of confidence that Mao Tse-tung launched the Socialist Education Campaign in the fall of 1962, a campaign with the ambitious objective (in the words of Chairman Mao) of "educating man anew and reorganizing our revolutionary ranks." As indicated earlier, the Socialist Education class struggle campaign initiated at this time comprises an integral, if formative, phase of the Cultural Revolution.

Although Mao's important speech to the Tenth Plenum has not been published, enough is known from extracts to identify the major problems addressed in this speech—problems which remain as central, motivating concerns of the Cultural Revolution. First, Mao warned of the danger of intellectual dissidence by pointing out "that a number of people were making use of the writing of novels to carry out anti-Party activities and were creating a climate in public opinion for the restoration of capitalism." [12] Next, Mao revealed his concern over the problem of China's youth—the generational problem of cultivating loyal successors to Mao's revolution—by emphasizing that "class education for youth must be strengthened to ensure that our nation will remain revolutionary and incorruptible for generations and for ever." [13] Finally, Mao indicated his resolve to re-establish socialist, collective controls over the economy (especially the rural economy) when he "repudiated the trend of 'going it alone' (i.e., the restoration of individual economy) which had been incited by the bourgeoisie and its exponents within the Party. . . ." [14]

Despite the fragmentary nature of the public record, the main thrust of this key address by Chairman Mao to the Tenth Plenum was clear. Since Mao's domestic and foreign policies had suffered obvious and severe defeats in the preceding three year period, it was imperative that a rationale be advanced to explain past failures and silence future criticism. This rationale was to explain failures and criticism of Party policies as largely the handiwork of "foreign and domestic class enemies" against whom it was now necessary to launch a nationwide "class struggle" campaign.

The first stage of this campaign, extending to mid-1964, was relatively moderate. In May 1963, a campaign to eliminate "harmful bourgeois influence and unhealthy phenomena" in literature and the arts was launched at a national conference of writers and artists. In December 1963, Chairman Mao issued another in the "series of extremely important instructions and stern criticisms of literary and art work" which the Chinese regime now characterizes as important milestones on the road to the Cultural Revolution. At a meeting of the All-China Federation of Literary and Art Circles, Mao complained that "socialist transformation has by now achieved very little effect" in the various fields of literature and art and termed "absurd" the fact that "many communists are enthusiastic in promoting feudalist and capitalist art but are not enthusiastic in promoting socialist art." [15]

The task of coping with the disillusionment and cynicism of China's youth, especially its educated youth, was even more formidable than that posed by the intellectuals. Since educational and job opportunities were sharply curtailed following the collapse of the Great Leap Forward, the almost insurmountable problem faced by the Party propagandists was to persuade these educated youth to sacrifice their careers and personal ambitions for the good of the revolution.

The solution advanced in the spring of 1963 was the full-blown propaganda campaign "to study the good example of Lei Feng." Intended to imbue China's youth with the "revolutionary spirit" and heroic self-sacrifice of the "extraordinary soldier" Lei Feng, a major objective of this campaign was to provide an ideological and moral substitute for material incentives in motivating China's youth.[16] In attributing all of Lei Feng's miraculous accomplishments "to earnest and repeated study of Chairman Mao Tse-tung's works," this campaign foreshadowed the recent phenomenon of Red Guards constantly carrying and consulting their red-bound *Quotations of Mao Tse-tung*. In exhorting China's youth to emulate soldier Lei Feng, it anticipated Mao's call to all sectors of Chinese society "to learn from the People's Liberation Army." And the failure of this campaign to achieve its objective (there were many reports at the time of students poking fun at Lei Feng as a paragon of virtue) would prompt Mao in time to abandon persuasion in favor of coercion (the violence and terror of the Red Guards) as the solution to China's youth problem.

The main focus of the Socialist Education Campaign in the year following the Tenth Plenum, was in China's rural areas where the "spontaneous tendency to capitalism" had developed to an alarming degree. Rural cadres, who were held responsible for this resurgence of capitalism, were now subjected to a "five antis" campaign, charged with permitting "individual farming" and engaging in corruption. The appearance of a new "antis" campaign signified a shift from ideological to political struggle, from persuasion to coercion. Although the campaign was apparently conducted on an experimental, piecemeal basis in 1963, refugee reporting testified to its violent nature with accounts of struggle sessions, public trials and beatings of erring cadres.

Of greater interest in tracing the origins of the Cultural Revolution, however, was the appearance at this time of Poor and Lower Middle Peasant Associations. Reviving the "peasant association" used during the land reform era (1950–52) to bully and suppress landlords and rich peasants, the regime began in early 1963 to form Poor and Lower Middle Peasant Associations for the express purpose of implementing, under Party control, this new tough rural rectification campaign.[17] The parallels between this organization and the organizations which would be created to carry out the Cultural Revolution—the Cultural Revolution teams, committees and congresses and their action arms, the Red Guards—are both numerous and striking.

The first and obvious similarity is that membership is determined by class origin, since by definition the urban and rural proletariat are the most reliable supporters of Mao's revolution. Second, the authority of these organizations is limited in that neither is empowered to remove Party or government leaders or (in theory) interfere in governmental functions. Third, and most important, the principal function of both organizations is to facilitate the purge and thought reform of erring Party cadres. In effect, these organizations are intended to serve as a kind of popular jury in judging Party cadres (who are summoned before them to engage in self-criticism), thus sparing the Party itself from the necessity of performing this chore and at the same time serving as a pretense of local democracy. Finally, after subjecting the cadres to criticism and self-criticism, the members of these organizations are then supposed to engage in the same process themselves; this is regarded as the ultimate stage of the rectification campaign.

At the same time that the Socialist Education Campaign in the countryside began to focus on iniquitous Party cadres, a new campaign inaugurated in the urban modern sector of Chinese society reflected the same distrust of the reliability and efficiency of Party cadres in China's towns and cities. This was the campaign initiated by Mao's call in December 1963 to "learn from the PLA," with all political, economic, and social organizations in China now directed to study and emulate the organizational, operational and ideological training methods of the People's Liberation Army. As subsequently revealed, Mao at this time ordered all departments of the national economy "to study the methods of the PLA, establish and strengthen political work and thus arouse the revolutionary spirit of the millions and tens of millions of cadres and masses on the economic front." [18] This injunction was followed literally, beginning in the spring of 1964, with the establishment in industry, transportation, trade and finance and all government departments of a political commissar system modelled on that of the PLA.

Although it was difficult at the time to grasp the purpose of this new political network, that purpose is much clearer in retrospect. As an early, vivid expression of his distrust of the conventional Party apparatus, it strongly suggests that Mao had already decided that his Party was shot through with incompetents, at best, or dissidents, at worst, and required a thorough-going purge. As this new political network came to be staffed increasingly by political cadres recruited from the PLA in 1964 and 1965, the groundwork was being laid for the emergence of Lin Piao and the PLA as dominant forces in Mao's Cultural Revolution.

Mao Steps Up the Attack

The Great Proletarian Cultural Revolution sweeping across China today was intimated by Mao Tse-tung [several] years ago in his July 14, 1964 polemic "On Khrushchev's Phoney Communism and Its Historical Lessons for the World." [19] Reflecting anxiety over the present status and future course of the Chinese revolution, Mao unveiled in this significant document a 15-point program designed to root out revisionism and prevent a restoration of capitalism in China. This theoretical pronouncement purported to be an authoritative Marxist-Leninist explanation of such assaults on the dictatorship of the proletariat in recent years as the Hungarian counter-revolution in 1956 and the rise of Khrushchev revisionism in the Soviet Union. The message was clear—

unless extraordinary measures were adopted, the same thing could and would happen in China too.

One of these extraordinary measures was to intensify the attack against China's intellectuals. The directive to escalate was provided by Mao at a June 1964 All-China Federation of Literary and Art Circles meeting when he charged that China's "literary workers" (and the publications under their control) had since 1949 "in the main failed to carry out the Party's policies"; had in recent years "fallen to the brink of revisionism"; and, failing earnest reform, "would inevitably become an organization like the Petofi Club of Hungary." [20] The import of this remarkable statement was that the real threat of "revisionism" in China, as seen by Mao, came not from intellectuals outside the Party (who were well known and easily dealt with) but from intellectual cadres within the Party, some of whom were obviously highly placed.

Since the Cultural Revolution is a direct outgrowth of this decision in mid-1964 "to launch a rectification campaign . . . on the front of literature and art," it is ironic that the man selected by Mao at this time to lead the initial phase was [Peking Mayor] P'eng Chen. P'eng was to purge the Party of intellectual dissidents by screening their literary and artistic output in the preceding few years. He would find (if he did not already know) that the most flagrant examples of "anti-Party and anti-socialist poisonous weeds" had appeared in publications of his own Peking Party committee. And while he was charged to ferret out high-level intellectual cadres opposed to Mao, he himself would be the first prominent victim.

A second extraordinary measure was acceleration and intensification of the program of "cultivating revolutionary successors" who could be trusted to carry on loyally after Mao had gone. Mao characterized this program as "an extremely important question, a matter of life and death for our Party and our country," and laid down five criteria in "On Khrushchev's Phoney Communism" to govern the selection and training of "revolutionary successors." Of these requirements, perhaps the most important was that they "come forward in mass struggles and are tempered in the great storms of revolution." When combined with the injunction that "they must especially watch out for careerists and conspirators like Khrushchev and prevent such bad elements from usurping the leadership of the Party and government at any level," these were the essential features of the Red Guard movement initiated two years later.

Mao's obsession with the problem of China's youth, especially educated youth, was further revealed in conversations with foreign visitors in the fall and winter of 1964–65. In talks with these visitors, Mao disclosed his distrust of educated youth in remarks about China's younger generation, a generation "which had never fought a war and never seen an imperialist or known capitalism in power" and which could in the future "negate the revolution." [21] The great weakness of China's youth, as Mao pointed out to these foreign visitors, was its lack of "combat experience." This "combat experience" would come in the largely contrived "class struggle," the terroristic attacks and the violent clashes of the Red Guard phase of the Cultural Revolution.

Encompassing the first two, the third extraordinary measure was the decision taken in mid-1964 to transform the Socialist Education Campaign into the "broadest, deepest socialist revolutionary movement since our Party came to power." Still focused primarily on rural areas, this new-style rural rectification campaign, called the "Four Clearances," was designed to uncover and punish cadre obstructionism and corruption in China's rural communes. A special feature was reliance on outside "task force cadres" or "work teams" to administer this campaign.

The fourth extraordinary measure, although initiated before the publication of "On Khrushchev's Phoney Communism," was Mao's plan to revitalize the propaganda apparatus in Party and government with political officers recruited from the People's Liberation Army. A definitive statement of the purpose and functions of the newly established political network in the economy and government was provided by Yang Shu-ken in February 1965 at a national conference for political cadres in trade and finance work.[22] Taking as his text Lin Piao's exposition of the "four firsts" at the October 1960 PLA political work conference (characterized as a "general summation of our Party's experience in conducting politico-ideological work over the past few years"), Yang stressed that the principal function of the new political network was "grasping both ends well"—that is, "to keep a firm grip on both the upper end, the thought of Mao Tse-tung and the policies and directives of the Party center, and the lower end, the ideological state of the broad masses of workers." With this formulation, the intended role for the new political network throughout government and the economy—as the transmission belt for Maoist thought and Party policies—was made clear. And with the disclosure that most of the some 200,000 ex-PLA officers and men at work in the trade and finance sector were staffing this new political network,[23] it appears in retrospect that the process of militarization of the Chinese Communist Party, a salient feature of the current Cultural Revolution, was well under way in early 1965.

The events of the spring and summer of 1965 in Communist China are also believed to provide an important clue to understanding the motivation and character of today's Cultural Revolution. The sharp escalation of the attack against domestic class enemies in the last six months of 1964 was followed by a noticeable lull. Indeed, there was an unmistakable shift at this time away from militant emphasis on "class struggle" and frugal living toward a softer, more conciliatory line. This was revealed first of all in semi-official approval for people to spend more money on better clothes, food and other consumer goods, and, even more strikingly, in a series of directives in mid-summer designed to ensure workers, peasants and students adequate rest and leisure time by reducing overtime schedules and spare-time political meetings.[24]

In seeking an explanation for this about-face, it seems clear that a major factor was concern over the rapid escalation of the U.S. war effort in Vietnam during the winter and spring of 1965, especially the decision in February to initiate large-scale bombing of North Vietnam on a regular basis. Since this was not playing the game of revolutionary war according to Mao's rules (i.e., it violated Mao's thesis of the sanctuary of revolutionary basis), it must have been an unexpected and worrisome development. The reaction, then, was de-emphasis of "class struggle" in order to conciliate and unite the population in the face of a possible war situation. And, in fact, the dominant theme of Communist China's domestic propaganda-political indoctrination campaign in the spring and summer of 1965 was that of "war preparations."

An important clue for understanding the motivation of the Cultural Revolution arises at this point. For, as recent Red Guard wall posters have revealed, Communist China's top leaders apparently reacted differently in the winter of 1965 in evaluating the gravity of the threat of war posed by U.S. escalation in Vietnam and especially the extent to which the domestic "class struggle" program should be soft-pedalled to meet that threat. Indicating that its authors had access to unpublished Party documents, a major 20-page wall poster issued in late November 1966 accused both Liu Shao-ch'i and Teng Hsiao-p'ing of "not giving sufficient support to the Maoist line after the opening of the rectification campaign, called the Socialist Education Movement, at the end of 1964."

There are indications in the public record, moreover, that Mao was displeased with the performance of some of his top lieutenants at a national work conference called by the Politburo in January 1965, at which a major Party document ("Some Current Problems Raised in the Socialist Education Movement in the Rural Areas") was drawn up under Mao's personal guidance. In the cryptic and somewhat obscure language of the August 21, 1966 *Red Flag* editorial, this document was designed to overcome "mistakes" in the implementation of the Socialist Education Campaign in 1964, "mistakes which looked 'Leftist' but were actually 'Rightist'. . . ." These "mistakes," as the *Red Flag* editorial went on to point out, constituted "opposition" to Mao's thought.

These disclosures provide valuable insight into one of the puzzling aspects of the Cultural Revolution—why it was considered necessary to extend the purge into the very highest echelons of the Chinese leadership to encompass such notorious hard-line "leftists" as Liu Shao-ch'i and Teng Hsiao-p'ing. Whether described as "not giving sufficient support" or as "opposition," whether labelled as "Leftist" or "Rightist" and after making due allowance for *ex post facto* exaggeration and distortion, it appears that Mao had already begun in the winter and spring of 1965 to entertain doubts about the loyalty of his top lieutenants in charge of Party affairs. When these doubts were strengthened by new signs of resistance at a crucial meeting of the Party center in September 1965, the Great Proletarian Cultural Revolution would begin. . . .

1. For a good discussion of this and other parallels between Mao and Stalin, see Arthur A. Cohen, "Mao: The Man and His Policies," *Problems of Communism,* September–October, 1966.

2. See David A. Charles, "The Dismissal of Marshal P'eng Teh-huai," *The China Quarterly,* No. 8 (October–December, 1961).

3. The Kao Kang-Jao Shu-shih "anti-party alliance" of the early 1950s had been directed at Mao's subordinates, Liu Shao-ch'i and Chou En-lai.

4. Lin Piao "March Ahead under the Red Flag of the Party's General Line and Mao Tse-tung's Military Thought," *Jen-min Jih-pao* (People's Daily), September 30, 1959.

5. See Liu Lan-t'ao, "The Chinese Communist Party is the Supreme Commander in Building Socialism," *People's Daily,* September 28, 1959.

6. *Kung-tso T'ung-hsün* (Bulletin of Activities), No. 6, January 27, 1961, p. 15.

7. *Ibid.,* No. 19, May 13, 1961, pp. 12–13.

8. *Ibid.,* No. 3, January 7, 1961, pp. 1–33.

9. *Ibid.*

10. See Kao Chu, "Open Fire at the Black Anti-Party and Anti-Socialist Line," *Kwang-ming Jih-pao* (Kwang-ming Daily), May 8, 1966.

11. "Teng T'o's 'Evening Chats at Yenshan' is Anti-Party and Anti-Socialist Double-Talk," *Kwang-ming Daily,* May 8, 1966. For a good discussion of intellectual dissidence in China at this time, see Harry Gelman, "Mao and the Permanent Purge," *Problems of Communism,* November–December, 1966.

12. *New China News Agency* (NCNA), July 30, 1966.

13. Hu Yao-pang, "Strive to Revolutionize the Youth of Our Country," *People's Daily,* July 7, 1964.

14. See editorial in *Hung Ch'i* (Red Flag), No. 11 (August 21, 1966).

15. *NCNA,* June 6, 1966.

16. See, for example, the article by Lo Jui-ch'ing, "Learn from Lei Feng," in *Chung-kuo Ch'ing-nien* (China Youth), March 2, 1963.

17. For a description of the role of the Poor and Lower Middle Peasant Associations, see Chang P'ing-hua, "We Must Rely on Poor and Lower Middle Peasants," *People's Daily,* November 2, 1964.

18. Quoted in Commentator article, "Political Work is the Lifeline of All Work," *Red Flag,* March 31, 1964.

19. Article by the editorial departments of *People's Daily* and *Red Flag,* July 14, 1964.

20. *NCNA*, June 6, 1966.
21. Interview with Edgar Snow, January 1965: *Washington Post*, February 14, 1965.
22. Yang Shu-ken, "Give a Prominent Place to Politics and Pay Close Attention to Upholding the 'Four Firsts,'" *Ta Kung Pao*, March 27, 1965.
23. *People's Daily*, May 18, 1965.
24. See, for example, the editorial "Link Labor and Leisure," in *People's Daily*, June 21, 1965.

THE CHINESE COMMUNIST PARTY IN THE
1960s: PRELUDE TO THE
CULTURAL REVOLUTION

Charles Neuhauser

. . . If anything is clear about the present upheaval, it is that the tensions and disputes that brought it into being did not arise overnight, but are deep-seated and have been growing throughout the 1960s.

Signs of malaise within the CCP were not lacking. The Ninth Party Congress, due to meet in 1963, was never convened. Following the Tenth Plenum in September 1962 the Central Committee did not meet in plenary session for nearly four years.[1] For almost the same length of time discussions of the Party *qua* Party, the specific self-criticism and adumbration of CCP strengths and weaknesses that are normally a feature of the press, were very largely absent from Chinese media. While unexplained absences of Party congresses and lack of Central Committee plena are by no means unknown in CCP history, such phenomena may well reflect the presence of unresolved issues at a very high level; the last such hiatus occurred in the early 1960s prior to the purge of Kao Kang.

But the CCP's troubles were not confined to the Party center. By 1960 the Party organizational structure was clearly in disrepair.[2] That the Great Leap Forward proved traumatic for the CCP hardly needs emphasis. Morale, already shaken by the all too apparent chasm between the promises of the Great Leap program and the resultant reality, was further eroded by the anti-rightist campaign of 1959.[3] Nor should it be forgotten that in many respects the CCP was suffering badly from growing pains. By mid-1961 the CCP comprised some 17 million members and most were relatively new recruits. No more than 20 per cent of all Party members in 1961—a mere 3.4 million—had joined the Party prior to the establishment of the Chinese People's Republic.[4] This huge mass of fairly new recruits undoubtedly included a considerable number of careerists, and among the remainder the level of ideological training often was not high. Furthermore, the Party continued to grow—perhaps to 20 million by the end of 1965.

Charles Neuhauser, "The Chinese Communist Party in the 1960s: Prelude to the Cultural Revolution," *The China Quarterly*, no. 32 (October–December 1967), pp. 3–36. Reprinted by permission of the publisher.

In a very real sense the Party could be said to be suffering also from an identity-crisis. One aspect of this was of course the steady loss of revolutionary élan as Party cadres became enmeshed in the increasingly complex bureaucratic and managerial problems of governing the country.[5] "Old cadres" who joined the Party while it was still struggling for mastery of China found their revolutionary experience increasingly irrelevant to the problems now confronting them; "new cadres" lacked this experience but also lacked the sense of total involvement with the Party that it imparted. Furthermore, the Party could not govern without the assistance of non-Party technical experts. These people were often given pride of place.[6] Pressures within the Party to reverse this trend played a part in the decision to embark on the Great Leap Forward. But in the subsequent period of retrenchment the trend toward technical expertise and separation of functions was once more resumed, only to be reversed again—partially and hesitatingly—in the period following the Tenth Plenum.[7]

Against this background of strain and difficulty the disputes of the 1960s were played out within the Party. The fact that there *were* disputes is of itself hardly surprising; the policy-making levels of the CCP had by no means always agreed unanimously. But the conflicts of the past several years eventually shook the Party to its foundation. In part this was a result of the disaster brought on by the Great Leap Forward. Far-reaching decisions of great importance were urgently required to retrieve the situation. Faced with a series of natural disasters, increasing economic dislocation and stagnation, and widespread disaffection, the Party relaxed its controls, retreated in the countryside, and lowered its goals in the industrial sector. This program was largely successful in the economic sphere, but though it alleviated the immediate political crisis, it created a host of new political problems.

The attitudes engendered by this period of relaxation placed expertise, bureaucratic rationalization and efficiency and pragmatism in commanding positions. Not a few CCP members in the upper and middle levels came to feel that precisely these qualities would guarantee that the 1959–60 collapse would not be repeated. For them the goal of the Chinese revolution became largely bound up with considerations of wealth and power: the growth of the productive and military capacity of the state, and a rise in the people's standard of living. But this emphasis on rationalization implied a general distrust of "revolutionary spontaneity," a relegation of purely ideological considerations to second place and a tacit admission that the philosophy and techniques of the Great Leap Forward had been mistaken. This view was by no means universally held, particularly among those whose prestige had been most closely bound up with the Great Leap experiment—above all Mao Tse-tung himself.

The issue as this second group saw it was in its simplest form the question of "revisionism"—the question of whether revolutionary fervor and momentum could be maintained over a long period of time, or whether China would in fact "change its color." . . .

It is tempting to see in these two divergent philosophies and conflicting areas of primary concern two clear-cut and self-conscious factions within the CCP, one represented by Mao Tse-tung, the other perhaps by the "rationalizing" bureaucrat, Liu Shao-ch'i. But reality appears to have been more complicated. What might be called the "Maoist" position seems reasonably well defined, at least in the period following the Tenth Plenum, but that of the "opposition" is more complex. Despite the many charges of "plotting" thrown up by the Cultural Revolution, there is very little evidence that Mao's opponents were acting in concerted, organized fashion for any extended period prior to 1966. While opposition to, and even sabotage of, several "Maoist" policies was real enough after 1962, it is possible that some of the "rationalizers" believed they were in fact carrying out the broad policy directives of the Chairman. However, given their preoccupation with order, efficiency, technical progress and similar concerns, in the process of "gearing down" these general directives they in fact distorted them. But this was a subtle process, and one that was probably not always immediately apparent to Mao himself.

The Eleventh Plenum resolution, not to mention subsequent events, makes it clear that Mao and the "Maoists" had eventually come to believe that revisionist rot was centered in the Party apparatus itself. What then had gone wrong with the Party? . . .

There appear to be three broad problem areas within the CCP in the 1960s: first, that of basic-level cadres, where the problems stemming from hasty recruiting, deficient ideological training and questionable motivation were most evident. . . . Another problem area was that of Party organization, primarily involving the middle levels of the CCP. In the early 1960s great emphasis was placed on the strengthening of the organizational sinews of the Party and on the importance of Party discipline. This emphasis, however, tended to multiply bureaucratic abuses within the CCP, and a "Maoist" attempt to counter this tendency through the device of allowing criticism of individual Party members by groups outside the CCP was strongly resisted by apparatchiks at the middle level of the Party.

The third problem involved the implementation of the many national campaigns introduced in the years following the Tenth Plenum. Opposition to the sloganeering and simplistic solutions to complex problems fostered by these campaigns cut across all levels of the Party but was concentrated in the middle and upper levels of the CCP, particularly in those Party organs concerned with propaganda and culture and with education. . . .

Intertwined with these problems was the crucial question of personal power. Party figures were able to resist "Maoist" pressures, often with considerable success because they were in a position to modify the "Maoist" programs while continuing to mouth the orthodox "Maoist" slogans. Indeed, the history of the CCP from mid-1964 and particularly since the start of the Cultural Revolution itself can be seen as an attempt on the part of Mao Tse-tung to reassert his personal authority over all aspects of Party policy and over all levels of Party organization. . . .

Basic-Level Cadres

In the wake of the extensive failures growing out of the Great Leap experiment, and especially with the introduction of the "agriculture in first place" slogan, the Party turned its primary attention to its basic-level cadres. These men were the infantry of the Party who of course encompassed the vast majority of Party members. Upper-level functionaries were frequently inclined to treat them with considerable contempt. . . . Most importantly, the basic-level cadres were accused of failure to understand properly the directives and policies of the Party Central—above all, failure to understand, and in turn make the masses understand, that pure communism could not be created overnight and that the transitional period would be long and painful. . . .[8]

In general the attack on the basic-level cadres was threefold: it focused on their relations with the masses, on their ideological understanding and adherence to the Party line, and on problems of their control and discipline. Few complaints were new, but the wide range of charges and the continuation of the attack over a considerable period was in itself somewhat unusual. Discussions of basic-level cadre problems showed great sensitivity to the unspoken accusation that the Party had pushed the general populace too hard during the Great Leap Forward. Numerous instances of "commandism" were cited, and cadres were charged with ignoring the complaints of the masses and of assuming the airs and prerogatives of pre-Liberation officials.[9] Cadres at the basic level were accused not only of failure to understand Party policy, but of failure to study CCP ideology, resulting in a crude understanding of even the most basic and accessible works of Chairman Mao, and of failure even to read Party directives.[10]

Concurrent with these charges was a drive towards relaxation and rationalization in the factories and countryside. The basic-level cadres in turn were urged to reward and defer to people with technical skills. They were to encourage the entrepreneurial and acquisitive instincts of the peasants and to avoid applying rigid formulas to problems of local resistance or local conditions requiring special handling.[11] The watch word "learn from the masses" in this period meant deference to local opinion and a general effacement of the cadres themselves. They were admonished to establish easy working relationships both with natural local leaders and with the general populace.[12]

These measures and admonitions reflected a profound distrust of the basic-level cadres themselves, reducing and circumscribing their direct leadership role. Concurrent emphasis on technical ability and expertise tended to erode further their activities. Production, rather than politics, was in command. . . . While ideological training was by no means abandoned—new Party schools for cadre training were established and a large number of teachers were accepted into the Party—it was not to interfere with production and regular work.[13] Continued insistence that basic-level cadres act strictly in accordance with higher-level Party directives and not take matters into their own hands restricted initiative at the lowest levels of the Party. . . .

The general economic recovery beginning in 1962 reinforced pressures to expand and deepen these "rightist" policies. In February of that year Ch'en Yün, a principal advocate of economic rationalization and opponent of the Great Leap policies, apparently put forward a proposal for further extension of the relaxation program which was discussed and evidently tentatively endorsed at high levels of the Party.[14] But those most committed to the Great Leap Forward, who had reluctantly endorsed relaxation as a necessary evil when the crisis of 1960 seemed to provide no alternatives to a drastic reorientation of state and Party priorities, found such relaxation intolerable in a period of economic recovery. Mao's reaction to Ch'en's proposals was negative in the extreme.[15] And in September 1962 the Tenth Plenum of the Central Committee brought the period of relaxation to an abrupt end.

The hallmark of the Tenth Plenum was of course an all-out attack on revisionism. The importance of class struggle was emphasized and a new effort at ideological rectification and education demanded. Basic-level cadres were told to abandon the relaxed procedures of the period of retrenchment. A Socialist Education Campaign was launched. The problems this policy reversal presented are illustrated by the experience of Lien-chiang county, Fukien.[16]

Lien-chiang county inaugurated a program of socialist education and ideological training almost as soon as the Tenth Plenum had concluded, but quickly discovered that problems at the basic level were so numerous that a new rectification campaign would have to be conducted before a more ambitious program could properly be launched. The first two months of 1963 were devoted to this task. The county Party committee insisted that it retain close control over the campaign; basic-level cadres were allowed little initiative and were told to refer all important matters to the county;[17] moreover, coercion was prohibited—"soft winds and gentle rain" was the order of the day. Nevertheless, struggle meetings were in fact convened, and several "extraordinary" deaths occurred, apparently by beating.[18] Perhaps more interesting was the reluctance of many basic-level cadres to go along with the new policies: the county Party committee was forced to keep a box score of the number of cadres (presumably many were non-Party members) who tried to resign, and of those who had been pressured into staying on.[19] The cadres opposed the new policies for four basic reasons: fear of engaging in "struggle" because they might be disciplined or lose face if the policy changed; fear that the populace might "retaliate" against them; fear that all that would come of the new movement would be further trouble with the masses; and above all, a cynical suspicion that the Socialist Education Movement was useless and would not change anything.[20]

The county committee also had great difficulty convincing the cadres that the practice of *tan kan,* "going it alone" in agricultural production rather than farming collectively, was a major error. Not only did many cadres indulge in this practice themselves; they argued that it created good management, stimulated production, was popular with the masses, and was in line with socialism because reward was equal to work and it created a good attitude among the people. Furthermore, the cadres resisted the counter-arguments of the county committee: as one remarked, "the higher-ups always talk about morality, but they have something different in their hearts. Their words and actions never coincide." [21]

The situation in Lien-chiang is illustrative of the tensions between the basic-level cadres and the general populace on the one hand, and the cadres and the higher levels of the Party organization on the other. . . .

Despite the rather generalized but unremitting exhortations that filled the press in the years after the Tenth Plenum, there was in fact no general "revolutionary upsurge" in the countryside. . . . The issues involved—whether the basic levels could be trusted to carry out policy, whether or not they needed close supervision from above or were in fact being unduly restrained by the dead hand of bureaucracy, whether the basic level contained an untapped reservoir of revolutionary potential or had to be coaxed and rewarded for performances and production—remained unresolved. There was certainly no denial that major problems existed among the basic-level cadres. But the crucial question of how to treat and utilize the great mass of poorly trained, under-educated and perhaps indifferently motivated Party members at the bottom of the pyramid remained unsettled until the spring of 1966.

Organization

If the Party's first concern in the crisis of 1960–61 was with its basic-level cadres, concern with the state of the Party organization followed as a close second. The policies of the Great Leap Forward, and in particular the moves toward decentralization that accompanied it, had tended to dislocate the Party command structure; thus, the first moves in organizational refurbishing were directed toward making the weight of the Party center felt more strongly at all levels of the CCP. To this end new regional bureaus were established in 1960. Unlike the regional bureaus that had existed in the early 1950s, the new bureaus were clearly organs of the Central Committee itself, and were obviously designed to facilitate the work and increase the power of the Central Committee Secretariat.

With the establishment of the regional bureaus came a strong assertion of Party discipline from the center. At the same time there was a concerted effort to clear and improve channels of communication both from the top down and in the opposite direction. If the basic-level cadres had been accused of failing to understand Party policies, the intermediate levels of the CCP—the provincial and county committees —were charged with failure properly to implement and supervise those policies.[22] Above all, the intermediate levels were accused of blocking and suppressing information needed by the center to formulate correct decisions.[23] "Learn from the masses" in this context meant supplying the policy-making organs at the center with specific and accurate information about conditions and attitudes at the working levels; it was specifically stated that without such information the Party could not make correct decisions.

At the same time, an effort was made to renovate and refurbish Party activity in cells and committees at all levels. The press insisted that Party meetings could not become mere ratifying sessions where Party work was hardly discussed. Nevertheless, emphasis was also increasingly placed on the importance of "personal responsibility" in Party work, and a clear distinction was frequently drawn between the "hard-core leadership elements" of the Party—that is, the Party secretaries—and other members of the CCP.[24] Such emphasis of course tended to vitiate any moves toward "democratization" of Party life in the committees, and in fact it seems likely that the role of the Party secretary was enhanced, rather than reduced, during this period. Reassertion of central authority, routinization and an increasing emphasis on discipline all tended to calcify further the bureaucratic aspects of Party life.

In an attempt to obviate the unhealthy tendencies of such a situation, new emphasis was placed on the Party control commissions. For the first time, these organs became an important feature of CCP organizational structure.[25] Unlike other Party officials, CCP members responsible for Party control reported upward directly through the control commission organs running parallel to the regular Party hierarchy, rather than through the various Party secretaries;[26] they were particularly concerned with behavior unbefitting a CCP member. Thus an independent check on members' activities was provided at all levels of the organization, but it was a check by a duly constituted organ of the

Party itself, operating according to carefully prescribed rules and procedures; disciplinary action could only be taken by regular Party organs at the next highest level. At the provincial level and above there was a close connection between the control commissions and the respective regular Party committees. Control was still exercised from the top down. . . .

These several tendencies found fullest expression in a propaganda campaign, running from the summer of 1961 to the autumn of 1962, calling on all CCP members to "learn from the Party constitution." In particular that part of the constitution pertaining to the Party's internal rules was stressed. It was repeatedly emphasized that the Party needed cohesive discipline, that the governing principle of the CCP was "subordination of the individual to the organization, subordination of minority to the majority, subordination of the lower level to the higher level, and subordination of the whole Party to the Central Committee." [27] Members could protest a proposed decision before it was ratified, but after it had been approved they could formally protest only through prescribed channels, and in the interim would have to carry it out.[28] Individual initiative was clearly circumscribed. Indeed, the recent charges against Liu Shao-ch'i that in the early 1960s he insisted that the individual Party member should in all circumstances subordinate himself to the Party organization is certainly true in the sense that this theme played a very large role in the Party propaganda of the period.

But the "democratic" side of democratic centralism was not totally ignored, although it received subordinate attention. It was in this connection that the theme of democratic discussion within the Party committee was raised. Still more interesting was the theme that on occasion the minority opinion might be the correct one and therefore could not be wholly ignored.[29] Almost certainly the reference here was to those "rightists" who had protested against the policies of the Great Leap period and were now seen to be at least partially correct. Many persons in this category were asking that disciplinary charges against them be dropped and were asserting themselves in intra-Party discussions at this time. Statements that their views should not be ignored tended to encourage them at all levels of the Party.

This trend was of course reversed at the Tenth Plenum, with its renewed stress on class struggle. The plenum decision called for greater interchange of senior personnel at the upper levels of both Party and state, as well as between the two hierarchies. Here once again the Party center was grappling with the intractable issue of the increasing bureaucratic rigidity of both the Party and state organizations. This trend would have to be reversed if the new effort of revolutionization of China that now can be seen to be foreshadowed by the plenum were to have any chance of success. The major effort in this direction, still more important than personnel changes which at best were carried out in only fragmentary fashion, was to be renewed emphasis on ideological indoctrination.[30] But the intermediate levels of the Party hierarchy tended to accept the view that ideological renewal was not meant for them as relatively senior members of the Party, often with a long history of revolutionary activity—it was meant for the relatively uninitiated and often far junior Party members at the lower levels. Recent charges made in the course of the Cultural Revolution that personnel at the provincial and county levels often considered ideological study as a mere formality and that some important Party figures did not even possess the selected works of Chairman Mao[31] are no doubt exaggerated, but there can be little doubt that the accusations contain more than a grain of truth. . . . The problem was not complacency. The need to deal with the problem of bureaucratic stultification was probably generally accepted, especially at the uppermost levels of the Party. The question was how this was to be done. . . . Party bureaucrats were willing to allow a degree of criticism of the basic-level cadres; but they were unwilling to see this criticism extended to the higher levels. The Party would criticize and discipline its own personnel through the recognized channels and procedures it had so recently strengthened; it was not ready to open the door to unbridled criticism from outside its own ranks. . . .

This resistance on the part of the Party bureaucracy was recognized [by the Maoists] in January, 1965. . . . Elements in the Party organization at the intermediate and upper levels as well as at the basic level were attacked. The rationale for this attack can unquestionably be traced in very large part to the continued resistance of the Party bureaucracy in 1963 and 1964 to the proposals for increased class warfare and above all to the plans for criticism of Party personnel by non-Party elements. . . .

Yet even after the campaign was fully under way, important elements within the Party continued to drag their feet. In January [1966] a number of articles in the *People's Daily* continued to present the conservative point of view, albeit in a muted and somewhat disguised form, on both the organizational question and that of the basic-level cadres. Was the real problem, an article on January 1 asks, "how to serve" or was it rather "whom to serve"? Was the issue a question of reforming one's "world outlook" or was it really a matter of reaching a better understanding of the desires of the masses and then trying to meet them?[32] This issue was drawn even more sharply in an article on January 17 which suggested that the problem of revolutionizing the countryside could best be met by a continued emphasis on . . . on-the-spot inspection and supervision by higher-level cadres over an extended period of time: "Why don't we leap forward again? Is it a lack of enthusiasm and drive in 'leaping'? Or is it that we don't know how to 'leap'?

This is worth pondering." [33] This put the issue between "rationalization" and "revolutionary enthusiasm" baldly and in basic terms. Indeed, on February 13 the *People's Daily* was still reporting resistance on the part of Party committees to the idea of mass criticism in open meetings.[34] This divergence in views was probably never resolved in the spring of 1966, although the campaign was soon supplemented and then swallowed up by even more violent attacks on Party members in the educational, literary and artistic spheres.

The Campaigns

These attacks were directed above all at Party figures connected with the CCP propaganda apparatus who were accused of opposing the many campaigns initiated in the years following the Tenth Plenum. The campaigns were a major hallmark of the stepped-up attack on revisionism inaugurated at the plenum. Important Party figures, and above all Mao himself, were convinced that this effort was crucial if the Chinese revolution was to recover its momentum. But apparently a very large section of the Party itself was less concerned with this issue than with the more mundane tasks of building and modernizing China in the sense of acquiring wealth and power for the state. They were afraid that the campaigns, like the Great Leap Forward, would disrupt, rather than advance, this effort. With the conspicuous exception of the Socialist Education Campaign all the campaigns in this period had a rather short life span. All seemed to fade out without reaching a real climax and conclusion. None seems to have been very successful, nor was any campaign sharply focused or clearly defined in the classic pattern. The actual victims of these campaigns appear to have been relatively few.

Of the several campaigns, the Socialist Education Campaign was the most important. It was a multi-faceted affair; three separate campaigns appear to have been conducted simultaneously under its general label. One was primarily an educational campaign directed at the broad non-Party masses in the countryside. A second, the *Ssu-ch'ing* (four cleanups) campaign, was a rectification campaign directed against rural Party cadres. The third, the *wu fan* (five antis), apparently ran concurrently in the urban areas, and seems to have been directed at bourgeois attitudes and elements in the cities.[35] Under any label, these campaigns were, in contrast to the classic pattern, extremely leisurely affairs. The Socialist Education and *Ssu-ch'ing* efforts were meant to run for from seven to nine years;[36] as late as February 1966 the Central South Bureau of the Party implied that the campaigns were far from completed in that region.[37] It would appear that the slow pace was meant to ensure that production was not to be disrupted. . . .

A major aspect of the Socialist Education Campaign was, of course, its emphasis on ideological purity. This involved many spheres including literature and the arts and Party propaganda. Mao Tse-tung drew attention to shortcomings in these areas at the Tenth Plenum;[38] and indeed a decrease in strident propaganda and a thaw in the cultural sphere had been a notable feature of the period of relaxation. This "little hundred flowers" episode had been welcomed and encouraged by important Party leaders.[39] The permissive attitude it engendered was less sweeping and open than the more famous Hundred Flowers period of 1956–57, but like the earlier period, it eventually emboldened critics to express rather basic disagreement with CCP policies and with the Party itself. But unlike the earlier period, some of the critics were either close to or actually within the bosom of the CCP itself: the famous left-wing writer Pa Chin called the Party's cultural overseers "men armed with hoops and clubs";[40] Party literary czar Chou Yang in August 1962 presided over a conference at which numerous dissenting opinions were expressed;[41] Shao Ch'ün-lin, himself a lieutenant of Chou Yang, in calling for writing about "middle characters" who were not fully committed to communism, suggested that CCP ideology as yet represented no more than a thin veneer overlaying traditional Chinese attitudes and assumptions.[42]

Criticism of this sort was undoubtedly what Mao had in mind when he attacked the cultural trends of the early 1960s at the Tenth Plenum. But in fact this blast did not entirely bring an end to "revisionist" practices. In November 1963 a conference on Confucianism praised the sage as an example to be followed by modern Chinese;[43] in both 1963 and 1964 K'ang Cho, another lieutenant of Chou Yang, attacked Party policies during the Great Leap Forward.[44] In fact Mao himself felt it necessary to strike out again at writers and intellectuals in December 1963.[45] Nevertheless, there was no serious criticism of those who had been most outspoken during the period of relaxation until the middle of 1964. . . .

The Cultural Revolution has thrown up a mass of detail about foot-dragging and outright resistance to the highly politicized atmosphere of the post-Tenth Plenum period. Unlike some charges relating to earlier periods, such as the attacks on Chou Yang for the policies he pursued in the 1930s,[46] these accusations of more recent "crimes" cannot be dismissed out of hand. In fact it would appear that Mao's rather querulous criticism of the state of cultural affairs was in large measure ignored, that Party officials did in fact "distort, revise and block" Chairman Mao's directives in this area.[47] Much of this resistance was concentrated in the Party's propaganda apparatus, which not only bore primary responsibility in this area, but also was charged more generally with making the new policies felt and understood. This resistance was largely passive, a mere slowing down of machinery, a diversion of pressure toward limited and relatively unimportant targets.[48]

It should be emphasized that this resistance was *within* the Party. There was no quarrel with the idea that the CCP should exert ultimate control over the cultural and intellectual sphere; the question was one of methods and degree. The old-line cultural commissars have been accused of advocating a "literature and art of the whole people." [49] This concept involved a dilution of the ideological content of artistic creations to make them more palatable to the general public. . . . But it also implied contempt for a kind of simplistic conformity, for a narrow-minded anti-intellectualism that grew out of the sweeping attacks on revisionism. . . .

This attitude was not confined to those concerned with culture and propaganda. It was also evident in the educational area, where in 1964 the "socialist successors" campaign, coupled with a series of educational reforms sought to root out all vestiges of revisionism in the schools and among the young. Here again we touch on a theme close to Mao Tse-tung's heart. . . . The problem was real enough, and it was directly related to China's need to modernize. China needed an educated elite, but as this group was trained it started to *act* as an elite —a tendency reinforced by deep-seated Chinese traditions, but one that cut off the new experts from the "masses" they were expected to "serve." Moreover, those best qualified for extended higher education often came from bourgeois backgrounds.

It was not until 1964 that the "socialist successors" campaign, aimed at intensively indoctrinating students with proper revolutionary attitudes, was initiated. But like the other campaigns, the "socialist successors" campaign never developed full momentum. Students in specialized fields, particularly in the sciences, were apparently exempted from much of the ideological pressure inherent in the campaign.[50] A "half-study, half-work" program was instituted to emphasize to students the value of manual labor, and proper class credentials were demanded for admission to institutions of higher learning. But while the evidence is mixed it seems reasonably certain that students from bourgeois backgrounds continued to be admitted to major institutions of higher learning, particularly the more prestigious universities. And the administrators of major educational institutions—often Party officials of considerable importance—tended to react to pressure for ideological conformity much as their counterparts in the cultural field did.[51]

The "socialist successors" campaign was not restricted merely to the schools and universities. It also played an important part in the work of the Communist Youth League (CYL). Here also great emphasis was placed on ideological conformity in the years following the Tenth Plenum, and here also considerable stress was placed on class background as a necessary prerequisite for membership in the CYL. But it is interesting to note that by 1965 emphasis on ideological training had distinctly fallen away; and in that year large numbers of new members were admitted without regard to class background. . . .[52]

Still another kind of campaign was endemic in the years 1963–65.

These were the emulation campaigns, of which the first, the Lei Feng movement, is the best known. . . . The figures selected for emulation in 1963–65 were all members of the PLA. This fact suggests the importance of perhaps the most interesting campaign of all, the "learn from the PLA" movement. . . . As the title of the campaign itself suggests, the PLA in these years became the paradigm of the proper "communist work style." . . . But the army was not merely a symbol, nor was it merely a kind of "pilot project" where political techniques were tried out before they were applied to society in general. . . . Rather, the PLA was important to Mao, and became the ideal to emulate, precisely because the army made the techniques and methods advocated by the Chairman work, while the Party did not.

The "learn from the PLA" campaign was concerned primarily with inculcating ideological purity, uprooting self-seeking and corruption, and transforming people's "world outlook." In this respect the campaign did not differ greatly from those we have been discussing. But in asking that the country learn from the PLA, the implication was clear that the Party had not been doing its job properly. The implied rebuke was certainly not lost on the Party bureaucracy. Moreover, "learn from the PLA" was not merely an abstract slogan. In 1965 army officers, many probably recently retired, began to assume posts in the propaganda sphere—an area long specifically reserved for and jealously guarded by the Party bureaucracy.[53] Numbers of civilians in the industrial sector were sent to PLA schools for training[54] and, even more important, army officers began to assume positions normally held by civilians, particularly in the trade and finance system. This development was related to the establishment early in 1964 of a network of "political work departments" clearly modelled on the PLA's political commissar system, running parallel to the regular hierarchy of bureaus in nearly all areas of governmental activity. These networks had no administrative duties but were designed to revitalize political work within the governmental machinery and to eliminate corruption. Once again the implied rebuke to the Party bureaucrats was unmistakable.

Precisely for this reason, the new and expanded role of the army created resentment among Party functionaries. Here was another challenge to their prerogatives and privileges, and once again they engaged in passive resistance. . . . But this quite natural resentment of the new role of the PLA did not mean that the Party as a whole was united in opposition to the army. Most PLA officers and the entire senior level of the army hierarchy were of course themselves members of the CCP. Resentment was probably centered in those areas most threatened by the new state of affairs: entrenched middle-level officials and those Party functionaries at all levels concerned with propaganda, education, and Party organization. Moreover, the PLA was not "usurping" state and Party functions. Its role was strictly political, not administrative, and its job was to supplement, rather than supplant, Party activity. And at all times the *Liberation Army Daily* made it clear that the PLA remained the "tool" of the Party.[55]

Nevertheless, many Party officials were undoubtedly aware of certain major difficulties in attempting to apply the methods of the military to the tasks of the Party. . . . Party officials were apparently unwilling to embrace fully the simplistic slogans of the campaigns or the methodology endorsed by the PLA. The result was a subtle sabotage of the campaigns themselves and continued stagnation within the Party. . . .

Independent Kingdoms

CCP literature both before and after 1949 is replete with denunciations of individuals and unnamed "certain comrades" who have attempted to establish "independent kingdoms" capable of resisting the general will of the Party. The Kao Kang case is merely the most conspicuous example of a much wider tendency, but Kao was nevertheless something of an exception because he was a member of the top Party leadership—a leadership that has generally been united in implementing Party decisions despite occasionally vigorous debates before the decision was actually taken. There is, however, some evidence that this cohesion began to show signs of strain in the summer of 1958.[56] And it was shortly after this that Mao Tse-tung, at the Wuhan Plenum of the Central Committee which endorsed the first retreat from the commune concept and halted urban communization, resigned as Chairman of the People's Republic of China. There is no evidence that Mao was forced to resign as the result of concerted pressure on the part of his colleagues in the Central Committee; rather, it seems likely that this was very largely a co-operative effort, in which Mao acquiesced, to disassociate the supreme leader from a set of policies that were already proving very difficult to apply in practice. . . .

Mao's resignation tended to formalize a distinction between "first line" and "second line" positions in the top leadership of the Party (with Mao in the "second line"), which the Chairman now claims had long existed. . . .[57] After the high tide of the Great Leap Mao did in fact play a less active and immediate role in the day-to-day affairs of Party and state, although his voice appears to have been decisive when he chose to intervene in policy debates. Indeed, the record presented by his present supporters seems to indicate that the Chairman very largely endorsed decisions made by others, especially during the period of relaxation, rather than actually participating in the discussions at which those decisions were reached.[58] At times it would appear that he was largely unaware of the content of major decisions issued in the name of the Central Committee. . . .

Indeed, as it has been frequently remarked, the cult of Mao itself fell on hard times at the height of the period of relaxation. The name of the supreme leader was invoked far less often, and with less ecstasy, than during the Great Leap Forward or in the period following the Tenth Plenum. . . .

In retreating from active participation in the daily formulation and implementation of policy after [1958], Mao to a considerable degree lost control of the Party machine. Moreover, the Chairman's advanced age and failing health of itself was bound eventually to affect his capacity for sustained work. In any event, as Mao ceased to oversee carefully and intimately the daily tasks of governing China, power at the highest levels of the Party tended to fragment and to gravitate into hands other than his. One repository of this fragmented power was undoubtedly Liu Shao-ch'i, who as the heir apparent, senior Vice-Chairman of the Party, and head of state, could speak with very great authority on the widest range of issues. Another was, quite naturally, the Party Secretariat, and in particular the Secretary General, Teng Hsiao-p'ing, as well as those secretaries, such as P'eng Chen, Lo Jui-ch'ing and Lu Ting-yi, whose responsibilities gave them an enormous and commanding voice in specific areas or "systems" within the Party machine. To a degree this situation was always present, if only in embryo; it became a crucial factor as major differences appeared between Mao and his supporters and those who felt the Maoist policies to be unwise. Once these differences had solidified Mao found it impossible to reassert his dominance in areas controlled by his opponents despite formal abolition of the distinction between the "first line" and "second line."

But this situation did not arise in full-blown form overnight; it developed gradually. Indeed, it seems possible that the participants in the tug-of-war at the top of the Party, including Mao himself, were themselves not fully aware how much their much varying approaches to problems had come to differ. For Mao's "opponents" did not oppose him directly. They mouthed the same slogans he advocated; they "waved the red flag to oppose the red flag." Where Mao called for arousing the masses, they proposed limits and controls; where Mao asked for criticism of the Party from without they suggested criticism within prescribed Party channels; where Mao called for revolution in education they noted the importance of expertise—but always in terms very similar to those used by Mao and his supporters. Nor need we suppose that this "opposition" was united among itself, for some were undoubtedly concerned with limiting the Maoist policies in one area, while others were more concerned with another. In general, however, where Mao advocated boldness, these "opponents" suggested caution. But for Mao caution itself was revisionist. Since both sides said very nearly the same thing, it required very careful examination of the actual implementation of policy to discover if the intent of that policy was in fact being thwarted. It was for this reason that from 1964 on—especially in PLA propaganda—emphasis was so heavily placed on the importance of the application of the thought of Mao Tse-tung "in practice." . . .

The summer of 1964 in fact might be considered a watershed in the post-Tenth Plenum Period. As we have seen, anti-revisionist doctrines were intensified in a number of areas. But in many respects this "revolutionary surge" was "leftist in form, but rightist in content," as recent propaganda has so stridently insisted. Education was only partly reformed; culture only slightly proletarianized; peasants were "aroused" only under restrictive Party supervision. Mao could no longer be unaware of the seriousness of the situation: revisionism had wormed its way into the Party Central itself. Mao's understanding of this situation might explain why no new Central Committee plenum was called at this time to deal with so serious a problem. In fact it seems likely that Mao simply did not have the votes to make his will prevail at such a plenum. . . .

Under these circumstances, at a Central Committee meeting in September [1965] Mao once again renewed the attack,[59] concentrating on the cultural sphere. . . . The issue of Mao's own position in the Party had been raised directly. From this departure we can date the real beginning of the Cultural Revolution. . . .

1. See *Survey of the China Mainland Press (SCMP)* (Hong Kong: U.S. Consulate-General), No. 3761, p. 3.

2. James R. Townsend, *Political Participation in Communist China* (Berkeley, Calif.: University of California Press, 1967), p. 192.

3. For evidence see *Collection of Documents Seized in Guerrilla Attack on Lien-Chiang, Fukien* (Taipei: Ministry of Defense, 1964) (Lien-Chiang Documents; in Chinese), p. 9.

4. Liu Shao-ch'i, "Speech on the 40th Anniversary of the CCP," in *Current Background (CB)* (Hong Kong: U.S. Consulate-General), No. 655, p. 1.

5. For an excellent discussion see Ezra Vogel, "From Revolutionary to Semi-Bureaucrat: the 'Regularisation' of Cadres," *The China Quarterly*, No. 29 (January–March 1967), p. 36.

6. *Ibid.*, p. 39.

7. Franz Schurmann, *Ideology and Organization in Communist China* (Berkeley, Cal.: University of California Press, 1966), p. 303.

8. *People's Daily*, October 31, 1960, in *SCMP*, No. 2379, p. 4.

9. *Nan-fang Daily*, November 26, 1960, in *SCMP*, No. 2416, p. 1.

10. *Ibid.*

11. *Nan-fang Daily*, October 7, 1960, in *SCMP*, No. 2380, p. 12.

12. *People's Daily*, March 4, 1961, in *SCMP*, No. 2455, p. 10.

13. *Nan-fang Daily*, October 7, 1960.

14. Liu Shao-ch'i, "Self-Criticism," *Mainichi Shimbun*, January 28, 1967.

15. *Ibid.*

16. The following discussion draws on materials from the *Lien-Chiang Documents, op. cit.*

17. *Ibid.,* p. 233.

18. *Ibid.*

19. *Ibid.,* p. 198.

20. *Ibid.,* p. 229.

21. *Ibid.*

22. *People's Daily,* July 21, 1961, in *SCMP*, No. 2550, p. 2.

23. *People's Daily,* October 31, 1960, in *SCMP*, No. 2379, p. 1.

24. *Nan-fang Daily,* November 26, 1960.

25. Paul Cocks, "The Historical and Institutional Role of the Party Control Commission in the CCP," manuscript in Harvard East Asian Research Center Library, pp. 32–41.

26. *Nan-fang Daily,* October 11, 1961, in *SCMP*, No. 2602, p. 5.

27. *Nan-fang Daily,* April 4, 1962, in *SCMP*, No. 2770, p. 3.

28. *Hung Ch'i (Red Flag)* July 16, 1962, in *Selections from China Mainland Magazines (SCMM)* (Hong Kong: U.S. Consulate-General), No. 326, p. 11.

29. *People's Daily,* September 20, 1961, in *SCMP*, No. 2591, p. 1.

30. *CB*, No. 691, p. 1.

31. *Hung Wei Pao* (Canton), October 4, 1966, in *SCMP*, No. 3804, p. 4.

32. "Cadres Both Old and New Must Be Educated Anew," in *SCMP*, No. 3616, p. 4.

33. "The 'Leap,' Something to be Learned," in *SCMP*, No. 3628, pp. 7–8.

34. "Correctly Sum Up Historical Experience, Wipe Out Individualistic Thoughts," in *SCMP*, No. 3648, p. 8.

35. "23 Articles," in R. Baum and F. C. Teiwes, *Ssu-ch'ing: The Socialist Education Movement of 1962–66* (Berkeley: Center for Chinese Studies, 1968), Appendix F, section 3.

36. *Ibid.,* sec. 11.

37. *Yang-ch'eng Wan-pao,* Canton, February 1, 1966, in *SCMP*, No. 3635, p. 1.

38. Philip Bridgham, "Mao's Cultural Revolution: Origin and Development" [see selection 2, above—Ed.].

39. See for example the speech by Ch'en Yi to the Peking Institute of Higher Learning in *Kuang-ming Daily,* September 3, 1961.

40. Shanghai *Wen-hsüeh,* No. 5, 1962.

41. *Yang-ch'eng Wan-pao,* Canton, July 17, 1966, in *SCMP*, No. 3750, p. 1.

42. *Wen-yi Pao,* No. 8/9, 1964.

43. *People's Daily,* January 10, 1967, in *SCMP*, No. 3863, p. 1.

44. *Yang-ch'eng Wan-pao,* July 17, 1966.

45. *New China News Agency (NCNA)*, May 27, 1967, in *SCMP*, No. 3905, p. 1.

46. See Merle Goldman, "The Fall of Chou Yang," *The China Quarterly,* No. 27 (July–September 1966), p. 132.

47. *NCNA*, May 27, 1967, in *SCMP*, No. 3950, p. 14.

48. *Red Flag,* July 1964, treats the "reform" of the Peking opera as an event of major significance. That "victory" in this limited sphere should be regarded as a major achievement is in itself a measure of the resistance within the Party.

49. *Red Flag,* May 1967.

50. Maurice Kelly, "The Making of an Intellectual," *Current Scene*, IV, No. 19, p. 11.

51. *Ibid.*

52. *China News Analysis*, No. 633, p. 2.

53. John Gittings, *The Role of the Chinese Army* (Oxford: Oxford University Press, 1967), p. 256.

54. *Ibid.*, p. 257.

55. "Politics Command Military Affairs, Politics Command Everything," in *SCMP*, No. 3644, p. 6.

56. *Communist China 1955–1959: Policy Documents with Analysis* (Cambridge, Mass.: Harvard University Press, 1965), pp. 38–42.

57. For a report of Mao's speech to an October 1966 meeting of the Central Committee, see *Yomiuri*, January 7, 1967.

58. See Liu, "Self-Criticism," *op. cit.*

59. Bridgham, *loc. cit.*

PART TWO

Perspectives on the Origins and Meaning of the Cultural Revolution

It is obviously much easier to describe the sequences of events which preceded—and culminated in—China's Cultural Revolution than it is to lend a coherent analytic interpretation to these events. In Part I the antecedents of the Cultural Revolution were traced to a series of economic, political, and organizational crises which arose in China in the half decade following the retreat from the Great Leap Forward. In Part II we shall be concerned with probing the causal links between these crises and the actual initiation of the Cultural Revolution. The common question to which five Western analysts of Chinese politics address themselves in this section is, "What was the Cultural Revolution really about?"

There is no single, universally shared consensus on the answer to this question. Broadly speaking, five main schools of thought have emerged. One such school, represented here by Franz Michael (pp. 52–59), sees the Cultural Revolution as a classical Machiavellian struggle for political power among the organized supporters and opponents of Chairman Mao Tse-tung. According to this view, the upheavals of 1966–68 had their origin in Mao's attempt to recapture power from Party "moderates" who had successfully wrested control of the CCP from him in the aftermath of the Great Leap.

A second school of thought, represented here by self-confirmed Maoist Gerald Tannenbaum (pp. 60–66), views the Cultural Revolution within a uniquely cultural context as a "class struggle" between the respective adherents of the "proletarian" and "bourgeois" world outlooks. In this view, the crisis of 1966–68 was occasioned by Mao's decision to launch a counter-attack against a group of firmly entrenched "bourgeois authorities" in China's literary, educational, artistic, and propaganda circles.

A third school, represented here by Richard Baum (pp. 67–77), regards the Cultural Revolution as a last-ditch attempt by the Maoists to revive and revitalize the CCP's puritanical ideological values in a postrevolutionary era characterized by the increasing secularization of Chinese society and by a consequent "erosion of ideology." In this interpretation, the main lines of conflict in China are seen to reside in the mutually contradictory imperatives of Maoism and modernization ("red" and "expert"). It is suggested that the Maoist vision of the "good" ("red") society may be fundamentally incompatible with the

49

social and economic requirements of the "modern" ("expert") society. A fourth school, represented here by Jack Grey (pp. 78–87), holds that the Cultural Revolution was primarily a contest for hegemony between the rival strategies for economic development put forward in the late 1950s and early 1960s by Mao Tse-tung and Liu Shao-ch'i, respectively. Mao, it is argued, advocated the simultaneous, balanced growth of industry and agriculture, decentralized administration of the economy, and widespread popular participation in economic planning and management. Liu, on the other hand, reportedly gave high priority to heavy industrial development, centralized administration, and strict Party control over planning and management. In this view, China's recent upheaval is regarded first and foremost as a manifestation of economic conflict.

Finally, a fifth school of thought, represented here by Robert Jay Lifton (pp. 88–94), sees the Cultural Revolution as symptomatic of a psychological quest for immortality on the part of China's aging leader, Mao Tse-tung. Mao is pictured as a man who, in his declining years, has become obsessed with the idea of establishing an undying spiritual legacy for future generations of Chinese leaders. And the Cultural Revolution, with its accent on youth and its near-hysterical glorification of the myth of Maoist infallibility, is thus viewed as a form of symbolic rebirth of the man and his revolution.

These five schools of thought—or perspectives—on the origins and meaning of the Cultural Revolution are by no means either wholly discrete or mutually exclusive. The concept of ideological renewal, for example, occupies a prominent (though subordinate) position in both the power struggle and psychic immortality schools, while the element of economic conflict can be readily discerned within each of the four remaining schools. Nevertheless, each of these schools offers a rather unique outlook on the rank-order—or "mix"—of the various factors that went into the making of the Cultural Revolution. Each, therefore, leads to a somewhat different conclusion on the essential nature and significance of the revolution.

It might be argued that yet a sixth school of thought exists, one that stresses the critical importance of foreign policy and military defense-related issues and cleavages in the genesis of the Cultural Revolution. (Here the conflicting perspectives of various Chinese leaders on such issues as the Sino-Soviet dispute, China's role in the Vietnam War, and the strategic requirements of Chinese national security are the three most frequently mentioned factors.) While it is undoubtedly true that fundamental questions of foreign policy and military strategy were seriously and acrimoniously debated within China on the eve of the Cultural Revolution (witness the Maoist purge of Army Chief-of-Staff Lo Jui-ch'ing in the winter of 1965–66), no serious scholar has yet suggested that such debates—or the intra-Party cleavages exposed by such debates—constituted the primary *raison d'être* of the subsequent upheaval in China. For this reason, foreign policy and military strategy are not treated as separate and distinct explanatory perspectives.

We are left with one important question. If each of the five schools of thought represented in this section has something to recommend it, then which of them is to be considered as the most valid, the most faithful reflection of reality? Happily for us, this is a moot point. For each of the five perspectives—political, cultural, ideological, economic, and psychological—is both logically and empirically defensible; and all, moreover, contain sufficient common elements so as not to be mutually exclusive or incompatible. Hence, our answer to the question of validity must be that *all* are substantially valid, since their differences lie more in the areas of emphasis and perspective than in any fundamental analytic contradictoriness. *De gustabus non est disputandum.*

THE STRUGGLE FOR POWER

Franz Michael

What is going on in China today is clearly a power struggle between the rival exponents of what are in essence two divergent Communist lines: one representing a pragmatic, rational communism moving forward or retreating within the confines of stages of development as hitherto understood by most Communist leaderships; the other, Mao's radical, utopian communism, which preaches the attainment of the same Communist goals by means of a short cut replacing economic and political rationality with blind belief in doctrine and reliance on force and the power of human will. This battle for supremacy began in 1958 when Mao Tse-tung abandoned all previously accepted principles of Communist development and started the Great Leap Forward as an all-out effort to achieve China's rapid advance toward communism. . . .

This departure from previous Communist practice was designed as much to advance China's position within the Communist world as to speed up the revolution at home. . . . The Great Leap Forward and the commune system of 1958 were designed not only to accomplish the rapid communization of China, but also, in the fantastic Chinese boasts of the time, to enable her to "bypass the Soviet Union on the way to communism."

We know today that this double-edged attack was virtually the product of Mao's own lone-handed scheming, and that it was forced upon a reluctant and to some extent divided Chinese Communist Party leadership. In three meetings called between December 1957 and March 1958 at Hangchow, Nanning and Chengtu, Mao had informed a group of Party leaders of his plans for the Great Leap Forward, adding at the third meeting the proposal to set up the commune system.[1] Mao's plans, however, immediately encountered opposition, the most outspoken objections coming, we are told, from the top military leaders. Marshal P'eng Teh-huai, a leading military member of the Politburo and Minister of Defense, supported by Huang K'o-cheng, Chief of Staff of the People's Liberation Army (PLA), are understood to have strongly resisted Mao's proposals with the argument that they were economically unfeasible and contrary to establish Communist concepts of staged development. Other Party leaders, however, did not openly voice their opposition, and Mao went ahead with his program without seeking any

Franz Michael, "The Struggle for Power," *Problems of Communism* 16, no. 3 (May–June 1967): 12–21. Reprinted by permission of the publisher.

formal endorsement by the official Party organs. Only in August 1958 was the new policy officially adopted by an enlarged Politburo meeting at Peitaiho, by which time the commune movement was already spreading over the country.

Rise of the Opposition

Mao's Great Leap Forward and the commune system proved catastrophic failures, causing famine and economic disaster in China. This disaster in turn led the more rational of China's leaders to come to the fore in order to salvage the situation. Thus, what had started as Mao's challenge to the Soviet leaders resulted in the reluctant emergence of an internal opposition to Mao.

The conflict began with a serious defeat for Mao. The failure of the Great Leap and the communes quickly became apparent, and the reaction set in at the end of 1958. On December 10, a Central Committee meeting decided on an initial retreat from the commune system. The exorbitant claims of the summer were abandoned. No longer were the communes said to be ushering in the first stage of communism. Payment was to be, in the main, according to work and in cash instead of according to need and in kind; some of the peasants' private property was restored; and families were again permitted to live together.

At the same time, however, another, even more crucial decision was officially announced: Mao Tse-tung—the author of the utopian Great Leap communes program—was stepping down from his post as Chairman of the Republic. As Mao had held this highest government position since the founding of the Communist regime in 1949, his resignation inevitably raised questions. The official explanation given was that Mao wished to relinquish his duties as chief of state in order that he might devote all his time to leadership of the Party, of which he remained Chairman. Nevertheless, it was widely suspected abroad even then that Mao's surrender of the chairmanship of the Republic was not voluntary, that it represented a demotion, and that it occurred as a result of strong pressures from within the Party leadership.[2]

Disclosures recently made by Mao's supporters in the Great Proletarian Cultural Revolution tend to confirm these suppositions and to show that Mao did in fact suffer a drastic loss of personal power in December 1958. Red Guard wall posters put on display in Peking in early January 1967 quoted Mao as having told the Party Central Committee in October 1966 with regard to his 1958 removal as Chairman of the Republic: "I was dissatisfied with the decision, but I could do nothing about it." The posters further quoted Mao as stating that on this occasion the opposition, headed by the newly-designated Chairman of the Republic, Liu Shao-ch'i, and Party Secretary-General Teng Hsiao-p'ing, "treated me as if I were their dead parent at a funeral" and thereafter "never bothered to consult me on vital matters." [3]

It may well be that Mao's colleagues were influenced by more than just their concern for the stability of Chinese development. There is no reason to exclude the possibility that Khrushchev, who had reacted strongly to the challenge to Soviet primacy implied in the Great Leap and commune programs, may have exerted pressure in China on the side of the opposition. . . .

There is strong evidence for believing that Khrushchev had a hand in the new assault on Mao's policies that developed in the summer of 1959. This attack was led by Defense Minister Marshal P'eng Teh-huai, who reportedly had already expressed opposition to Mao's Great Leap policy when it was first discussed the year before. At the Central Committee meeting at Lushan in August 1959, P'eng again attacked this policy and its effects on the army, which Mao wanted to use as a political weapon to put pressure on the communes. In P'eng's view, the army should remain a professional force and should rely on the nuclear cover and military equipment provided by China's Soviet ally. The attack was mounted with the apparent foreknowledge of Khrushchev, whom P'eng had met in the Crimea prior to the Central Committee meeting, and seems to have been directed not merely against Mao's policies but against his very position of leadership. According to an authoritative study of the Lushan proceedings, Mao answered the threat against him with an emotional speech in which he declared that if the army deserted him he would go back to the villages, recruit another army, and fight all over again. . . .[4]

At the Lushan meeting, Mao managed in the end to carry the day when a majority of the Central Committee stood by him. P'eng Teh-huai and Army Chief of Staff Huang K'o-cheng were purged, and with them fell some forty other high-ranking military figures and a number of lesser Party leaders. Mao not only won the fight but gained—in the newly purged army under the leadership of Lin Piao (who became Defense Minister)—an instrument for his attempt to regain full power.

P'eng's failure and Mao's victory also severed the link between Khrushchev and the Chinese opposition to Mao. Those Party leaders who were inwardly opposed to Mao's reckless internal policies nevertheless stood by him in his crucial fight against the army opposition backed by Khrushchev, and from then on the opposition at home parted ways with the opposition abroad—at least for the time being and for the official record.

Mao's Program Dismantled

But the internal battle over Mao's policy continued. Removed from practical control of state affairs, Mao had to stand passively by as, step by step, his grandiose programs were dismantled. His successor as Chairman of the Republic, Liu Shao-ch'i—who is regarded today as Mao's chief opponent in the Party leadership—was a reluctant dragon who never directly attacked Mao's prestige or claim to leadership. But, without abandoning its slogans, Liu led the retreat from Mao's extreme programs through a series of practical measures. . . .

In January 1961, Liu issued a "12-point emergency directive regarding rural work," which restored the peasants' right to cultivate private plots and to sell their produce in "free" markets, and which stipulated that labor should be given more rest than they had been allowed under the frenzied mobilization of the Great Leap Forward.[5] In the same month, the Central Committee endorsed a so-called "8-character charter" designed to adjust the economy to the growing crisis, which by that time had reached extreme proportions.[6] In May 1961, Liu issued a number of regulations that signified a general retreat from Mao's 1958 policies. Sixty articles provided for a drastic decentralization of the communes, restoring production authority to the smaller-size collectives; and seventy dealt with the reestablishment of normal procedures in industry. . . .[7]

The curtailment of [Mao's] political power at home after 1958 prevented him from continuing to press the radical program of communization which he hoped would justify his claim to supreme leadership of the Marxist-Leninist world movement. If, in Mao's view, his domestic program was related to his claim for world leadership, the question urgently arises as to the connection, if any, between Mao's external and internal opposition, all indiscriminately denounced as "revisionists" by Mao and his followers.

Moscow and the Chinese Opposition

What contact or cooperation has there been between the Soviets and Mao's domestic opposition? That there was some connection at the beginning of the internal and external conflict has already been indicated. Mao's demotion in 1958 and P'eng Teh-huai's attack on Mao in 1959 were, at least in some ways, related to the Soviet opposition to Mao's line. But after Mao had survived P'eng's challenge to his position and continued in Party control—though reduced in political power—the other Party leaders seem to have closed ranks behind him, at least vis-à-vis Moscow. Of those Chinese leaders recently affected by Mao's purge, only a very few are on record as having opposed the conflict with Moscow. Aside from some minor figures, the only important victim of the current purge who can be regarded as having leaned toward Moscow is Lo Jui-ch'ing. (Although Lo became Army Chief of Staff after the purge of 1959 and was therefore presumably loyal to Mao, there are at least some indications that he may later have come to view the conflict with Moscow as prejudicial to the Chinese military.[8]) Mao's principal opponents within the Party leadership, Liu Shao-ch'i and Teng Hsiao-p'ing, on the other hand, are certainly on record as having attacked Soviet "revisionism" as bitterly as Mao himself.[9] If Liu and Teng, on the one hand, and the Soviet leaders, on the other, were on common ground in opposing Mao's utopianism, why has there been no sign of cooperation between them, but rather hostility?

Two explanations seem possible. One is that even if Liu and Teng and their followers were opposed to the recklessness of Mao's domestic policies, their organizational solidarity and patriotism impelled them to support him once he was under fire from Moscow. . . .

Another possible explanation of the absence of any overt rapport between Mao's Chinese opponents and Moscow could be that, if such collusion did exist, it would obviously have been foolhardy and dangerous to let it become known publicly; rather, it would have been all the more necessary for the Chinese oppositionists to pay lip service to the doctrinal attacks against their actual or potential supporters in Moscow. The problem at hand was to keep Mao from rocking the boat at home. An open division within China would endanger not only Mao's opponents but also the very stability of Party rule, as indeed it has in the present struggle.

The absence of any known collusion between Mao's chief opponents and Moscow has not, however, deterred Mao's supporters in the current internal struggle from voicing such accusations against the opposition. Recent Red Guard wall posters have accused by name General Yang Shang-k'un, a member of the Central Party Secretariat; Lu Ting-yi, purged chief of the Party's Propaganda Department; P'eng Chen, purged Politburo member and Peking Party First Secretary; Lo Jui-ch'ing, purged Army Chief of Staff; and finally the son of Liu Shao-ch'i, of having conspired with the Soviet Ambassador in Peking. Yang Shang-k'un was even accused of "placing listening devices behind Chairman Mao's back and handing secret information to the Soviet Ambassador." [10] True or not, this accusation probably reflects Mao's conviction that his battle against "revisionism" both in Moscow and at home is one and the same. . . .

Mao's Counterattack

After weathering the attack from P'eng Teh-huai and his associates at the Central Committee meeting in the summer of 1959, Mao began his comeback by building up the myth of his ideological leadership. In the years immediately after destalinization, his personal role had been less emphasized in Chinese Party pronouncements in line with the general Communist tendency to stress collective leadership. But, by the end of 1959, Mao's personality cult was again on the rise, eventually coming to surpass anything that Stalin, or for that matter Hitler, had practiced at the height of their power. Mao became not only the "greatest Marxist-Leninist theorist of the epoch" but also the prophet in whose writings could be found the answer to all problems. . . .

Why did the opposition in China tolerate and even participate in this cult of worship, which to sophisticated Chinese must have been rather nauseating? The fact is—as the Maoists themselves have acknowledged—that there were many who did not accept the cult and even tried to combat it in subtle and devious ways. In China, political attacks have traditionally been carried out on several levels and through resort to hidden meanings and allusions. Satire, symbolism, and double meanings have been used to express ridicule or opposition which, if stated directly, would not only appear crude but would also be dangerous for the speaker or writer. Careful students of Chinese Communist literature have felt for some time that writings which ostensibly catered to the adulation of Mao were composed with tongue in cheek by authors known for their skill in political satire.[11] Hence, it is not surprising that Mao's current drive to stamp out the opposition began in late 1965 with accusations against the writers and key figures of the Wu Han group,[12] and later was extended to editors of newspapers and propaganda officials—all accused of using or permitting the use of symbolism and allegory in plays and essays to denigrate Chairman Mao's thought. If many of these charges were trumped up, some unquestionably contained a measure of truth.

But the principal political leaders of the opposition—Liu Shao-ch'i, Teng Hsiao-p'ing and others—played along with the Mao cult, at least on the surface. To indulge Mao's appetite for personal glorification may well have appeared to them a minor concession as long as they could keep practical matters of policy in their own hands.[13] Yet it was precisely this hero cult that Mao used as a major weapon for his reconquest of power. Without it Mao could scarcely have exploited the authority of his "thought" to revive the radical utopian revolution of the Great Leap, with the added feature of a Cultural Revolution that was to eliminate all remnants of the past and bring China close to the intellectual climate and institutional setting of the Communist millennium. . . .

Situation and Outlook

Looking back over the course of events in Communist China since 1958, the present spectacle of madness and chaos appears as the natural climax to Mao's losing battle to impose his brand of radical, utopian communism at home and to assert his claim to world Communist leadership abroad. Having built up his power in China as a trained Communist who knew better than his rivals how to achieve Communist ideological goals in the context of Chinese conditions, Mao eventually became a maverick in his own Party and in the world Communist movement. In his last stand, he had to rely on his own sycophantic court clique, on his presumably loyal but politically ambitious followers in the army leadership, and on the excitable young members of the Red Guard, who represent the roughest elements of the adolescent and post-adolescent student youth.[14] Against Mao stood some of the Party's most seasoned leaders, men who had been his close associates through decades of revolutionary struggle, and who had sought after the Communist victory of 1949 to keep China on a reasonable course of socialist development but were forced by Mao's own scheming into a position of resistance that finally led to open conflict.

Mao's battle appears, then, as the desperate comeback attempt of an aging and mentally declining man who could not accept the loss of his real political power in China and the defeat of his grandiose ambitions for world Communist leadership. Rather, he would himself lead the attack to tear down the very structure of which he had been the chief architect. Even if his utopian schemes of Communist development at first seemed to produce results, they could scarcely support, in the long run, a working form of government, Communist or any other. . . .

1. This resumé of developments within the CCP in 1957–58 is based mainly on an article written by Ting Wang, a former CCP official now living in Hong Kong, and published in the independent Hong Kong Chinese-language newspaper *Ming Pao* (Oct. 23–24, 1966) under the title "*I-chiu-liu-i nien ti chung-kung tang-nei chan cheng*" (The Communist Internal Party Struggle of 1961). The author, who had personal knowledge of the events described, corroborated the substance of his published account in a personal interview with the present writer. The account is also consistent with what was officially reported at the time concerning Mao's whereabouts and activities.

2. See Franz Michael, "Khrushchev's Disloyal Opposition: Structural Change and Power Struggle in the Communist Bloc," *Orbis* (Philadelphia), Spring 1963, pp. 64–65.

3. Tokyo dispatches published in *The New York Times*, Jan. 6, 1967 (pp. 1–2), based on Japanese press correspondents' reports from Peking.

4. See David A. Charles, "The Dismissal of Marshal P'eng Teh-huai," *The China Quarterly* (London), Oct.–Dec. 1961.

5. See Ting Wang, *loc. cit.;* also *Kung Fei "Jen-min Kung-she" Tzu-liao Ch'uan-chi* (Taipei), Vol. V, October 1961.

6. The charter stressed the need to increase agricultural production and outlined a "three-level" (commune, production brigade, and production team) ownership system for the communes. See Ting Wang, *loc. cit.*, and *Peking Review*, Jan. 27, 1961, pp. 3–5.

7. Ting Wang, *loc. cit.*

8. See article by Lo Jui-ch'ing, "Carry the Struggle Against the US Imperialists Through to the End in Memory of the Victory over the German Fascists," in *Hung-ch'i* (Peking), May 10, 1965; also, Lo's statement at the Chinese People's Republic anniversary celebrations on October 1, 1965.

9. It should be noted, however, that Liu, at a Peking rally on July 22, 1966, in support of the Vietnamese Communists, made a speech in which, unlike all the other speakers, he omitted any attack on Soviet "revisionism." See *Jen-min Jih-pao*, July 22, 1966; *Peking Review*, July 29, 1966, p. 6.

10. See story in *The Washington Post,* Jan. 20, 1967 (p. 1), citing Reuters and Yugoslav news agency reports.

11. E.g., Vincent Shih, "Satire in Communist Literature," unpublished manuscript scheduled to appear in book form in 1967 or 1968.

12. Yao Wen-yüan, "On Hai Jui Dismissed From Office," *Wen Hui Pao* (Shanghai), Nov. 10, 1965; also, *Peking Review,* No. 18, pp. 5–10. For details of the attacks on Wu Han, Teng T'o, and others, see Harry Gelman, "Mao and the Permanent Purge," *Problems of Communism,* November–December 1966.

13. It may be noted that Liu, though never the object of a personality cult such as that built up around Mao, nevertheless enjoyed a visible share of personal popularity. According to information received from foreign eye-witnesses, cheers for "Chairman Liu" were interspersed with those for "Chairman Mao" at the CPR anniversary celebrations in Peking on Oct. 1, 1965, and eye-witnesses also saw placards for Liu as well as for Mao in a procession at Soochow as late as September 1966.

14. See *China News Analysis* (Hong Kong), No. 26, Nov. 11, 1966.

CHINA'S CULTURAL REVOLUTION: WHY IT HAD TO HAPPEN

Gerald Tannenbaum

. . . Why is a *cultural* revolution necessary to save and propel forward the new society? Chairman Mao has said: "It must not be assumed that the new system can be completely consolidated the moment it is established, for that is impossible. It has to be consolidated step by step. To achieve its ultimate consolidation, it is necessary . . . to carry on constant and arduous socialist revolutionary struggles . . . on the political and ideological fronts." Here Chairman Mao is referring to culture, because included within this general term are ideology, social thought, world outlook, customs and habits, political points of view as expressed through art, films, theatre, dance, fine arts, education, literature and other departments which compose the superstructure of society.

The fact is that for seventeen years after Liberation, particularly in the field of culture, Chairman Mao's line of thought was not carried out and encountered stubborn resistance. Through his lieutenants, Liu Shao-ch'i was able to make the cultural sphere his bastion, from which he launched incessant attacks against the dictatorship of the proletariat. . . .

Base and Superstructure

Going to the crux of the problem, what was in question was the relationship between the economic base and the [cultural] superstructure. The decisive element is that once the economic base has undergone a fundamental change, such as it had in China, the superstructure must follow course. If the base is new but the culture remains as of old, sooner or later it will subvert the base. The old culture will be working for the restoration of the old relations of production. It sprang into being to serve the former ruling classes; it will continue to serve them if given the chance, even under the conditions where the economic base has been changed. Culture must catch up with the new economic base. If it does not, it will obstruct the further development of the socialist economy, and in the end destroy it. Therefore, the carrying out of the

Gerald Tannenbaum, "China's Cultural Revolution: Why It Had to Happen," *The Great Proletarian Revolution: What Really Did Happen in China* (Eastern Horizon Press, 1969), pp. 1-27.

Great Proletarian Cultural Revolution is essential in determining whether or not the socialist revolution can be maintained, whether or not it can be advanced. Not only cultural questions are involved, but life and death political questions. This accounts for the prolonged nature of the struggle, its heat and depth. Two ways of life are locked in mortal combat.

Bourgeois in Arts

The opponents of Chairman Mao, the Party and socialism were well entrenched in Chinese culture. . . . From the very beginning after Liberation there was an acrimonious contest in all the cultural fields between the feudal and bourgeois ideology of these people and the proletarian ideology which had come out of the old Liberated Areas, nurtured in the War of Resistance against Japan and the War of Liberation and which was in conformity with Chairman Mao's directives issued in his famous "Talks at the Yenan Forum on Art and Literature" (May 1942). The old ideology still had great strength and its proponents were ever making a concerted effort to attain the upper hand. This was especially evident during the three difficult years (1959–61) when China faced an incredible succession of natural disasters and the culpability of the Soviet Union which suddenly withdrew its experts and tore up hundreds of contracts, at the same time demanding the repayment of loans from the Korean War and other outstanding debts, some dating back to Czarist times! This fearful pressure was purposely applied just at the moment when the right opportunists inside the Party led by P'eng Teh-huai mounted an attack against Chairman Mao Tse-tung at the Lushan Meeting of the Party Central Committee in 1959. Supported by Liu Shao-ch'i, P'eng and his cohorts were shouting for Chairman Mao to relinquish his top Party post and let them take over. This assault was defeated and P'eng was removed as Minister of Defense, but the bourgeois headquarters behind him was not rooted out and it then mobilized all its forces in the sphere of culture to continue the attack against the proletarian line and to fight for the rehabilitation of P'eng. During these years all sorts of feudal and capitalist ideas held sway on the stage, screen and in the publications of China. It was then that the Peking opera *Hai Jui Dismissed from Office* appeared, written by Wu Han, a bourgeois historian who had crawled into the Party. This was a thinly disguised exposition berating Chairman Mao for ousting P'eng Teh-huai, and as Chairman Mao later pointed out, the play was a political dissertation against the Party and socialism, because the emphasis was on "dismissal from office," which spoke for the line of the bourgeois headquarters. This sudden rash of activity with its reactionary content aroused the concern of some people at that time, but Chairman Mao saw it as a natural phenomenon growing out of the existence of classes in society. He advocated struggle against these erroneous and harmful cultural expressions so that the people could be educated and immunized against them. . . .

The Crisis

These attacks on the proletarian headquarters in the Party showed how the superstructure could be utilized to wreck the socialist economic base, and this is what was intended. In reply, in September of 1962 at the Tenth Plenary Meeting of the Central Committee, Chairman Mao raised his slogan: "Never forget class struggle!" Again, on December 12, 1963, he posed the question: "Isn't it absurd that many Communists are enthusiastic about promoting feudal and capitalist art, but not socialist art?" Less than a year later, on June 27, 1964, he warned that the various artist organizations had slid right down to the brink of revisionism and were surely headed for a reactionary future, on the pattern of the Petofi Club, which had played such a nefarious role in the Hungarian counter-revolution of 1956. This last statement threw a scare into the Chou Yang gang,[1] who felt that to ignore it would be too dangerous. Thereupon they held a phony rectification movement among the cultural circles, with Chou flailing himself where it did not hurt and pleading that his errors were a matter of miscomprehension rather than his taking a bourgeois political line meant to counter Chairman Mao's proletarian line in culture. But Chou and his gang having thus been manoeuvering for thirty years, so little faith could be placed in their words. Besides, the times had changed radically; this was a period of crisis, when the threat to the dictatorship of the proletariat had reached a critical point, when the bourgeois headquarters was ready to stage a take-over, a *coup d'état*. It was a moment of life and death struggle between the two lines, and it was under such circumstances that Chairman Mao decided to carry out the Great Proletarian Cultural Revolution, to save the Chinese revolution, to dig out the root of revisionism in China, the bourgeois headquarters inside the Party, and to give this very new and extremely important lesson to revolutionaries all over the world.

Intellectuals

Many so-called China "experts" have interpreted the Cultural Revolution as an attack against Chinese intellectuals prompted by Chairman Mao's personal distrust of them. This kind of nonsense is pernicious because in the first place it deliberately conceals the class content of the Cultural Revolution; and in the second, it tries to raise intellectuals above classes, as if they represent a classless truth.

What are the facts? We have just seen that the Cultural Revolution is a struggle between the proletariat and the bourgeoisie, between the socialist and capitalist roads, between the proletarian and bourgeois headquarters in the Party. When investigating the Cultural Revolution it is imperative to start from this premise. Otherwise it will never be properly understood.

As for the intellectuals, in their pursuit of the "truth" they invariably carry with them a class point of view. As Chairman Mao has written: "In class society everyone lives as a member of a particular class, and every kind of thinking, without exception, is stamped with the brand of a class." The intellectuals' interpretations of phenomena are seen through the eyes of this or that class, colored by their upbringing, education, world outlook and source of employment. In the old societies they work for, and in the interest of, the bourgeoisie, so they are called bourgeois intellectuals. There is nothing incorrect about this designation whatsoever. Therefore, it is not strange that in the new society, intellectuals should be the objects of thought reform, enabling them to shift their stand to the side of the proletariat, to allow them to make their maximum contribution to the building of socialism. In China, since Liberation there have been several movements to remold the thinking of intellectuals. In many cases, individuals made a successful transition. In others not, and where this happened, aside from personal stubbornness due to a bourgeois world outlook, too often it was because these people were protected by the bourgeois headquarters inside the Party. On many occasions such intellectuals were allowed to join the Party, even though their qualifications fell far short of the minimum for Party members. These people, especially the artists and writers, were in extremely sensitive positions. They were remolding public opinion, and if they persisted in their bourgeois outlook, they were like time bombs inside the Party. . . .

Chairman Mao on Art

In various documents and speeches, Chairman Mao has laid out a very explicit road for the development of proletarian culture. He starts out by showing that there is no such thing as ". . . art for art's sake, art that stands above classes, art that is detached from or independent of politics." This being the case, the artists must decide which class their art will serve. In the struggle for liberation and under socialism, art and literature must be for the masses of people, must be for the workers, peasants and soldiers (people's fighters) and must be put to use in their cause. . . . Chairman Mao called for all artists and writers to go deep among the workers, peasants and soldiers for long periods in order to change their world outlook, so as to identify with their audience completely and without reservation. . . .

In other words, artistic works must appeal to the workers, peasants and soldiers and be inspired by their life and struggles. At the same time, the legacy of culture from the past as well as from foreign cultures had to be handled correctly. These must be assimilated critically, taking what is beneficial to the present struggles of the workers, peasants and soldiers, but not hesitating to discard what is harmful to the new society nor to make changes in the forms the better to present the new content, in order to propel history forward. . . .

This creation of new things involves both destruction and rebuilding. The old must be torn asunder so the new can be built. This is not a peculiarity of China's Cultural Revolution; throughout history every ruling class has operated similarly: initially grasp power over politics and economics, then deal with the cultural heritage. . . . In China, the laboring people are the ruling classes. Led by their Communist Party and using the doctrines of Marxism-Leninism and the thought of Mao Tse-tung, they have the right and duty to make a thorough break with the old culture and traditional concepts, to evolve their own new culture and through this make their ideology the dominant one.

Unavoidable Battle

The battle is absolutely unavoidable. In analyzing the societies man created up to the era of socialism, whether it be slave, feudal or capitalist, the common characteristic they all have is rule by the exploiting classes, whose purpose in life is to foster and protect their private property. The culture from the past is the result of several thousand years of class ideology which argued and fought for private ownership. . . .

With the appearance of socialism, we have the disappearance of private ownership of the means of production, replaced by public ownership. Everything eventually belongs to the people. "Self" is no longer the end all and be all. It is merged in "public" or "collective." People of a new and higher quality with original thinking have to emerge. They have to shed the limitations of "self" and achieve the freedom and limitless horizons of "public" or "collective." Here ideology and culture play decisive roles. Therefore, to consolidate the socialist system, a new culture must arise, and in order to open the way the culture of the bourgeoisie and all exploiting classes must be destroyed. We must not look upon these old forms and their content as innocent relics of the past. They represent classes, exploiting classes, and their influence under conditions of socialism would be to revive the old power of private ownership, something which took centuries of bitter and costly struggle in terms of human life and treasure to get rid of. If one fears the destruction of such things and opposes it, he places himself as an obstacle to revolution, as a roadblock to human progress. He will end up suppressing revolution and the revolutionary masses. The people then would have no other recourse but to regard and treat him as an enemy. . . .

Portraying the ordinary working people as heroes, the new art and literature inspires its viewers to remold themselves in thought and action, to become people of courage, foresight and with the objective of building the new world. They will place the general welfare first, and their own advantage second. . . . Their sole aim will be to build and defend socialism and communism. They will be out to revolutionize the world, to eliminate all suffering and oppression.

Man and Machine

Such culture must be closely aligned with actual life. This does not mean simply a pictorial replica of daily events, but a probing into the basic questions of how to build the new society as reflected through the personalities of ordinary but great people. For example, in the world communist movement and in China two political lines have appeared for constructing socialism and communism. One is the way of the modern revisionists in the Soviet Union, who have revised Marx and Lenin, putting machines, mechanization and material incentives in first place. The other is that of Chairman Mao Tse-tung, which recognizes the importance of the material and mechanization but which places revolutionizing of the people's ideology in first place. In this concept MAN is the most vital element, the decisive factor. Without man there would be no machines to begin with. Seen in their true light, machines are mere extensions of human faculties. Therefore, prime attention is given to man's ideology, to lifting his level of political comprehension and identification, to revolutionizing his thinking in class terms so that he is willing to serve the people and thereby fulfil himself. Revolution is used to lead mechanization, to stimulate it and make it rise to ever higher stages.

The conflict between these two lines is a sharp class struggle. It affects not only ideology but extends into the political and economic fields. Depending upon which line wins supremacy, the questions of "self" first or society first, forward to socialism and communism or backward to capitalism, holding high the revolutionary flag or letting it drop into the mire of revisionism, are decided. These are not ordinary questions. The fate of mankind is held in abeyance. Unless they are decided in a correct way, all the political and economic progress initially won by the socialist revolutions in the world will be lost. How can culture stand aside and not comment on this struggle and take a definite class stand for revolution, for the people?

The Next Generation

It was not until Mao Tse-tung brought this question to the attention of all revolutionaries that its importance was thoroughly recognized. Up till then the emphasis in countries where the working people had won power had been on political and economic construction. Ideological construction was relegated to a lesser position and in most instances was neglected, with the mechanical application of classics from home and abroad. The more revisionist a Communist Party became, the further away from revolution culture drifted until it was floundering in a sea of shop-worn antiques and imported decadence. To go on in this way is to cultivate the grave diggers for the dictatorship of the proletariat!

Chairman Mao's creation of the Great Proletarian Cultural Revolution to systematically solve the question of ideological construction opens an entirely new era in the recognition and conscious utilization of the precept that the broad masses are the makers of history. The theory and practice of extensive democracy by vast groups of people, which Marx and Lenin envisioned, has now been put into effect. The Chinese people are engaged in a period of great criticism, great debates and great mass actions. This is a schooling in the principles of Marxism-Leninism and the thought of Mao Tse-tung that defies the imagination. Workers, peasants, soldiers, students and revolutionary intellectuals have become not only the builders of society but also its critics and theoreticians. They learn about revolution by engaging in it. They learn how to safeguard their most precious possession: the dictatorship of the proletariat. And from the eye of this turbulent political and ideological storm have emerged many young leaders, thereby assuring that the Chinese revolution will have "red successors" for the next several generations. This is an event of incalculable significance for the whole world. . . .

There is a Chinese saying: "A tree may prefer the calm, but the wind will not subside." Whether we wish it or not, class struggle will be an objective fact as long as classes themselves exist. This law of development denotes the certitude of class contradictions and conflicts being the center of political life in human society for an undetermined period. This is why the present Cultural Revolution *had* to take place in China. . . .

---

1. Chou Yang was Chairman of the All-China Federation of Literary and Art Circles, and was generally regarded as China's "Culture Czar" prior to his purge in the early stages of the Cultural Revolution—ED.

IDEOLOGY REDIVIVUS

Richard Baum

In the fall and winter of 1962–63, the Chinese Communist Party (CCP) launched a nationwide movement of politico-ideological education and indoctrination designed to rekindle the sputtering flame of China's revolution and to immunize the Chinese people against the pernicious virus of Khrushchev's apostate "revisionism." At first limited in scope and cautious in tempo, the movement gradually gathered momentum until the entire nation was caught up in a frenzy of ideological revivalism, unprecedented in both scale and intensity—the Great Proletarian Cultural Revolution. This article proposes to consider the origins of China's ideological revival and to develop a theoretical framework which will relate the revivalist movement to certain generic processes and problems that characterize a modernizing Marxist-Leninist society.

The situation in 1963, on the eve of China's ideological revival, can be summed up briefly: domestically, a partial recovery from the severe economic dislocations of the "three hard years" of 1959–61 was coupled with a potential threat to the political hegemony of the CCP in the form of the rise of an incipient "new class" of bureaucrats and technicians. Internationally, a severe deterioration of Sino-Soviet relations was linked with increasing Chinese restiveness over the progressive *embourgeoisement* of the Soviet Union and over the decreasing international militancy of the Soviet Communist Party.

The relatively liberal economic policies adopted by the CCP in 1961–62, in the aftermath of the disastrous Great Leap Forward, had in effect granted broad decision-making autonomy to local production units. This meant that industrial, commercial, and agricultural "experts"—managers, administrators, and technicians—were given a relatively wide zone of discretion in meeting their contractual obligations to the state. Moreover, the reinstitution of private plots and trade fairs in the agricultural sector served to remove a certain segment of the nation's economic activity from direct supervision by organs of the state and Party. Finally, renewed emphasis in this period on piece-rate systems of remuneration and on material incentives in general meant that the egalitarian-collectivist ideals of the Party were being diluted for considerations of expediency.

Richard Baum, "Ideology Redivivus," *Problems of Communism* 16, no. 3 (May–June 1967): 1–11. Reprinted by permission of the publisher.

Understandably, such economic concessions to "bourgeois individualism" had a beneficial effect on the morale—and hence on the productivity—of workers and administrators alike, since prior to 1961 ultimate authority for production-related decisions had been vested in local and regional Party committees, most of which were long on manipulative skills but woefully lacking in managerial and technological competence. But if the "liberalization" of 1961–62 was thus conducive to economic rationality, the reduced authority of the Party committees soon led to the emergence of an incipient "instrumentalism"—the substitution of a largely apolitical production and managerial ethic for the consummatory ethic of the "command economy." As a result, the Party's control over the economic life of the country came to be increasingly challenged by the rise of a "new class" of semi-autonomous managers, administrators, and technocrats, and by the resurgence of vestigial "rural capitalism." [1]

A second major feature of the domestic scene in 1963 was the growing apprehension of the CCP leadership over the trend toward bureaucratization within the Party itself. Many Party cadres had assertedly become "divorced from the masses"—that is, they had become immersed in paperwork and formalistic office routines and had neglected their duties as opinion leaders and propagandists among the masses. Moreover, it was acknowledged that many officials and cadres had been guilty of *pen-wei chu-yi* (literally, "departmentalism"), a catch-all term of derogation referring to such unorthodox practices as the establishment of protective interpersonal relationships among mutually vulnerable officials and the promotion of private ("vested") interests in disregard of the interests of the state or of the masses. [2]

Worried lest these manifestations of increasing bureaucratism lead to a "routinization" of the revolutionary functions of the Party—and consequently to a weakening of political controls—the CCP in the spring of 1963 launched a frontal attack—in the form of a nationwide Socialist Education Movement—on those cadres who "indulge in idleness and hate work, eat too much and own too much, strive for status, act like officials, put on bureaucratic airs, pay no heed to the plight of the people, and care nothing about the interests of the state." [3] In conjunction with this verbal attack, the Party initiated a campaign to dislodge cadres and officials from their offices and send them out to live and work among the masses. The rationale behind this *hsia-fang* (literally, "downward transfer") was Mao Tse-tung's doctrine of "revolutionary practice"—i.e., that only by taking active part in class struggle, production struggle, and scientific experimentation could a cadre or official truly learn to "love the masses and put collective interests above selfish interests." [4]

Concurrently with these disturbing domestic trends in the direction of instrumentalism in the economy and bureaucratism in the Party, the dominant feature on the international scene in 1963 was the marked deterioration of Sino-Soviet relations. Once "comradely" and "fraternal," these relations reached a new low in July following the acrimonious dissolution of high-level CCP-CPSU negotiations held in Moscow. Beginning in late July, the Chinese Communists stepped up their verbal attacks on Khrushchev, calling him a "stooge of imperialism" and an "enemy of the people of the world." [5]

The fact that the intensification of the CCP's attack on revisionism abroad coincided with its attack on bureaucratism and instrumentalism at home is suggestive of a functional connection between these phenomena. . . . What this notion implies is that, far from being merely fortuitous, the appearance of certain heterodox tendencies in developing Communist societies—tendencies such as bureaucratism, instrumentalism, and so on—may actually be causally related to the historical transition of these societies from the relatively undifferentiated stage of radical social mobilization and revolution to the more organizationally complex stage of economic rationalization and technological innovation.[6] This notion is, of course, a familiar one to students of comparative communism and has served as a theoretical underpinning for several interpretive studies of the ostensible "erosion of ideology" in the Soviet Union.[7]

According to this view, which may be termed the generational hypothesis, revisionism is the ideological reflection of the declining relevance of revolutionary norms and values to the solution of qualitatively new, post-revolutionary socio-economic problems. Translated into the language of contemporary social science, the generational hypothesis holds that as a value-oriented social movement becomes institutionalized—or "routinized"—with the passage of time, a certain amount of cultural strain is generated between traditional ideological prescriptions and new social structures and cognitive perspectives.[8] As this cultural strain (as, for example, between the contradictory imperatives of a fundamentalist religion and a maturing industrial order) becomes more intense, there is a natural tendency for traditional doctrines to lose much of their positive content—a situation which is manifestly favorable to the emergence of new behavioral norms and cognitive perspectives.[9]

When viewed in this light, the phenomenon of revisionism becomes readily explainable as a latent function of the modernization process itself. But to say this is not to imply that revolutionary doctrines, once they have become functionally anachronistic, will be automatically and voluntarily discarded. For doctrines have a way of resisting social change, and doctrinaires alter their beliefs only with the utmost reluctance. This is all the more true if the doctrine in question happens to serve the ancillary function of legitimating the special status and authority of a particular social group or stratum—such as a Communist party.

The distinguished French political philosopher Raymond Aron, commenting on the ideological dilemma faced by the CPSU, remarked that while it is difficult to maintain a faith, it is more difficult still to do without one. The truth of this maxim is nowhere better illustrated than in the characteristically ambivalent attitudes of Soviet and Chinese Communist leaders toward the modernization process. On the one hand, modernization is positively valued as a social goal, for modernization means economic development and economic development means national power. On the other hand, however, modernization entails bureaucracy, instrumentalism, and the consequent attenuation and ritual sterilization of ideological principles. Damned if they do and damned if they don't, the leaders of the CPSU and the CCP have thus been forced to steer a not altogether happy course between the Scylla of modernization-cum-revisionism and the Charybdis of atavism-cum-orthodoxy.

Faced with such a heads-you-win, tails-I-lose proposition, it is little wonder that Communist elites have been unable to resolve satisfactorily the fundamental contradiction between the values of "red" and those of "expert." The prototypical "red" is the mass-oriented cadre, the combat leader, the highly indoctrinated jack-of-all-trades. He is the "line" officer whose task is to unify and lead the masses to implement predetermined policies and directives. His goal is human solidarity; his vision is of a spiritually integrated *Gemeinschaft;* his forte is the manipulation of human relations; his outlook is typically utopian and fundamentalist. The prototypical "expert," on the other hand, is the management-oriented technocrat, the professional administrator, the highly skilled specialist. He is the "staff" officer whose task is to specify operations, to allocate available resources efficiently, and to ensure the effective coordination of the division of labor. His goal is technical rationality; his vision is of a functionally integrated *Gesellschaft;* his forte is scientific management; his outlook is typically secular and pragmatic.[10]

Ideally, of course, Party leaders would like to combine the best qualities of each of these prototypes into a single individual (the so-called "new Communist man") who would be both red and expert. But since the weight of accumulated evidence indicates that ideological fervor tends to diminish in proportion to the acquisition of technical and administrative skills, such a goal would appear, in the long run, to be unattainable.[11]

In the short run, however, there are at least three ways in which a party that monopolizes the instruments of coercion, the channels of social mobility, and the media of mass communications can attempt to control, if not the causes, then at least some of the more undesirable consequences of social change. The first of these involves the atomization and intimidation of potentially unreliable groups and strata through the systematic application of terror. The problem with this method, which was used by Stalin to consolidate his control over the Soviet *apparat* in the 1930s, is that it may have certain unintended consequences that are ultimately counterproductive.[12]

A second instrumentality available to Communist elites involves the principle of cooptation—the exercise of social control through manipulation of incentives and deprivations. By establishing political and ideological criteria for the career advancement of upwardly mobile individuals—particularly the "new class" of engineers, managers, and administrators—the Party can discourage deviant behavior and ensure at least a modicum of "redness" among those who, by virtue of their educational and vocational backgrounds, are most likely to be influenced by heterodox ideas.[13] But the victory thus gained must ultimately prove to be a Pyrrhic one. For despite the outward manifestations of political loyalty on the part of upwardly mobile individuals, and despite their ostensible acceptance of the dominant ideological ethos, a certain displacement of goals will occur. That is, those values which are *consummatory* for the Party will tend to become merely *instrumental* for the ambitious careerist.[14]

If the technique of cooptation, like that of terror, thus proves to be an insufficient guarantee against the "erosion of ideology," a third instrumentality is available to a totalitarian party. This method, which involves a spiritual regeneration of the masses, lies at the heart of the phenomenon which I have termed "ideological revivalism."

Populism vs. Professionalism

One of the more striking differences in the respective approaches of Soviet and Chinese Communist leaders to the problems of economic and social development is the markedly greater commitment of the Russians to the goal of professionalism, to the creation of a rational, highly differentiated bureaucratic apparatus, and to a degree of operational autonomy for "expert" hierarchies, particularly in the industrial, state-administrative, and military spheres. By contrast, the Chinese have increasingly demonstrated a profound distrust of vertically integrated bureaucracies, highly trained professionals, and narrow economic specialists, and have instead adopted a "populist" approach to social change which calls for the horizontal integration of society on the basis of subjectively mobilized masses under the direct, combat-style leadership of "red" cadres.[15]

Among the various reasons which have been advanced to account for this divergence, two are particularly relevant to our present discussion. The first is the more highly developed scientific, technological, and industrial resource base of the Soviet Union in contrast to the relatively "backward" or "underdeveloped" economic structure of Communist China (a contrast which, incidentally, helps to explain the many difficulties encountered by the CCP in attempting mechanically to emulate the Soviet model of industrialization in the early 1950s). The second is the deeply ingrained revolutionary romanticism of the present Chinese leaders—the so-called "spirit of Yenan"—which is intrinsically hostile to excessive reliance on material resources and technical hierarchies, and which instead stresses the developmental potential of the "human factor"—i.e., subjective leadership, conscious activism, moral rectitude, and *esprit de corps*.[16]

The point to be made here is that, given the similar desires of the Soviet and Chinese elites to maximize economic development while at the same time minimizing the ideologically corrosive effects of social change, the technique of coopting upwardly mobile technological and administrative personnel is, *ceteris paribus,* more apposite to the highly differentiated, highly bureaucratized Soviet system, while the contrary technique of ideological revivalism is manifestly more congenial to the less differentiated, "massified" Chinese system.[17]

The term "revivalism" is defined in Webster's as "the tendency or desire to restore religious principles following a period of relative decline or indifference." The three critical conditions of a revival, then, are *religiousness, relative decline,* and a desire for *restoration.* In the preceding pages, we have dealt with the latter two elements. In order to complete the circle and establish the relevance of the revivalist metaphor to the present inquiry, it is now necessary to turn to the concept of religiousness itself.

Parallels between communism and religion have frequently been drawn, and it has become commonplace to refer to Marxism-Leninism (-Stalinism-Maoism) as a "secular religion" or "political religion."[18] This convention rests on the (often unarticulated) assumption that all fundamentalist ideologies, whether transcendental or humanistic in perspective, may be treated as "value-oriented beliefs"—and hence as functional equivalents—so long as they envision a regeneration of self and society and provide a comprehensive hierarchy of values and behavioral norms.

A recently published study in the field of the sociology of religion employs the term "value-orientation" to denote those special kinds of all-encompassing perspectives which make an absolute claim upon the allegiance of all who partake of their vision of reality.[19] In a similar vein, the author of a major work on the theory of collective behavior argues that all value-oriented beliefs have in common a preoccupation with the moral bases of social life and an overriding concern with nature, man's place in nature, and man's relation to man.[20] In this sense, then, the Communist *Weltanschauung* would seem to fall within the same category of beliefs as the other great cosmic doctrines of history, both religious and secular.

Sects and Secularization

But there is an even more immediate sense in which the religious metaphor is appropriate to the present analysis, and this relates to the propensity of value-oriented movements to become routinized over time. In this connection, students of religious organization have frequently noted the near-universal tendency for protest-oriented *sects* to evolve into establishment-oriented *denominations*.

Sects, which are the characteristic organizational form of value-oriented movements in their initial, enthusiastic stage, are identified by the following traits. They are voluntary associations, and membership is by proof to sect authorities of some claim to personal merit—such as knowledge of doctrine or affirmation of a conversion experience. Their self-conception is one of an elect, a gathered remnant, possessing special enlightenment. Exclusiveness is emphasized, and sects are usually organized around a charismatic leader to whom is attributed a "gift of grace," and from whom the inner circle of disciples receive spiritual inspiration. The disciples, in turn, are expected to live austere lives, shunning worldly possessions and material perquisites. And finally, sects accept, at least as an ideal, the egalitarian priesthood of all true believers.[21]

For a variety of reasons, some of which have already been mentioned in another context, fundamentalist sects are seldom able to maintain their original values and their pristine character in the face of changing external or internal social conditions. As the sect begins to encounter the exigencies of sustaining itself over long periods of time, it gradually loses its exclusiveness and egalitarian character and increasingly displays the characteristic traits of an established church, or denomination. It begins to employ formalized procedures of entry; breadth and tolerance are emphasized. Its self-conception becomes unclear, and its doctrinal position unstressed. It begins to accept the standards and values of the prevailing culture. A hierarchically organized, professional priesthood arises. Personal charisma is attenuated and progressively replaced by the "charisma of office." The evangelism of the outsider declines; denominational services become formalized, and spontaneity disappears. Finally, individual commitment grows weaker as the intimate community of *believers* evolves into an impersonal society of *members*.[22]

The obvious point to be made here is that many of the major elements of the Chinese Communist Party's "Yenan style" of social organization and leadership correspond rather closely to the dominant ethical imperatives of the sectarian *Gemeinschaft,* while the organizational and leadership principles of the CPSU bear more than a superficial resemblance to the ethos of the denominational *Gesellschaft*. Moreover, the various factors which tend to cause sects to evolve into denominations are of precisely the same etiological order as the factors which we have identified as being among the major sources of revisionism—i.e., the internal differentiation, bureaucratization, and professionalization of the *apparat;* the ritual sterilization of doctrinal prescriptions; and the gradual acculturation of the movement to prevalent external norms and values.

Herein, then, lies one possible key to understanding the phenomenon of ideological revivalism in Communist China. For if our analogy is at all relevant, the CCP now stands at the threshold of denominationalism. Its pristine sectarian values have already begun to suffer dilution from the "corrupting" influences of its secular environment; the Party itself has become increasingly bureaucratized and differentiated; and its charismatic appeal and sense of mission have faded along with memories of its past revolutionary heroics.

With the example of Soviet revisionism confronting them as an augury of the future, the Chinese Communists have, in the past three years, been engaged in a desperate race against time, a frantic struggle to "sectarianize" the society before the society can "denominationalize" the Party. And what lends this sectarian revival an even greater sense of urgency is the fact that the process of routinization coincides with the historical epoch of the "changing of the guard"—the period of declining health and activity of the charismatic founder and the maturation of a second generation of "professional" clerics.[23]

The Road Ahead

The People's Republic of China, barely seventeen and a half years old, now faces squarely the universal crisis of adolescence: the crisis of *identity*. The twin forces of modernization and denominationalism seem destined to attenuate many of the more radical tenets of the Maoist faith. The social structure of the Chinese nation likewise seems destined to evolve further in the direction of bureaucratic professionalism, secularism, and instrumental rationality—ideological revivalism notwithstanding.

It is a primary axiom of cultural anthropology that when the behavior enjoined by ideal value-patterns departs too radically from that which is suitable under actual socio-economic conditions, the value-patterns themselves will change. There is no small irony in this, for it is the very success of the Chinese Communists in overcoming the inherited conditions of economic backwardness and social disintegration that spells the ultimate doom of the Party's "Yenan spirit" as an operational ethos. It has rightly been observed that "what they [the Chinese Communists] call 'revisionism' is here to stay, for it is the essence of the industrial society that they have sought to mold."[24]

The CCP has, in the past, demonstrated a remarkable ability to assess pragmatically its successes and failures and to alter its policies accordingly. This is one of the built-in advantages of Mao's dialectical conception of society, which views everything in terms of the fluid interplay of contradictory principles. If today the Party leadership chooses to emphasize one particular social contradiction (e.g., the contradiction between "red" and "expert"), and to give major stress to one particular aspect of this contradiction (e.g., "red"), then certain strains and imbalances are likely to arise—as indeed they have arisen. But such strains and imbalances can be—and have been in the past— reduced by a subsequent shift of policy in the direction of the golden mean. Hence, what appears in the short run to be a fanatical and irrational outburst of political and ideological violence may in the long run appear as merely a single episode in the pendulum-like dialectic of social development. Assuming that Mao and his colleagues are not utterly mad, we may thus anticipate that the present tense mood of revivalism will likely be followed by a relatively calm period of reassessment and readjustment.

But to what extent can this developmental dialectic continue to operate on the fundamental sociological assumptions provided by "the thought of Mao Tse-tung"? To what extent is the Maoist vision of the "good" society reconcilable with the structural and normative imperatives of the "modern" society? The thrust of our analysis has been that there remain a great many unresolved (if not unresolvable) contradictions between the two. Mao is undoubtedly correct in anticipating troubled times for the second generation of leadership in Communist China.

1. The contradiction between "instrumentalism" and "ideologism" lies at the heart of many of the policy controversies which have occurred in China since 1957. On the liberalization measures of 1961–62, see Franz Schurmann, *Ideology and Organization in Communist China*, Berkeley, University of California Press, 1966, pp. 163–67 and *passim*; also Schurmann, "China's New Economic Policy—Transition or Beginning," *The China Quarterly* (London), January–March 1964, pp. 65–91.

2. These deviations bear a close resemblance to the phenomenon of *semeistvennost* ("familyness") which has frequently been noted in connection with the "erosion of ideology" in the Soviet Union. See, e.g., Joseph Berliner, *Factory and Manager in the USSR*, Harvard University Press, 1957.

3. *Hung Ch'i* (Red Flag: Peking), No. 13–14, 1963, p. 11.

4. For further documentation of China's Socialist Education Movement, see Richard Baum and Frederick C. Teiwes, *Ssu-Ch'ing: The Socialist Education Movement of 1962–66*, Berkeley, University of California, Center for Chinese Studies, 1968.

5. See, for example, *Peking Review*, No. 31, Aug. 2, 1963. For a capsule summary of

important developments in the Sino-Soviet dispute in 1963, see H. Arthur Steiner, "China to the Left of Russia," *Asian Survey*, Vol. IV, No. 1 (January 1964), pp. 625–37.

6. For the purposes of this discussion, we shall adopt Professor Benjamin Schwartz's limited, non-teleological definition of modernization as "something approximating Max Weber's conception of the process of rationalization in all those spheres of social action—economic, political, military, legal, educational—which lend themselves to the application of *Zweckrationalität* (i.e., instrumental rationality). It involves the sustained attention to the most appropriate, 'rational,' and efficient methods for increasing man's ability to control nature and society for a variety of ends. . . . It tends to involve the notion of a highly developed division of labor of 'functional specificity' with the corollary that men should have a degree of autonomy and authority within their various spheres of competence. It also involves a stress on norms of universality rather than ascription, and thus should involve social mobility—the opening up of careers to talent. . . . It may also involve a sober respect for objective conditions. The technocrat and, for that matter, the professional bureaucrat will be very conscious of the limits imposed by his materials and by the imperatives of the situation in which he operates." See Schwartz, "Modernization and the Maoist Vision," *The China Quarterly*, No. 21, January–March, 1965, pp. 3–19.

7. See, e.g., Leopold Labedz, "Ideology: The Fourth Stage," in Abraham Brumberg, ed., *Russia Under Khrushchev*, New York, F.A. Praeger, 1962, pp. 46–66; and Zbigniew Brzezinski, "The Soviet Political System: Transformation or Degeneration?", *Problems of Communism*, No. 1, 1966, pp. 1–15.

8. See Karl Mannheim, *Ideology and Utopia*, New York, Harcourt, Brace and World, 1936, pp. 100–01, for an early formulation of the generational hypothesis.

9. On the subject of the situational determinants of normative and cognitive orientations, particularly in the context of social change, see Talcott Parsons, *The Social System*, New York, Free Press, 1964, Chapter XI and *passim*. See also Chalmers Johnson, *Revolutionary Change*, Boston, Little, Brown, esp. Chapters III and IV.

10. These ideal-typical profiles of the "red" cadre and the "expert" technocrat are adapted from Schurmann, *Ideology and Organization* . . . , pp. 69–70, 99–100, 231–34.

11. "Once [a society] 'takes off' in social development, the social justification for an essentially ideological political system decreases, . . . while such social groups as the new industrial elite or the new technological intelligentsia may begin to crave for the stability inherent in a more instrumental political system. . . . The almost parallel development of industrial economy and technology has produced a degree of social complexity which is now reducing the appeal of purely doctrinal programs in the more developed countries. . . ." (Zbigniew Brzezinski and Samuel P. Huntington, *Political Power: USA/USSR*, New York, Viking Press, 1965, p. 73.)

12. "The endless belt of irresponsible denunciation begins to destroy the nation's treasury of needed skills. The terror apparatus grows on the stuff it feeds upon and magnifies in importance until it overshadows and depresses all the constructive enterprises of the state. . . ." (Merle Fainsod, *How Russia is Ruled*, Cambridge, Harvard University Press, 1963, pp. 441). There are some indications that the recent Red Guard movement has precipitated a similar demoralization in China.

13. For a further discussion of the cooptative technique, see Fainsod, "Bureaucracy and Modernization: The Russian and Soviet Case," in J. La Palombara, ed., *Bureaucracy and Political Development*, Princeton University Press, 1963, pp. 233–67.

14. Since positive identification with the manifest goals of the Party increases his chances for professional advancement, the careerist will be motivated to conform to officially prescribed norms of conduct and communication. However, since the official ideology may be *substantively* irrelevant to the performance of his professional duties, his demonstrations of faith will tend to become mere hollow incantations. On the appearance of this phenomenon in the Soviet Union, see Alfred G. Meyer, "The Functions of Ideology in the Soviet Political System," *Soviet Studies*, No. 3, January 1966, pp. 273–85.

15. For an elaboration of this contrast, see Schwartz, *loc. cit.*

16. For a discussion of the historical roots of this "man over material" syndrome, see Richard Baum, "Red and Expert: Political-Ideological Foundations of China's Great Leap Forward," *Asian Survey*, Vol. IV, No. 9 (September 1964), pp. 1048–57.

17. This is not to say that cooptation and revivalism are necessarily exclusive techniques. Indeed, the Soviet as well as the Chinese leaders have utilized both methods at times. The question is simply one of relative structural suitability.

18. See, e.g., Raymond Aron, *The Opium of the Intellectuals*, New York, Norton, 1962; Jules Monnerot, *Sociology and Psychology of Communism*, Boston, Beacon Press, 1960; and David E. Apter, *The Politics of Modernization*, Chicago, University of Chicago Press, 1965.

19. Charles Y. Glock and Rodney Stark, *Religion and Society in Tension*, Chicago, Rand McNally, 1965, p. 9.

20. Neil J. Smelser, *Theory of Collective Behavior*, New York, Free Press, 1963, pp. 120–22.

21. Adapted from Bryan R. Wilson, "An Analysis of Sect Development," *American Sociological Review*, Vol. XXIV, February 1959, pp. 13–15. A similar list of attributes appears in the pioneering work of Joachim Wach, *Sociology of Religion*, Chicago, University of Chicago Press, 1944, pp. 196 ff.

22. Wilson, *loc. cit.*

23. On the subject of succession crises faced by charismatic sects upon the death of the founder, see Wach, *op. cit.*, pp. 137–41.

24. John W. Lewis, "Revolutionary Struggle and the Second Generation in Communist China," *The China Quarterly*, No. 21 (January–March 1965), p. 146.

THE ECONOMICS OF MAOISM

Jack Gray

The Cultural Revolution was explicitly about cultural change, but it took the form of a struggle for political power. The policy implications generally were less prominent than the struggle itself, and among these the implications for economic policy made a relatively late entry.

Mao Tse-tung's ideas, moreover, and the manner in which he expresses them, tend to obscure the economic implications of his theory and of the practice which springs from it. "Politics takes command" seems at first sight a denial of the primacy of economic growth. "A great spiritual force can be turned into a great material force" seems to be an un-Marxist insistence on the possibility of transcending by political and ideological means the constraints of economic facts and economic laws. Mao's recent attacks on "material incentives" seem to Westerners a rejection of the most obvious and powerful means of stimulating economic enterprise. It is this sort of epigrammatic expression of the decisive importance of "ideological revolution" which has led to the Soviet denunciation of Mao Tse-tung as a voluntarist, an anti-Marxist who believes that the human will, by some magic, can wish away objective facts, and the Soviet charge has been taken up and elaborated in the West.

It may be that Mao Tse-tung's prescriptions for economic and social change have little in them that is immediately recognizable as "economics," but the record of the Cultural Revolution itself leaves little doubt of the importance of economic policy within it. The movement which led to the Great Proletarian Cultural Revolution began with the Communiqué of the Tenth Plenum of the Eighth Central Committee, September 1962, which, as far as internal affairs are concerned, dealt almost entirely with economic policy. The two great models of Maoist organization, carefully nurtured since then and widely publicized, were both economic enterprises, one industrial (the Tach'ing oil field) and the other agricultural (the Tachai Production Brigade). From 1963 until 1965 there were growing signs, behind the ideological exhortations which filled the press, that the real preoccupations were with economic organization. . . .

There can be no doubt of Mao's preoccupation in recent years with

Jack Gray, "The Economics of Maoism," *China After the Cultural Revolution* [A selection from *The Bulletin of the Atomic Scientists*] (New York: Random House, 1969), pp. 115–42. Copyright © 1969 by the Educational Foundation for Nuclear Science. Reprinted by permission of Random House, Inc.

problems of economic growth, and there is no obvious case for asserting that he is primarily interested in politics and ideology. It might still be true, of course, that his interpretation of the conditions necessary for successful economic growth neglected economic analysis. It is certainly true that there is nowhere in his works any detailed attention given to problems of costs, the precise definition of effective incentives, and the alternative use of resources. And it is certainly not a sufficient explanation of his sketchy treatment of such themes to say that he leaves them to the technical economist. It is clear that he regards them as of secondary importance in the process of economic growth in a country such as China.

Mao's Writings

To some extent Mao's apparent indifference to economic questions becomes exaggerated in Western minds because attention has so far been unduly concentrated upon his writings before 1949, conveniently translated in the four volumes of his *Selected Works*. Other parts of Mao's writing, especially of his writing since 1949, have been neglected, including almost everything of economic relevance. . . .

It is not possible to elaborate here on Mao's economic ideas, but before considering the economic implications of the Cultural Revolution, it may help to put forward a hypothesis concerning them which may assist the reader in understanding what follows.

An examination of Mao's writings suggests three points of importance in the economic sphere:

1. Mao has always insisted that the emphasis of work in economics and in public finance must be on the increase of production. Taxation and state procurement must be subordinated to and dependent upon increased production. In this, he is not simply making moral noises, but reacting strongly against the static, tax-collecting tradition of Chinese administration (both traditional and Nationalist), against the counterproductive procurement policies of Stalin, and against the strong tendency of the cadres to inherit the worst of both.

2. He has always attached very great importance to material incentives in economic policy. In the perpetual tension throughout the history of Chinese Communist administration since 1927, between economic rationality and doctrine or between economic rationality and social justice, Mao has usually been on the side of economic rationality, insisting that economic and social policies could not hope to succeed unless they were successful in raising personal incomes.

3. He has always emphasized the importance of entrepreneurship at least as strongly as any economist working on the problems of India or of Latin America. This is obscured for the Western reader only by the fact that in the West, "entrepreneur" implies an individual operating in more or less free market conditions. Mao's entrepreneurs are collec-

tives, or more precisely individuals working through collectives. In spite of this, he meets the Western economist in the value which he attaches to willingness to innovate, willingness to take risks, and effective forethought. These are the qualities of the heroic leaders of the Tachai Production Brigade and of a thousand other economic enterprises, agricultural and industrial, which have been presented as models over the years since the "transition to socialism" and planned economic growth began in 1953. One is of course at liberty to doubt how far the collective system of China can go in producing a high level of these entrepreneurial qualities; but there can be no doubt that maximizing these qualities within that system is one of Mao's preoccupations—perhaps his greatest and most constant preoccupation in the economic field.

In order to see how far these considerations have influenced the course and the consequences of the Cultural Revolution, one must evade as far as possible the general statements made by Mao and his supporters, and look at the problem in a concrete form. Mao addresses himself to the grass-roots: to half-educated sons of workers and peasants, to subliterate lower-level cadres, and to the still largely illiterate masses. He is therefore more concerned to express himself in memorable slogans than in statistical tables. The slogans provide texts which his local supporters then elaborate in concrete terms, largely by verbal communication. This present study is deliberately based largely upon publications in Chinese specialist journals, where one might expect that Mao's case would be put in its most sophisticated form; but even there, especially as the Cultural Revolution gathered strength, the slogan, the epigram, and the mnemonic soon came to dominate what was published. It is only by taking one important practical issue and examining it that one can bring Maoist economics down to reality.

Tenth Plenum Policy

One key issue in the struggle which was developing over economic policy and organization after 1962 was the question of the best means to achieve the mechanization of Chinese agriculture. The Communiqué of the Tenth Plenum put forward a new economic policy expressed in the formula: "Take agriculture as the foundation of the economy, and industry as the leading factor." This was a reaction to the agricultural disasters of the preceding three years. It looked forward not simply to giving agriculture priority in economic planning, and to the fullest possible use of industry to equip agriculture, but also to two specific policies: first, the transformation of agricultural technology by the development of mechanization, electrification, water conservancy, and the use of chemical fertilizers; and second, concentration upon the creation of areas of stable high yields as a defense against the natural disasters which had so damaged the economy between 1959 and 1961.

In relation to this, the Tenth Plenum reasserted much more strongly than any previous statement the idea that class struggle must be expected to continue after the foundation of the socialist state. The context showed, and subsequent comments confirmed, that renewed class struggle was closely related to the new policy of transforming agricultural technology. The full resources of the collectives would have to be mobilized for investment in agriculture if the new plans were to be realized; the diversion of savings and labor into the private sector which had been permitted to flourish increasingly since 1959 would have to be curtailed.

Behind this decision by the Central Committee lay two issues which might (in spite of the resounding phrases in which this new consensus was expressed) give grounds for renewed and fundamental disagreement. First, it is very probable that the reassertion of collectivist agriculture was not accepted with equal wholeheartedness by all the leaders. The form (the small cooperative represented by the production team, or the very large collective represented by the commune?) was not defined, nor was the degree to which the private sector would be reduced. Second, nothing was said about how collective resources would be mobilized: in the form of local savings directly invested by the collective as in the communes of 1958; or by increased taxation and procurement making possible greater central investment in agriculture by the state?

Tractors and Peasants

In relation to the new economic policy, the question of agricultural mechanization and how it could be achieved was of fundamental importance. The crux of agricultural mechanization is the tractor. In 1952–53, the first tractor stations appeared in China. They were operated by the state and fees charged for their services to the farmers. That some of China's leaders were unhappy from the beginning about this acceptance in China of the Soviet organization of agricultural mechanization is now revealed by quotations from remarks reported to have been made by K'ang Sheng (now one of the hard-core Maoist group) in 1954 after his return from a tour of inspection of the Soviet Union:

"Collective farms in the Soviet Union have many machines, but output is nevertheless low, and costs are high. . . ." And on the Chinese imitation of the Soviet Union's tractor stations: "This is the problem that must be solved: how to link the tractors to the peasants. . . . If tractor stations continue to be run in their present form . . . they will become disguised tax-collectors, and will hold the peasants to ransom, as the Soviet tractor stations do. . . ."

Consequently, when collectivization had been rapidly completed in 1956 under pressure from Mao Tse-tung, backed by a conference representing not only the Party leadership but the provincial, municipal,

and regional authorities throughout China, experiments were conducted in Manchuria and in North China in permitting the collectives
to run their own tractors. In March 1958 (we are now informed by Red
Guard sources) at a conference at Chengtu in Szechuan, Mao Tse-tung
advocated that agricultural mechanization should be carried out
through the collectives themselves, buying the equipment out of their
own resources and operating it on their own account. Although this
decision was apparently suppressed by the Party's right wing, when the
communes were formed later in the same year, seventy percent of the
existing tractors were handed over to them. . . .

Communal Mechanization

The recommendation of the Chengtu Conference of March 1958 that
the collectives themselves should take the initiative in mechanization
was, it is claimed, suppressed until "some people discovered it" in 1965.
Mao's only victory in this issue was to secure in 1963 the establishment
of a Ministry in whole and sole charge of agricultural mechanization, a
measure which he had sought since 1956. It was, however, short-lived,
and was perverted from its intended purpose of providing guidance to
communal mechanization, into the centralized manufacture of equipment within the system of state operation then being evolved by Liu
Shao-ch'i and P'eng Chen. This was a centralized and monopolistic
system, culminating in 1965 in a proposal to change the various economic ministries into trusts, of which the China Tractor and Internal
Combustion Company was one. They hoped eventually that these
public trusts would operate directly under the state Economic Commission, outside the control of the Party committees at all levels, and outside the control of local government bodies, and that the operations
of these trusts would be judged by their profitability.

As far as the problem of agricultural mechanization is concerned, the
crisis came in early 1966. Mao Tse-tung (Red Guard sources state) took
up a report on the problem prepared by the Hupeh Provincial Committee, a report favorable to his own views, and requested that it be
given nationwide Party circulation. Liu Shao-ch'i refused to circulate
the report, or Mao's accompanying comments, until the Central Committee had given its opinion. He gave P'eng Chen the task of drafting
this opinion. P'eng Chen did so, and he also edited Mao's own comments, cutting out Mao's warnings against rigid centralization, and also
(which was both significant and infuriating) cut out his condemnation
of Soviet agricultural policy. Within days, Lin Piao's troops turned
P'eng Chen out of his office, and the Cultural Revolution became a
struggle for political power.

A subsidiary issue was the fate of Mao's attempt to organize and
guide the peasants to develop their own "intermediate technology" by

systematic improvement of existing tools. In 1958, he had called for research stations in every province. In 1959, he put forward a plan for units in every county, in which scientists, technicians, local black-smiths, and carpenters would be associated with veteran farmers in working out new tools suitable for their locality. The Liu faction took no interest in this, believing that such an intermediate technology could at best have only a temporary importance, and they persisted more and more in pursuing "bigness, modernity, completeness, and newness."

We have, of course, only the Maoist story of these events. Although a rapid check back through the documentation of the years in question certainly shows that a muted struggle on these lines was going on, we have no access to any full statement of the opposition's case. We have to work, for the present, with what the Maoists chose to quote of it in the course of their attacks. If these quotations (which are very repetitive and sometimes contradictory) are organized into something as near to logic as they will permit, the argument is broadly as follows. . . .

The Liu administration seeks to get rid of political and administrative interference in economic organization; to improve efficiency by concentrating production, cutting out small inefficient enterprises, and standardizing products; to avoid wasteful investment by putting the operation of the industry on the clear and simple basis of profit and loss; to avoid wasteful use of resources by keeping the operating and repair, as well as the manufacture, of agricultural equipment in skilled hands. The means they chose to apply were those which were at the same time being experimented with in other Communist countries at much the same time.

The Maoist view, however, emphasizes the following points:

1. The peasants will not take an interest in mechanization or try to exploit its possibilities fully unless and until they have the machines at their own disposal, so that they can "regard the machines as a dependable force for the all-round development of production in a planned manner," instead of regarding them as something foreign which they call on, if at all, only when hard-pressed in the busy season. The idea that tractor stations themselves should take the responsibility for directing local agricultural production is emphatically rejected.

2. Reliance on state investment for mechanization would mean, in one form or another, increased procurement of agricultural produce to pay for mechanization, through centralized institutions remote from the peasants. It would "drain the pond to catch the fish."

3. State operation of equipment provides no "educational fallout."

4. Centralized monopoly of the industry deprives the local communities of one of their most obvious lines of industrial growth: service to local agriculture. This and the previous point are combined in the statement that the movement for the improvement of farm tools which

Mao sought to maintain "promoted local industry and handicrafts and also helped people to free their minds from superstitious attitudes and dogmatism about agricultural mechanization."

5. Using profit as the criterion of efficiency in the operation of agricultural machinery stations will tend to concentrate development in the richer areas and leave the poorer and remoter areas untouched, thus widening the gap (already politically important) between the richer and the poorer areas of China.

6. The dependence of the peasants on mechanization provided by skilled technicians and workers from outside would widen the existing social gulf between urban workers and rural peasants.

To sum up these points, Mao is opposed to the monopolization of agricultural machinery by the state on the grounds that it would increase the state's procurement needs and add to the peasants' burden; that it would impoverish the development of the local economies by minimizing the opportunities of the peasant communities to master modern technology and to develop local industry; and that it would tend to increase rather than diminish two existing social gulfs—that between city workers and the rural farming population, and that between the richer and poorer parts of China.

Of these points, clearly the most important in his mind is the question of education through participation. "The important question is the education of the peasants," is one of Mao's most frequently quoted aphorisms. Applied to the question of agricultural mechanization, it means that the peasants will not accept, or fully use, or pay for, agricultural mechanization unless they can be brought to appreciate its full possibilities in the amelioration of their own lives. It also means that this appreciation will be developed only by inducing the villagers gradually, through their own efforts toward an intermediate technology, to mechanize out of their own resources and to operate the machines with their own hands, in a milieu in which local industry, agricultural mechanization, agricultural diversification, and the education (both formal and informal) growing out of these activities mutually enrich each other. . . .

The reason which Mao is said to have advanced for this policy was that the peasants would learn to appreciate the nature of the relationships among individual, collective, and state interests—and the crux of this was an appreciation of what industry could do for them—only if they developed and operated industry for themselves. He had already made it clear that he regarded the state bureaucracy as the biggest obstacle to the growth of an appreciation among the population generally of the basic identity of individual and communal interests which the Party's economic planning was supposed to enshrine.

This was the basic argument behind the Great Leap Forward and the communes, and the examination made here of the problems of agricultural mechanization shows that, for Mao, the argument still stands. . . .

Reaction against Soviet Model

It is possible to approach Mao's ideas and policies in a questioning, rather than a dogmatic, spirit, and to judge them on their merits. They may then be seen to represent a reaction against the Soviet model at almost every point.

The first and perhaps the most important contrast to be made concerns agricultural procurement. On this there does not appear to be much dispute in China. While the *étatist* policies of the Liu administration are opposed by Mao partly because they seem to imply an increase in procurement, it is notable that throughout the period during which the controversies have been going on, with the means of publicity at first firmly in the hands of Liu's administration and then in the hands of the Maoists, past levels of procurement are not an issue. Even at times when the most liberalizing elements in China have been able to make their voices heard, this has remained true. (This tends to confirm work done in the West on the subject.) Even those who advocated between 1959 and 1961 that the family and not the collective should be assessed for taxation and state purchases did not go on to argue that the burden ought to be lightened. It seems to be accepted in China that procurement prices, even if they are inevitably below free market prices, cover production costs and leave a profit. The Chinese have not "drained the pond to catch the fish."

As far as capital for agricultural development is concerned, we have seen evidence that Mao Tse-tung prefers to encourage the collectives to invest for themselves rather than increase state investment. The funds for such investment are expected to come from increased production of agricultural produce and—not least—from successful diversification of the local economy through handicrafts, animal husbandry, and afforestation, according to the possibilities of the area. Such diversification has played an important part in increasing local capital accumulation since the very beginning of the organization of agriculture in 1953.

As far as talent is concerned, and this is to Mao the most fundamental point, he believes in diversification, work-study education, a drive for the spread of scientific attitudes through the "democratization" of science, and—at a level nearer to coercive measures—the sending of educated youth in enormous numbers down to the villages to make their lives there. In general the maximization of education opportunities, with this in mind, will prevent the villages from being drained of talent and enterprise, and will develop latent talent to the fullest extent.

The implications of all this are that the collectives will be run by peasant cadres for the peasants, and not dominated, as in the Soviet Union, by urban bureaucrats and technicians.

Finally, Mao seeks to avoid the Soviet problem that lack of consumer goods leads to lack of incentive to market agricultural produce by encouraging local economic diversification.

These are the features of the system of cooperative production which Mao seeks to develop. He may not be right, but it would be difficult to argue that he is irrational. The only argument which could prove his ideas irrational would be the argument that collective incentives, through the shared profits of cooperative working, must in all circumstances prove ineffective.

Class Struggle

The question remains, however, that if Mao Tse-tung puts forward this essentially economic argument, based upon incentives and how to make these incentives effective by education, why then does he feel obliged to justify his policies by non-economic slogans such as "let politics take command," and why does he feel obliged to emphasize that a class struggle is involved?

There are two quite distinct phenomena involved in what Mao now characterizes as class struggle, and although neither of them is class struggle in the classical Marxist sense, they certainly represent certain Chinese social realities.

The first phenomenon is the crystallization in China after the revolution of a "new class" in the sense in which this phrase has been used by Djilas, composed of Party administrators, managers, and technicians. There is a wealth of evidence (from first-hand observers in China) of mandarin-like behavior by cadres, of privileged schools for the sons of cadres, and all the other depressingly predictable signs of the formation of a new and hereditary ruling class perpetuating many of the attitudes of their predecessors. This is the fundamental point of Mao's resistance to the extension of state enterprise. It is a political and social point rather than economic, but Mao draws from it the economic lesson that if such a ruling group hardens out, it will put an insuperable obstacle in the way of the development of the abilities and sense of responsibility of the mass of the population on which economic vigor in the last analysis depends.

The second phenomenon is that within the collectives some individuals (whom Mao believes to be a small minority) have the means to participate profitably in the private sector and the free market which grew rapidly after 1959. It is obvious that at Chinese standards of income and saving, collective enterprise is unlikely to succeed without the participation of the more prosperous and the more skilled. Their concentration upon enterprise and private profit is therefore a mortal drain on collective resources, and must be stopped. His condemnation of Soviet procurement policy can be assumed to have the corollary that the private sector in the Soviet Union was a necessity of life when the whole economy was organized on the basis of exploiting the collective to the point where collective agricultural operations were carried on at a steady loss and maintained by sheer force. Clearly if Mao's conception of the collective was successfully applied, there would be no such necessity in China. The limitation and eventually the elimination of the private sector he therefore regards as both necessary and justified. "Class struggle" in the countryside is directed at removing this obstacle to collective investment and enterprise.

To prevent the growth of these two social phenomena, the new class of technocrats and the new class of private-sector operators, politics must take command. If these new cleavages in Chinese society are prevented, and the ring held for the development of collective entrepreneurship, then Mao believes that "a great spiritual force will be transformed into a great material force": the masses of China will at least become aware of the infinite possibilities of material progress through modern technology and large-scale social organization, and will launch a massive war for the control and exploitation of nature, before which they have lived precariously throughout history. . . .

It is perhaps in the idea of the "destruction of the three great differences"—among industry and agriculture, town and country, and mental and manual labor—that Mao's point of view on social and economic change is best summed up. In Karl Marx's own writings, the elimination of these social gulfs was expected to follow the creation of communism: it was a characteristic of the final classless Utopia. In Mao's thought, their elimination becomes instead the most critical step toward successful economic development in his own underdeveloped country, a step now planned in detail.

The argument in China does not, of course, involve free enterprise as one of the choices. The alternatives at present are represented by the policies of Mao and those which he ascribes to Liu Shao-ch'i, both Communist and equally alien to Western ideas of economic organization. Westerners, fortunately, do not have to make the choice, but we have an interest in the results. If Mao Tse-tung's social and economic program should prove successful in solving the problems of ignorance, fear, and social disunity, which he regards as fundamental obstacles to rapid economic growth, we cannot but remember that half of the world suffers bitterly from the existence of similar obstacles, and his solution —if a solution it should prove to be—might have very wide application.

THE DEATH OF THE LEADER

Robert Jay Lifton

Central to China's recent crisis, I believe, is a form of anxiety related to both the anticipated death of a great leader and the "death of the revolution" he has so long dominated. This death anxiety is shared by leader and followers alike, but we do best to focus for a time upon the former.

It is impossible to know Mao's exact physical or mental state. But let us assume, on the basis of evidence we have, that the seventy-four-year old (born on December 26, 1893) man has generally been vigorous, that he has experienced rather severe illness in recent years, and that he has always been a man of strong revolutionary passions. We can go a bit further, however, especially on the basis of a valuable interview with him conducted by Edgar Snow, perhaps the American who over the years has been closest to Mao, in January 1965.[1]

Snow found Mao alert, "wholly relaxed," and impressive in his stamina during their four-hour meeting.[2] He also found him "reflecting on man's rendezvous with death and ready to leave the assessment of his political legacy to future generations." Indeed, Snow's general description of the interview suggests a man anticipating, if not preoccupied with, death. Snow reports Mao to have said that "he was going to see God."[3] And when Snow responded by reassuring Mao that he seemed to be in good condition that evening, Mao Tse-tung "smiled wryly" and expressed some doubt, again saying that he was "getting ready to see God very soon."

We need not dwell on Mao's rather striking use of the theological idiom, other than attributing it to a combination of playfulness and perhaps an unconscious inclination—on the part of a man who early in his life had renounced rural supernatural beliefs in favor of Marxist-scientific ones—to hedge his bets a little. When Snow questioned him on the matter, he denied any belief in a deity but observed rather whimsically that "some people who claimed to be well informed said there was a God. There seemed to be many gods and sometimes the same god [when called forth for self-serving political purposes] could take all sides."

More important from our standpoint are the reminiscences that immediately follow—about family members who had died, about his career as a revolutionary, and about the "chance combination of reasons" that had caused him to become interested in the founding of the Chinese Communist Party. Involved here is an old man's nostalgic need to review has past life in relationship to his forthcoming death. That is, death is seen as a test of the quality of one's overall existence. And in the face of a threat of total extinction one feels the need to give form to that existence—to *formulate* its basic connectedness, its movement or development, and above all its symbolic integrity or cohesion and significance.

Prominent among these reminiscences is Mao's sense of being an *eternal survivor*—his recollections of both his brothers having been killed, of the execution of his first wife during the Revolution, and the death of their son during the Korean War. Mao commented that it was "odd" that he had escaped death, that although he was often prepared for it "death just did not seem to want him." He described several narrow escapes from which he emerged unscathed, including one in which he was "splashed all over with the blood of another soldier."

Mao seems to be telling us that his death is both imminent and long overdue. What he considers remarkable is not that so many family members and revolutionary comrades (the two categories become virtually inseparable) have died around him, but that he has in each case been spared. We recognize the survivor's characteristically guilt-laden need to contrast his own continuing life with others' deaths.[4]

For Mao is surely the survivor *par excellence,* the hero of a truly epic story of revolutionary survival, that of the Long March of 1934–1935, in which it is believed that more than 80 percent of the original group perished along a six-thousand-mile trek in order that the remainder—and the Revolution itself—might stay alive. To transcend his guilt, the survivor must be able to render significant the death immersions he has experienced—and in Mao's case, done much to bring about. This kind of survivor formulation faces both ways: justification of the past and contribution to the future.

Thus, for a man in Mao's position—of his age and special commitments—the affirmation of a sense of immortality becomes crucial. *The overwhelming threat is not so much death itself as the suggestion that his "revolutionary works" will not endure.*

We sense the passion behind his apparent calm as he goes on, during the same interview, to describe the "two possibilities" for the future: the first, the "continued development of the Revolution toward Communism"; and the second, "that youth could negate the Revolution and give a poor performance: make peace with imperialism, bring the remnants of the Chiang Kai-shek clique back to the Mainland and take a stand beside the small percentage of counter-revolutionaries still in the

country." The first is an image of continuous life; the second of death
and extinction, of impaired immortality. What he said next—"Of
course he did not hope for counter-revolution. But future events would
be decided by future generations. . . ."—is unexpectedly stark in its
suggestion of negative possibility. He is, in other words, far from certain
about the fate of his revolutionary works, about the vindication of his
own life.

The Death of the Revolution

Mao's ultimate dread—the image of extinction that stalks him—is
the death of the revolution. When he speaks of the possible "poor performance" of the young, his overriding concern is that the immortal
revolutionary legacy will be squandered. As he pointed out to Snow
[in 1965], "those in China now under the age of twenty have never
fought a war and never seen an imperialist or known capitalism in
power." His fear is not simply that the young are too soft, but that they
may be incapable of sharing and perpetuating the world view that
created the revolution. For that world view was based upon his and his
generation's specific experience, and as he goes on to say about the
young, "They knew nothing about the old society at first hand. Parents
could tell them, but to hear about history and to read books was not the
same thing as living it." That is, in such unknowing hands the sacred
thing itself—the Revolution—could be abused, neglected, permitted to
die.

Such "historical death" can, for the revolutionary, represent an "end
of the world," an ultimate deformation and desymbolization.[5] It may
cause anxiety similar to or even greater than that associated with the
idea of individual death. Actually, the two forms of death anxiety
become inseparable: if the revolution is to be extinguished, the dying
revolutionary can envision nothing but the total extinction of his own
self. . . .

But why now? Why the current crisis in revolutionary immortality?
There is much evidence that the Cultural Revolution represents the
culmination of a series of conflicts surrounding totalistic visions and
national campaigns, of an increasing inability to fulfill the visions or
achieve the transformations of the physical and spiritual environment
claimed by the campaigns. . . .

When the disparity between vision and experience became manifest,
we suspect earlier confidence in China's revolutionary immortality must
have been severely undermined even among those closest to Mao who
had in the past shared most enthusiastically in his vision. Whether one
attributed the Great Leap's failure to insufficient revolutionary zeal
(as Mao did) or to an excess of the same (as did Liu Shao-ch'i and other
"pragmatists"), all came to feel anxious about the life of the revolution. . . .

The Quest for Rebirth

The activist response to symbolic death—or to what might be called unmastered death anxiety—is a quest for rebirth. One could in fact view the entire Cultural Revolution as a demand for renewal of communist life. It is, in other words, a call for reassertion of revolutionary immortality.

Without losing sight of antagonisms among individual leaders, we do well to consider the significance of the "cultural" in this unique "revolution." We may speak of culture, in its broadest anthropological sense, as an accumulation of significant symbols, or, as Clifford Geertz has recently written of "symbolic sources of illumination" which each man requires "to put a construction upon events, to orient himself to 'the ongoing course of experienced things.' " [6] Mao seems to have a similarly inclusive view of human culture, but unlike Western anthropologists he feels compelled to regulate its tone and content, at least within his nation, and to take steps to alter it radically when it seems to be moving in undesirable directions.[7] A cultural revolution anywhere involves a collective shift in the psychic images around which life is organized. In Maoist China, however, it has meant nothing less than *an all-consuming death-and-rebirth experience, an induced catastrophe together with a prescription for reconstituting the world being destroyed.*

The "total mobilization of faith" (in Mark Gayn's phrase) involved in this prescription for rebirth has been peculiarly autistic. For more than a year the Chinese turned in upon themselves, performing actions required by their inner states or those of their leaders, however inappropriate or repugnant these actions may have seemed to a perplexed and fascinated outside world. In this sense the Cultural Revolution moves in the direction of what I propose to call *psychism*—the attempt to achieve control over one's external environment through internal or psychological manipulations, through behavior determined by intro-psychic needs no longer in touch with the actualities of the world one seeks to influence.[8] I shall have much to say about such psychism as a predominant element in the Cultural Revolution's Maoist call to life.

The agents of this attempted rebirth, the Red Guards, reveal much about its nature. The tenderness of their years—they have included not only youths in their early twenties or late teens but children of thirteen and fourteen—has been striking to everyone, and then much too quickly attributed to political necessity alone. The assumption here is that, having alienated most of the more mature population by his extreme policies, Mao had no choice but to call upon the young. But I believe that one must look beyond such explanations (whatever their partial truth) to the wider symbolism of the Red Guard movement. . . .

The formation of the Red Guard was in fact closely tied in with an attack upon teachers, university officials, and educational policies, beginning at Peking University in May–June 1966. This focus upon education has been part of an effort to bring about a shift in qualities of mind that are to be esteemed and rewarded. More important than newness as such (*past* revolutionary virtues were honored) has been an association with youth and vitality. And the human targets selected by the young militants for mental and physical abuse were, in contrast, referred to as "old fogies of the landlord and bourgeois class," "the revisionist clique of old men [on the Peking Party Committee]," and, a bit later, as "old men in authority" and "old gentlemen who follow the capitalist road." The Red Guards themselves were heralded as young people who had "declared war on the old world." But in their attack upon old age and decay they were, psychologically speaking, declaring war upon death itself.

The special aura of the Red Guard had to do not only with its youth but with its class purity. Its members were presented to the general public as an elite organization of youngsters charged with cleansing the entire nation. One could be admitted to their number, at least during those early days, only if one came from a family of workers, of poor (or "middle") peasants, of revolutionary cadres, or of members of the People's Liberation Army. With the rapid expansion of the Red Guard into a mass movement, these standards were inevitably relaxed, but its purity was nonetheless constantly contrasted with the "Five Black" categories of people selected for attack: landlords, rich peasants, counter-revolutionaries, "bad elements," [9] and rightists.

From this standpoint the August 18 [1966] rally launching the Red Guard becomes a momentous historical occasion. Western viewers of an official film of the event shown in Hong Kong and elsewhere were so impressed with the intensity of mass emotion and primal unity evoked that they have compared it to *The Triumph of the Will*, the Nazis' famous film of Hitler at Nuremberg. One of these observers, Franz Schurmann—noting the extraordinary dawn scene of a million people gathered in the great square singing "The East Is Red," Mao Tse-tung powerful in his presence though walking slowly and stiffly (and thereby encouraging rumors of severe illness), then moving out among the masses on the arm of a teen-age girl—went further and spoke of the formation of a "new community." I would suggest that this new community, in a symbolic sense, is a *community of immortals*—of men, women, and children entering into a new relationship with the eternal revolutionary process. An event of this kind is meant to convey *a blending of the immortal cultural and racial substance of the Chinese as a people with the equally immortal Communist revolution.*

On other occasions as well the Red Guard could convey an image of young people touched by grace, bestowing their anointed state upon everyone around them. A Chinese-speaking Westerner who moved freely among thousands of Red Guards during a visit to Canton in January 1967 described to me an extraordinary scene of "children of thirteen to eighteen with beautiful faces," enjoying themselves enormously and looking "exhilarated" as they chanted, sang, and exhorted one another with the sayings of Mao Tse-tung, all against a backdrop of innumerable pictures of their great leader. While there were a few older supervisors among them, the general image created was not unlike that of a children's crusade. They were a mass of youngsters unified by a transcendent vision, so infused with a sense of virtue as to be almost beatific—politicized "flower children" of the Cultural Revolution.

But the Red Guards, as everyone knows, have also had another face. Theirs has been the task of inducing the catastrophe, of (in their own words) "breaking and smashing," or initiating widespread agitation and disruption while spreading the message that this was what the country required. They became a strange young band of wandering zealots in search of evil and impurity. And during the first year of their existence virtually nothing and no one in China escaped their verbal or physical abuse—including at moments even Mao Tse-tung, in whose name all of their actions were carried out. Repeatedly identifying themselves as "anti-bureaucratic" and "anti-authority," the Red Guard became the means by which the Maoists undermined the very Party and state structure they had so painfully labored to create over the entire course of the Chinese Revolution. The Red Guard's symbolic mission was to "kill" virtually everything in order to clear the path for national rebirth, leaving only Mao and his Thought as the stuff of that rebirth. . . .

1. The interview was held on January 6, 1965. See Edgar Snow, "Interview with Mao," *The New Republic*, February 27, 1965.

2. Snow also states that "One of the chairman's doctors informed me that Mao has no organic troubles and suffers from nothing beyond the normal fatigue of his age"; and points out that an interview of that kind, coming as it did at the end of "strenuous weeks" devoted to the National People's Congress, "might have been more speedily terminated by a sick man." But he describes watching Mao, after seeing Snow to his car, "brace his shoulders and slowly retrace his steps, leaning heavily on the arm of an aide." Subsequent observations on his health differ, but they suggest that from 1965 through 1967 he was neither completely well nor totally incapacitated. The infrequency of his public appearances and his even rarer public speeches, together with a certain amount of observed bodily rigidity, have led to speculation that he might be suffering from some kind of arteriosclerotic condition, or possibly a form of paralysis agitans (Parkinson's disease). Such conditions could affect the mental state, both through organic damage and compensatory efforts to deny incapacity, with related changes in symbolic organi-

zation of thought. But if dysfunction were present it would probably take the form of exaggeration or even caricature of prior psychological tendencies rather than the sudden appearance of totally new ones.

3. Snow presents Mao's statements in close-third-person paraphrase, rather than direct quotation, in accordance with an agreement he made with Mao's aides. He was able to check his own recollections with a written record kept by one of the Chinese who had been present.

4. There is a suggestion here also of the survivor's sense of "reinforced invulnerability," of having met death and, by means of a special destiny, conquered it. It is this sense that permits the survivor to enter into the myth of the hero, as we shall see to be the case with Mao. But I have found that such feelings can be fragile, and can readily reverse themselves to expose a heightened sense of vulnerability concealed beneath. [R. J. Lifton, *Death in Life: Survivors of Hiroshima* (New York: Random House, 1968), Chapter XII.]

5. All of these terms refer to symbolic death, through loss of viable relationship to the forms and symbols which sustain psychic life.

6. Clifford Geertz, "The Impact of the Concept of Culture on the Concept of Man," *Bulletin of the Atomic Scientists,* April 1966, p. 6.

7. The idea that the state and its officials should manage the cultural tone of society—should supervise the songs people sing, the rituals they follow, the principles by which they live—goes far back in Chinese tradition. It is an aspect of the holistic view of man in his relationship to state, society, and nature that persists in communist practice.

8. "Psychism" is an admittedly awkward coinage, but it seems the best term for the phenomenon I wish to describe. Other related words, such as "autism," "psychologism," and "voluntarism" have specific meanings and would be misleading. The concept is relative, and to say that the Cultural Revolution moves in the direction of psychism is by no means to claim that everything its leaders and followers say or do fits into this category.

9. A rather loosely used term, which in earlier campaigns has referred to various undesirable local types—including those who have connections with the underworld or with remnants of secret societies (prominent in traditional and pre-Communist China), and those who do not engage in productive work.

PART THREE

The Cultural Revolution in Progress— Trends and Developments

> At present, our objective is to struggle against and overthrow those persons in positions of authority who take the capitalist road, to criticize and repudiate the reactionary bourgeois academic "authorities" and the ideology of the bourgeoisie and all other exploiting classes, and to transform education, literature and art, and all other parts of the superstructure not in correspondence with the socialist economic base. . . .

With these words, the CCP Central Committee announced to the world in August, 1966, the overall goals of the Cultural Revolution (see pp. 99–106). Thus began the "active" phase of the Cultural Revolution, a phase which was to last almost three years. During this time the Chinese body politic would undergo a series of profound convulsions, resulting in the erosion of political authority and the near paralysis of political institutions.

In preceding sections we have examined the background and origins of Mao Tse-tung's "last revolution." In this section we turn to an examination of the course of the Cultural Revolution itself—the particular events and general trends of the movement. Mao's decision to launch the Cultural Revolution probably came in September, 1965, at a meeting of the Party Central Committee. At that time, Mao's suspicions about the loyalty of certain top Party leaders were apparently confirmed; and he personally appointed a "Group of Five" leading Party officials to investigate and report on "bourgeois influences" in academic and literary circles.

For the next several months the Cultural Revolution, still an embryonic movement, was conducted in near-total secrecy. A few subtle references appeared in the press about the initiation of attacks on a handful of leading figures in the literary world, such as playwright (and Peking Party figure) Wu Han; but apart from this, the nature and dimensions of the Cultural Revolution remained concealed from public view. And it was only with the purge of Peking Mayor P'eng Chen (who was, ironically, the leader of Mao's "Group of Five") and the "reorganization" of the Peking Party committee in May, 1966, that the broader purposes of the Cultural Revolution were revealed.

With the publication of a series of major editorials in the *People's Daily* in early June, the public phase of the GPCR was launched. This phase initially witnessed a series of sharp attacks on "bourgeois authorities" in the educational system. During the summer months of 1966 large numbers of Party-led "work teams" were sent down to educational and cultural institutions to investigate and criticize.

In August the scope of the movement was broadened to include all "bourgeois representatives" in China's major cities and leading "capitalist roaders" in the Party. With the convocation of the Eleventh Central Committee Plenum in early August, the adoption by that body of the celebrated "16 Point Decision" (see pp. 99–106), the discrediting of the work teams as "counter-revolutionary," and the formal debut of Mao's "revolutionary little generals"—the Red Guards, the Cultural Revolution entered a more violent and disruptive phase.

Soon the impact of "leftist" attacks in Peking, Shanghai, and other major cities spread to the provinces, as Red Guards were sent out on a nationwide campaign to engage local Party committees in "great debates." Violence broke out in many areas when these latter committees, acting in self-defense, resisted the young "intruders" and hastened to set up their own, proestablishment Red Guards. So great was the ensuing turmoil that top Maoist leaders, including Defense Minister Lin Piao and Mao's wife Chiang Ch'ing, reluctantly ordered a clamp-down on Red Guard excesses and brought in PLA political instructors to help "discipline" the unruly youngsters. Thus begun the cycle which would characterize the entire Cultural Revolution—the wavelike alternation of violent, "leftist" periods when Red Guards and other "revolutionary" elements rose to the fore with the backing of radical leaders in Mao's "Cultural Revolution Group," and periods of retrenchment and consolidation when the "leftists" would be restrained and the PLA called in to restore order.

In 1967, as the Cultural Revolution progressed, the swing between extremes grew more pronounced. Antiestablishment rebels widened the scope of their attack to include not just "bourgeois power holders" but power holders of all political stripes in virtually every authoritative political institution in China. At the same time, the rebels became plagued by internal bickering, factionalism, and anarchist tendencies. In response to the increase of unprincipled disruption caused by the rebels, the PLA was called into the fray to restore order and play a supervisory role in ensuring the continued functioning of economic and state administrative organs and enterprises. As a result of the army's entry into the realm of civil politics and administration, the power of the military increased considerably in the latter half of 1967 and 1968. And when new governing structures—the "revolutionary committees" —were set up to replace the largely paralyzed and discredited system of Party committee leadership at every level, PLA leaders emerged as a dominant political force in the provinces.

With the convocation of the Twelfth Central Committee Plenum in October, 1968, and the subsequent Ninth Party Congress in April, 1969, the cycle of radicalism and restraint, chaos and control, was broken. By then, the fractious Red Guards had been disbanded and sent down to the countryside to be "reeducated" by the peasants; and the conservative influence of military leaders had been firmly established in the provinces. At the Party Congress, a new Draft Constitution of the CCP was adopted which legitimized the leadership of Mao Tse-tung and his designated successor Lin Piao, and repudiated the "renegade, traitor, and scab" Liu Shao-ch'i. With the adjournment of the Congress in late April, 1969, the Cultural Revolution for all intents and purposes came to an end, to be followed by a prolonged period of "Party building" and "consolidation."

There is widespread agreement among outside observers on many of the trends and developments which occurred during the three-year period 1966–1969. However, certain questions pertaining to this period remain to be answered definitively. For example, was the Cultural Revolution under the firm control of Mao and his supporters? Philip Bridgham (pp. 107–20 and 121–41) argues affirmatively, claiming that each successive stage of the movement throughout 1966 and 1967 was launched by Mao personally, or with Mao's tacit approval. Richard Baum (pp. 142–58) and Ralph Powell (pp. 159–73) adopt a somewhat different view, arguing that at least by 1967 the Cultural Revolution had generated a momentum of its own, unleashing forces and energies that could not be fully controlled by anyone. In support of this latter thesis, Baum points to the fact that many of Mao's ostensibly hand-picked lieutenants in both the original "Group of Five" and its successor, the "Central Cultural Revolution Group," were themselves purged at various stages of the movement. Bridgham gives ground on the question of Maoist control when he acknowledges that the Maoist rebels may have "succeeded too well, destroying the Party and government control apparatus without providing an effective substitute."

Some disagreement also exists on the question of whether the military actually achieved a position of effective political power during the Cultural Revolution. Bridgham argues that although the PLA played an increasingly important role in civil politics, the army was frequently hamstrung by its inability to use force to carry out its will and by the continual (Maoist) demand that military leaders engage in "self-criticism." Baum and Powell, on the other hand, argue that although the PLA was frequently called upon to exercise restraint in the settlement of local political disputes and factional conflicts, military officers did in fact exert a dominant influence in the determination of China's post-Cultural Revolution political order.

One possible explanation for these divergences of viewpoint lies in the varying time perspectives of the observers. The selections in Part III were written and organized in chronological fashion, with Bridgham concentrating almost exclusively on events and developments in 1966 and 1967, Baum on 1968, and Powell on 1969. Thus Bridgham's observations on the degree of Maoist control over the Cultural Revolution and on the political role of the PLA may have held true for the period with which he was primarily concerned, while Baum and Powell's observations may be more relevant to subsequent periods.

Beyond a wide range of questions pertaining to China's domestic political institutions and processes, the Cultural Revolution opened up a series of questions affecting China's foreign policy, economic policy, and educational and cultural policies. The intensification of the Sino-Soviet dispute in 1968–69 and the negative impact of the Cultural Revolution on China's diplomatic relations with her neighbors in East and Southeast Asia, particularly in 1967, are but two of the international ramifications of China's recent upheaval. And within China, the introduction of numerous economic and administrative reforms in the latter stages of the Cultural Revolution—including movements to decentralize industrial, commercial, and educational and public health services—contained the seeds of what the Maoists promised would be a new "leap forward" in China's socialist construction. Although these various developments are not treated separately or at length in the present volume, a selected bibliography has been appended to this collection to assist those readers who wish to pursue further questions relating to the impact of the Cultural Revolution on various sectors of Chinese society and on China's foreign relations.

DECISION OF THE CENTRAL COMMITTEE OF THE COMMUNIST PARTY OF CHINA CONCERNING THE GREAT PROLETARIAN CULTURAL REVOLUTION*

1. A New Stage in the Socialist Revolution

The Great Proletarian Cultural Revolution now unfolding is a great revolution that touches people to their very souls and constitutes a new stage in the development of the socialist revolution in our country, a deeper and more extensive stage. . . . At present, our objective is to struggle against and crush those persons in authority who are taking the capitalist road, to criticize and repudiate the reactionary bourgeois academic "authorities" and the ideology of the bourgeoisie and all the other exploiting classes and to transform education, literature and art and all other parts of the superstructure that do not correspond to the socialist economic base, so as to facilitate the consolidation and development of the socialist system.

2. The Main Current and the Zigzags

The masses of the workers, peasants, soldiers, revolutionary intellectuals and revolutionary cadres form the main force in this Great Cultural Revolution. Large numbers of revolutionary young people, previously unknown, have become courageous and daring pathbreakers. . . . In such a great revolutionary movement, it is hardly avoidable that they should show shortcomings of one kind or another, but their main revolutionary orientation has been correct from the beginning. This is the main current in the Great Proletarian Cultural Revolution. . . .

Since the Cultural Revolution is a revolution, it inevitably meets with resistance. This resistance comes chiefly from those in authority who have wormed their way into the Party and are taking the capitalist road. It also comes from the old force of habit in society. At present, this resistance is still fairly strong and stubborn. However, the Great Proletarian Cultural Revolution is, after all, an irresistible general

---

"Decision of the Central Committee of the Communist Party of China Concerning the Great Proletarian Cultural Revolution," *Peking Review*, no. 33 (August 12, 1966), pp. 6–12.

* Adopted on August 8, 1966; commonly known as the "16 points."–ED.

trend. There is abundant evidence that such resistance will crumble fast once the masses become fully aroused.

Because the resistance is fairly strong, there will be reversals and even repeated reversals in this struggle. There is no harm in this. It tempers the proletariat and other working people, and especially the younger generation, teaches them lessons and gives them experience, and helps them to understand that the revolutionary road is a zigzag one, and not plain sailing.

3. Put Daring Above Everything Else and Boldly Arouse the Masses

The outcome of this Great Cultural Revolution will be determined by whether the Party leadership does or does not dare boldly to arouse the masses.

Currently, there are four different situations with regard to the leadership being given to the movement of Cultural Revolution by Party organizations at various levels:

(1) There is the situation in which the persons in charge of Party organizations stand in the vanguard of the movement and dare to arouse the masses boldly. . . . They advocate the big-character posters and great debates. They encourage the masses to expose every kind of ghost and monster and also to criticize the shortcomings and errors in the work of the persons in charge. This correct kind of leadership is the result of putting proletarian politics in the forefront and Mao Tsetung's thought in the lead.

(2) In many units, the persons in charge have a very poor understanding of the task of leadership in this great struggle, their leadership is far from being conscientious and effective, and they accordingly find themselves incompetent and in a weak position. They put fear above everything else, stick to outmoded ways and regulations, and are unwilling to break away from conventional practices and move ahead. They have been taken unawares by the new order of things, with the result that their leadership lags behind the situation, lags behind the masses.

(3) In some units, the persons in charge, who made mistakes of one kind or another in the past, are even more prone to put fear above everything else, being afraid that the masses will catch them out. Actually, if they make serious self-criticism and accept the criticism of the masses, the Party and the masses will make allowances for their mistakes. But if the persons in charge don't, they will continue to make mistakes and become obstacles to the mass movement.

(4) Some units are controlled by those who have wormed their way into the Party and are taking the capitalist road. Such persons in authority are extremely afraid of being exposed by the masses and therefore seek every possible pretext to suppress the mass movement. They resort to such tactics as shifting the targets for attack and turning

black into white in an attempt to lead the movement astray. When they find themselves very isolated and no longer able to carry on as before, they resort still more to intrigues, stabbing people in the back, spreading rumors, and blurring the distinction between revolution and counter-revolution as much as they can, all for the purpose of attacking the revolutionaries.

What the Central Committee of the Party demands of the Party committees at all levels is that they persevere in giving correct leadership, put daring above everything else, boldly arouse the masses, change the state of weakness and incompetence where it exists, encourage those comrades who have made mistakes but are willing to correct them to cast off their mental burdens and join in the struggle, and dismiss from their leading posts all those in authority who are taking the capitalist road and so make possible the recapture of the leadership for the proletarian revolutionaries.

4. Let the Masses Educate Themselves in the Movement

In the Great Proletarian Cultural Revolution, the only method is for the masses to liberate themselves, and any method of doing things on their behalf must not be used.

Trust the masses, rely on them and respect their initiative. Cast out fear. Don't be afraid of disorder. Chairman Mao has often told us that revolution cannot be so very refined, so gentle, so temperate, kind, courteous, restrained and magnanimous. . . .

Make the fullest use of big-character posters and great debates to argue matters out, so that the masses can clarify the correct views, criticize the wrong views and expose all the ghosts and monsters. In this way the masses will be able to raise their political consciousness in the course of the struggle, enhance their abilities and talents, distinguish right from wrong and draw a clear line between the enemy and ourselves.

5. Firmly Apply the Class Line of the Party

Who are our enemies? Who are our friends? This is a question of the first importance for the revolution and it is likewise a question of the first importance for the Great Cultural Revolution.

Party leadership should be good at discovering the Left and developing and strengthening the ranks of the Left, and should firmly rely on the revolutionary Left. During the movement this is the only way to isolate thoroughly the most reactionary Rightists, win over the middle and unite with the great majority so that by the end of the movement we shall achieve the unity of more than 95 percent of the cadres and more than 95 percent of the masses.

Concentrate all forces to strike at the handful of ultra-reactionary bourgeois Rightists and counter-revolutionary revisionists, and expose and criticize to the full their crimes against the Party, against socialism and against Mao Tse-tung's thought so as to isolate them to the maximum. . . .

Care should be taken to distinguish strictly between the anti-Party, anti-socialist Rightists and those who support the Party and socialism but have said or done something wrong or have written some bad articles or other works.

Care should be taken to distinguish strictly between the reactionary bourgeois scholar despots and "authorities" on the one hand and people who have the ordinary bourgeois academic ideas on the other.

6. Correct Handling of Contradictions among the People

A strict distinction must be made between the two different types of contradictions: those among the people and those between ourselves and the enemy. . . .

It is normal for the masses to hold different views. Contention between different views is unavoidable, necessary and beneficial. In the course of normal and full debate, the masses will affirm what is right, correct what is wrong and gradually reach unanimity.

The method to be used in debates is to present the facts, reason things out, and persuade through reasoning. Any method of forcing a minority holding different views to submit is impermissible. The minority should be protected, because sometimes the truth is with the minority. Even if the minority is wrong, they should still be allowed to argue their case and reserve their views. . . .

In the course of debate, every revolutionary should be good at thinking things out for himself and should develop the communist spirit of daring to think, daring to speak and daring to act. On the premise that they have the same main orientation, revolutionary comrades should, for the sake of strengthening unity, avoid endless debate over side issues.

7. Be on Guard against Those Who Brand the Revolutionary Masses as "Counter-Revolutionaries"

In certain schools, units, and work teams of the Cultural Revolution, some of the persons in charge have organized counter-attacks against the masses who put up big-character posters against them. These people have even advanced such slogans as: opposition to the leaders of a unit or a work team means opposition to the Party's Central Committee, means opposition to the Party and socialism, means counter-revolution. In this way it is inevitable that their blows will fall on some really revolutionary activists. This is an error on matters of orientation, an error of line, and is absolutely impermissible. . . .

In the course of the movement, with the exception of cases of active counter-revolutionaries where there is clear evidence of crimes such as murder, arson, poisoning, sabotage or theft of state secrets, which should be handled in accordance with the law, no measures should be taken against students at universities, colleges, middle schools and primary schools because of problems that arise in the movement. To prevent the struggle from being diverted from its main objective, it is not allowed, whatever the pretext, to incite the masses to struggle against each other or the students to do likewise. Even proven Rightists should be dealt with on the merits of each case at a later stage of the movement.

8. The Question of Cadres

The cadres fall roughly into the following four categories: (1) good; (2) comparatively good; (3) those who have made serious mistakes but have not become anti-Party, anti-socialist Rightists; and (4) the small number of anti-Party, anti-socialist Rightists.

In ordinary situations, the first two categories (good and comparatively good) are the great majority.

The anti-Party, anti-socialist Rightists must be fully exposed, hit hard, pulled down and completely discredited and their influence eliminated. At the same time, they should be given a way out so that they can turn over a new leaf.

9. Cultural Revolutionary Groups, Committees and Congresses

Many new things have begun to emerge in the Great Proletarian Cultural Revolution. The cultural revolutionary groups, committees and other organizational forms created by the masses in many schools and units are something new and of great historic importance.

These cultural revolutionary groups, committees and congresses are excellent new forms of organization whereby under the leadership of the Communist Party the masses are educating themselves. They are an excellent bridge to keep our Party in close contact with the masses. They are organs of power of the Proletarian Cultural Revolution.

The struggle of the proletariat against the old ideas, culture, customs and habits left over from all the exploiting classes over thousands of years will necessarily take a very, very long time. Therefore, the cultural revolutionary groups, committees and congresses should not be temporary organizations but permanent, standing mass organizations. They are suitable not only for colleges, schools and government and other organizations, but generally also for factories, mines, other enterprises, urban districts and villages.

It is necessary to institute a system of general elections, like that of the Paris Commune, for electing members to the cultural revolutionary groups and committees and delegates to the cultural revolutionary congresses. The lists of candidates should be put forward by the revolutionary masses after full discussion, and the elections should be held after the masses have discussed the lists over and over again. . . .

The cultural revolutionary groups, committees and congresses in colleges and schools should consist mainly of representatives of the revolutionary students. At the same time, they should have a certain number of representatives of the revolutionary teaching staff and workers.

10. Educational Reform

In the Great Proletarian Cultural Revolution a most important task is to transform the old educational system and the old principles and methods of teaching.

In this Great Cultural Revolution, the phenomenon of our schools being dominated by bourgeois intellectuals must be completely changed.

In every kind of school we must apply thoroughly the policy advanced by Comrade Mao Tse-tung, of education serving proletarian politics and education being combined with productive labor, so as to enable those receiving an education to develop morally, intellectually and physically and to become laborers with socialist consciousness and culture.

The period of schooling should be shortened. Courses should be fewer and better. The teaching material should be thoroughly transformed, in some cases beginning with simplifying complicated material. While their main task is to study, students should also learn other things. That is to say, in addition to their studies they should also learn industrial work, farming and military affairs, and take part in the struggles of the Cultural Revolution as they occur to criticize the bourgeoisie.

11. The Question of Criticizing by Name in the Press

In the course of the mass movement of the Cultural Revolution, the criticism of bourgeois and feudal ideology should be well combined with the dissemination of the proletarian world outlook and of Marxism-Leninism, Mao Tse-tung's thought.

Criticism should be organized of typical bourgeois representatives who have wormed their way into the Party and typical reactionary bourgeois academic "authorities," and this should include criticism of various kinds of reactionary views in philosophy, history, political economy and education, in works and theories of literature and art, in theories of natural science, and in other fields.

Criticism of anyone by name in the press should be decided after discussion by the Party committee at the same level, and in some cases submitted to the Party committee at a higher level for approval.

12. Policy Towards Scientists, Technicians and Ordinary Members of Working Staffs

As regards scientists, technicians and ordinary members of working staffs, as long as they are patriotic, work energetically, are not against the Party and socialism, and maintain no illicit relations with any foreign country, we should in the present movement continue to apply the policy of "unity, criticism, unity." Special care should be taken of those scientists and scientific and technical personnel who have made contributions. Efforts should be made to help them gradually transform their world outlook and their style of work.

13. The Question of Arrangements for Integration with the Socialist Education Movement in City and Countryside

The cultural and educational units and leading organs of the Party and government in the large and medium cities are the points of concentration of the present Proletarian Cultural Revolution.

The Great Cultural Revolution has enriched the Socialist Education Movement in both city and countryside and raised it to a higher level. Efforts should be made to conduct these two movements in close combination. Arrangements to this effect may be made by various regions and departments in the light of the specific conditions.

The Socialist Education Movement now going on in the countryside and in enterprises in the cities should not be upset where the original arrangements are appropriate and the movement is going well, but should continue in accordance with the original arrangements. However, the questions that are arising in the present Great Proletarian Cultural Revolution should be put to the masses for discussion at a proper time, so as to further foster vigorously proletarian ideology and eradicate bourgeois ideology.

In some places, the Great Proletarian Cultural Revolution is being used as the focus in order to add momentum to the Socialist Education Movement and clean things up in the fields of politics, ideology, organization and economy. This may be done where the local Party committee thinks it appropriate.

14. Take Firm Hold of the Revolution and Stimulate Production

The aim of the Great Proletarian Cultural Revolution is to revolutionize people's ideology and as a consequence to achieve greater, faster, better and more economical results in all fields of work. If the masses are fully aroused and proper arrangements are made, it is possible to carry on both the Cultural Revolution and production without one hampering the other, while guaranteeing high quality in all our work.

The Great Proletarian Cultural Revolution is a powerful motive force for the development of the great productive forces in our country. Any idea of counterposing the Great Cultural Revolution against the development of production is incorrect.

15. The Armed Forces

In the armed forces, the Cultural Revolution and the Socialist Education Movement should be carried out in accordance with the instructions of the Military Commission of the Central Committee and the General Political Department of the People's Liberation Army.

16. Mao Tse-tung's Thought Is the Guide for Action in the Great Proletarian Cultural Revolution

In the Great Proletarian Cultural Revolution, it is imperative to hold aloft the great red banner of Mao Tse-tung's thought and put proletarian politics in command. The movement for the creative study and application of Chairman Mao Tse-tung's works should be carried forward among the masses of the workers, peasants and soldiers, the cadres and the intellectuals, and Mao Tse-tung's thought should be taken as the guide for action in the Cultural Revolution.

In this complex Great Cultural Revolution, Party committees at all levels must study and apply Chairman Mao's works all the more conscientiously and in a creative way. In particular, they must study over and over again Chairman Mao's writings on the Cultural Revolution and on the Party's methods of leadership. . . .

Party committees at all levels must abide by the directions given by Chairman Mao over the years, namely that they should thoroughly apply the mass line of "from the masses and to the masses" and that they should be pupils before they become teachers. They should try to avoid being one-sided or narrow. They should foster materialist dialectics and oppose metaphysics and scholasticism.

The Great Proletarian Cultural Revolution is bound to achieve brilliant victory under the leadership of the Central Committee of the Party headed by Comrade Mao Tse-tung.

MAO'S "CULTURAL REVOLUTION": ORIGIN AND DEVELOPMENT, Part 2

Philip Bridgham

... According to the authoritative Chinese reconstruction, the Great Proletarian Cultural Revolution originated at a Central Committee meeting in September 1965 when Chairman Mao issued the call "to criticize bourgeois reactionary thinking." [1] ... Mao Tse-tung found top Party leaders at this meeting questioning the desirability of pursuing a harsh, divisive domestic "class struggle" campaign at a time of national isolation and danger.

When this display of resistance strengthened his earlier suspicions of disloyalty, Mao apparently temporized and then decided not long after to initiate a rectification-purge campaign of a new type—directed at "old comrades" and "high-ranking cadres" holding positions of authority—designed to make the Chinese Communist Party once more responsive to his will. It is in this sense, then, as a final test of the loyalty and trustworthiness of his old "comrades-in-arms," that Mao's Cultural Revolution can best be understood. ...

Evidence of what Mao considered dissidence and disaffection in the Politburo at this time has been provided by a Chinese embassy defector who had access to secret Party documents explaining the Cultural Revolution. According to these documents, P'eng Chen declared at a national conference of provincial Party propaganda cadres in September "that everyone in the face of truth was equal, that everyone should be given freedom to speak, and that even if the Chairman [Mao] is wrong, then he too must be criticised." At the same conference, Lu Ting-i (then Director of the Central Committee Propaganda Department) was reported as delivering a speech in which he made critical remarks directed at Stalin but actually intended for Mao.[2] Again, allowing for distortion, the central charge—that these two Chinese Communist leaders were advocating more freedom for China's intellectuals than Mao was willing to tolerate—is believed to be true.

With this evidence of disaffection among his top "old guard" advisers, Mao then turned to his long-trusted military leader Lin Piao for advice and support in cleansing the Party of intellectual dissidence and

Philip Bridgham, "Mao's 'Cultural Revolution': Origin and Development," *The China Quarterly*, no. 34 (April–June, 1968), pp. 6–37. Reprinted by permission of the publisher. Part 1 of this article is reproduced above, pp. 17–30.

dissidents. Others to whom he turned at this time (or not long after) in planning this greatest of all Chinese Communist rectification-purge campaigns probably included Ch'en Po-ta (his former Political Secretary), Chou En-lai, K'ang Sheng (a long-time intelligence specialist), T'ao Chu (the powerful Central-South Regional Bureau First Secretary) and, last but not least, his wife, Chiang Ch'ing. Mao was forced to plan and run the campaign outside normal Party channels; apparently he created his own extra-Party organization and channels of communication at an early stage of the Cultural Revolution, with those performing leading roles destined to replace the purge victims.

Operating on his own, Mao instructed the Shanghai Party Committee in November 1965 to launch a political attack (in an article by Yao Wen-yüan appearing in the November 10 issue of the *Wen Hui Pao*) on Wu Han (a deputy mayor of Peking) and, by extension, on Wu Han's boss, P'eng Chen. . . .

P'eng's sense of political danger must have intensified sharply when on November 29 the attack by the Shanghai committee was endorsed by the *Liberation Army Daily*, the organ of the People's Liberation Army and of its commander, Lin Piao. To add to his uncertainty and insecurity, P'eng was probably unable to gain access to Mao, who, no doubt intentionally, had just left Peking for an extended five-month sojourn in East and Central-South China. P'eng's conduct at this point is susceptible of two, possibly related, explanations. First, he may already have sought out Mao following the initial attack of November 10, at which time he received limited, if ambiguous, assurances of support. On the other hand, he may have felt, along with the other principal figures in charge of Party cultural and propaganda work, that he had no alternative but to fight back in self-defense.

In either event, P'eng Chen and his supporters did resist and succeeded, moreover, in temporarily warding off the attack. Even in late December after Wu Han published a self-criticism (admitting historical error but not political culpability), there were still a number of intellectuals bold enough to speak out publicly in his defense. Then, for a period of nearly three months, the political attacks against Wu Han (and his defenders) ceased.

To understand the reason for this hiatus it is necessary to identify and discuss the second component of Mao's strategy in launching the Cultural Revolution in November 1965. This second component appeared in a five-point directive on the work of the People's Liberation Army for 1966 issued by Lin Piao on November 15, 1965.[3]

The significance of this directive, seemingly restricted in application to China's armed forces, for the unfolding of the Cultural Revolution was not at first apparent. Beginning in January and becoming more evident in February and March, however, Chinese Communist publications disclosed that this directive was being used to carry out a nationwide rectification-purge campaign of a new type encompassing not only the PLA but the Chinese Communist Party as well. The first novel feature of this campaign was that it was directed at leading cadres (Party secretaries), beginning at the county level and extending through the provinces and municipalities up to and including the powerful regional bureaus of the Party. Another was that the criterion for testing the loyalty and fitness of Party officials at all levels was their attitude toward "the thought of Mao Tse-tung"—whether (to cite the first of Lin Piao's five points) they "regarded the works of Mao Tse-tung as the highest instructions" in all aspects of their work. A third feature was the surprisingly candid admission that there were large numbers of senior Party officials who questioned the value of Mao's works in providing solutions to their problems. A common complaint was that these "leadership cadres have erroneous ideas of attaching much importance to professional matters and little to politics" (i.e., the study of Mao's thought). More specifically, their attitude toward placing Mao's thought in command was described as "outwardly compliant and inwardly disobedient." . . .[4]

Most unusual of all, however, was the fact that this high-level Party rectification-purge campaign apparently was being carried out under the auspices of Lin Piao's five-point directive. The prominent role of the PLA and Lin Piao in this campaign was revealed in an important February 12 speech by Wang Jen-chung, the first secretary of Hupeh Province. Entitled "Give Prominence to Politics and Put Mao Tse-tung's Thinking in Command of Everything," this speech contained a lengthy exposition of "Chairman Mao's call on the whole Party to learn from the PLA." Specifically, Party cadres were "to learn from the PLA how to give prominence to politics, how to carry out political and ideological work properly, and how to creatively study and apply Chairman Mao's works. . . ."

There were clear signs by the end of March that Mao's Cultural Revolution was designed to test the loyalty not only of P'eng Chen and other leaders in Peking but the entire Party apparatus as well. Mao was dissatisfied with the results obtained in the high-level rectification-purge campaign and was now turning openly to a new leader (Lin Piao) and a new organizational weapon (the PLA) in an effort to impose his will on an apathetic Party and society.

Shortly thereafter, on April 18, Lin Piao's organ, the *Liberation Army Daily*, publicly launched the Cultural Revolution in a major editorial entitled "Hold Aloft the Great Red Banner of Mao Tse-tung's Thinking and Take an Active Part in the Great Socialist Cultural Revolution" and followed this up with an equally important editorial on May 4, "Never Forget Class Struggle." Setting forth authoritative guide-lines, these editorials forecast a number of the major developments in what might be called the first stage of Mao's Cultural Revolu-

tion, which would last until the convening of the Eleventh Plenum of
the Central Committee in early August.

First, these editorials made clear that Mao had conferred a leading
role on the PLA ("the most loyal tool of the Party and the people, and
the mainstay of our proletarian dictatorship") in implementing the
Cultural Revolution. . . . Next was the revelation that there would be
a thoroughgoing rectification-purge of China's literary and art circles
("We must re-educate the cadres in charge of literature and art and reorganize the ranks of writers and artists"). The editorials revealed,
moreover, that the purge would encompass the entire "superstructure"
or "ideological sphere" and would be directed with special force at
" 'scholars,' 'specialists' and 'professors' who oppose the Party and socialism" in the realm of ideology. Finally, it is clear in retrospect that
these editorials intimated the purge of highly placed Party leaders depicted as "right-opportunist elements within the Party" whose collabo-
ration with "anti-Party, anti-socialist elements" had "posed a serious
danger." The shrill and vindictive tone of the second editorial clearly
foreshadowed the ensuing violence of the Cultural Revolution with
the ominous prediction of a "life and death struggle" against these class
enemies.

In fact, the first group of leading "right-opportunist elements within
the Party" had already been seized preparatory to launching the public
phase of the Cultural Revolution. Although subsequently branded
. . . as members of a "counter-revolutionary clique" which aimed at
"usurping the leadership of the Party, army and government so as to
restore capitalism," it seems more probable that their alleged crimes
were individual rather than conspiratorial in nature. The common
bond uniting these leaders appears to have been not an organizational
connection, but one of passive resistance to the application of Mao's
increasingly simplistic and narrow-minded ideas within their respective
spheres of responsibility. . . .

The purge of Lo Jui-ch'ing, Communist China's second-ranking military leader who disappeared in late November 1965, is a case in point.
One clue to the mystery of Lo's dismissal is to be found in the admission that there were those who opposed implementing the Cultural
Revolution in the armed forces. . . . The charge that Lo and others
had sought to minimize the disruptive impact of Mao's thought on
army building (featuring political indoctrination and productive labor)
and on the combat-preparedness of the PLA at a time of national
danger, is credible.

The main political target of the first phase of the Cultural Revolution, however, was P'eng Chen. Since he was both powerful and prestigious, it had been necessary for Mao to move cautiously in planning
and executing his downfall. By late March, the time had come to spring
the trap set the preceding November with the initial attack on Wu

Han. In seeking to defend his governmental and Party apparatus against attack, P'eng and his deputies exposed, in the words of an authoritative Chinese recapitulation of the P'eng affair, "their revisionist nature." The Chinese account disclosed Mao's strategy of entrapment and went on to say:

> But the full exposure of their revisionist nature required a certain course of time and certain "soil and weather" conditions. Even a poisonous snake comes out of its hole under certain weather conditions. The moment these poisonous snakes came out of their holes, they were captured by Chairman Mao and the Party Central Committee and immediately set upon by the broad masses of Party cadres and people.[5]

With the principals out of the way, the time had come to transform Mao's Cultural Revolution from a secret behind-the-scenes stratagem designed to test the loyalty of high-ranking Party leaders into a massively publicized nationwide campaign. In keeping with this new phase, P'eng Chen's dismissal was publicly revealed in a June 3 announcement that the Peking municipal committee had been reorganized and was now headed by a new first secretary, Li Hsüeh-feng.

In a series of important editorials beginning on June 1, the *People's Daily* proclaimed the objectives of the new public phase of the Cultural Revolution and the methods necessary to achieve them. The ultimate goal was presented as positive and constructive—"to arouse the enthusiasm of the people and broaden their horizon about the future by means of the great thought of Mao Tse-tung and our great just cause, so that they will unswervingly march ahead." Before this could happen, however, it was necessary to "wipe out all monsters and freaks," to purge all those in Chinese society who had been opposed to Maoist policy and thought. That the first stage of the Cultural Revolution would be both destructive and violent was revealed in the following passage in the June 4 [*People's Daily*] editorial: "Without destruction, there will be no construction. . . . Messrs. bourgeois 'authorities' describe us as 'men of dynamite' and 'clubs.' That's right. . . . We shall smash anyone who tries to oppose the Party and socialism . . . and oppose Mao Tse-tung's thought."

The first task, as indicated in the title of another editorial, was to "Take Over the Cultural Front Controlled by the Bourgeoisie." This was the signal for a massive purge of educators, journalists, writers, artists, composers, publishers and the entire Party propaganda apparatus from top to bottom—all held responsible for the disease of "bourgeois ideology" which had infected the mind of China.

The main thrust of the campaign at this stage, however, was directed at China's educational system, especially the universities, which Mao considered a major breeding ground of dissident thought in China. In order to cleanse thoroughly these Augean stables, a six-month vacation was decreed for all students and new criteria for the selection of students were announced which stressed class background and political reliability. The time had come to provide China's youth with the "combat experience" which Mao had previously termed essential for "cultivating revolutionary successors." The ensuing struggle was waged not only against university administrators and professors but against "bourgeois" students as well. . . .

With information from published reports, wall posters, and the recent confessions of some of the principals involved, it is possible to reconstruct the development of the Cultural Revolution in China's universities (especially those in Peking) during June and July. It seems clear, for example, that the sending of Party "work teams" to administer the Cultural Revolution was an accepted practice, one which had been employed extensively in the earlier Socialist Education Campaign. This being the case, the subsequent foisting of responsibility for this decision on Liu Shao-ch'i and Teng Hsiao-p'ing as a fundamental policy error can only be construed as part of a larger design to discredit and blacken their reputations.

The fact that 90 per cent of the "work teams" committed fundamental errors of "direction and line" (as Mao, according to a wall poster, would subsequently assert) was unmistakable evidence that they had not received clear guidance on how to conduct the revolution. Lacking these directives, they employed the customary techniques of China's rectification-purge campaigns, particularly those used in the preceding Socialist Education Campaign. Although violence had always been an integral part of past campaigns, it had been controlled and confined to preselected targets. One of the errors of the work teams, then, was an attempt to restrict the scope and degree of violence with which the "proletarian left" attacked defenseless educators and teachers in China's schools and universities. Despite this effort, there is abundant evidence of widespread systematic terrorization of China's intellectuals at this time, with students forcing their professors to kneel, beating them, and in one eye-witness account, "painting their faces with chalk and ink, taunting them and spitting at them, all in the name of Chairman Mao." [6]

A far more serious error committed by many work teams was the confusion of "friends" and "enemies." At a time of near anarchy on many university campuses, the work teams apparently sided with the majority of students to suppress the "revolutionary left." The best known example of this phenomenon occurred at Tsinghua University in Peking, where Madame Liu Shao-ch'i was a prominent member of the Party work team. In her confession, Madame Liu discloses how her team first labelled its critics as "troublesome schemers" and "false leftists" and then, after a period of "students struggling against students," resorted to strong political repression." [7]

It was at this juncture of events in a middle school attached to Tsinghua University that China's Red Guard organization was born. Organized as a fighting force of the "revolutionary minority," this first Red Guard unit in its first wall poster proclaimed its "right to rebel . . . in order to oppose a revisionist leadership." When Mao Tse-tung wrote a letter shortly thereafter conferring his blessing on the revolutionary action taken by this Red Guard unit at Tsinghua ("We warmly support all who stand in your position in the cultural revolutionary movement both in Peking and throughout the country"), the stage was set for inaugurating a higher-level phase of the Cultural Revolution. The great significance of the events at Tsinghua University in July is that they provided a pattern soon to be extended to encompass the entire country, with Red Guards issuing forth from the campus "to rebel" against a new and more formidable type of "revisionist leadership"—the Chinese Communist Party apparatus itself.

The Red Guards

The Eleventh Plenary Session of the Eighth Central Committee of the Communist Party of China was held in Peking from August 1 to 12, 1966. In a series of historic decisions, this plenum ratified Mao's choice of a new successor leadership headed by Lin Piao, adopted a 16-point decision concerning the Great Proletarian Cultural Revolution [see above, pp. 99–106—ED.] and issued a communiqué approving all of Mao's domestic and foreign policies in the four-year interval since the Tenth Plenum. Six days later, on August 18, Chairman Mao publicly revealed the new heir-apparent, Lin Piao, and the new organization created to carry out his Cultural Revolution—the Red Guards. . . .

Although the Red Guards were not mentioned by name, their purpose and functions were clearly spelled out in the August 8 Central Committee decision. They were referred to as "large numbers of revolutionary young people, previously unknown, who have become courageous and daring pathbreakers," and were identified as the vanguard in carrying out the threefold objective of Mao's Cultural Revolution: (1) "to struggle against and crush those persons in authority who are taking the capitalist road"; (2) "to criticize and repudiate the reactionary bourgeois academic 'authorities' and the ideology of the bourgeoisie"; and (3) "to transform education, literature and art, and all other parts of the superstructure that do not correspond to the socialist economic base. . . ." Red Guards were recruited primarily on the basis of militancy and revolutionary zeal (membership was restricted to representatives of the "five red classes" of workers, poor and lower-middle peasants, revolutionary cadres and revolutionary martyrs). In certain respects they were well suited to discharge the most important task assigned them, that of serving as a combat force, as the "army" of

Mao's Cultural Revolution. But the very same qualities of pugnacity, naïveté and fanaticism of its youthful members would soon split the Red Guard organization, gravely impairing its effectiveness as an instrument to assist in purging the Party.

The Red Guards were ideally suited to carry out their first assignment (conveyed by Chairman Mao during his symbolic meeting with the revolutionary masses on August 10 in Peking): "to pay attention to state affairs and carry out the Great Proletarian Cultural Revolution to the end." This was the launching of a reign of terror in China's cities in the last 10 days of August directed at "open representatives of the bourgeoisie." . . . Bands of teenage Red Guards set about systematically attacking individuals and institutions symbolizing bourgeois, feudal or foreign influence and ransacking homes in search of incriminating evidence. The same acts of violence, brutality and degradation previously directed at educators in China's schools and universities were now committed publicly against defenseless victims. . . .

The second enemy selected for attack—"those within the Party who are in authority and are taking the capitalist road"—was much more formidable. An additional cause of difficulty was a defective strategy of attack. This strategy was an attempt to apply on a nationwide basis the experience gained in implementing the Cultural Revolution in July and August at the universities in Peking. A special feature of this pattern of events had been the testing of the performance of Party work teams in administering the Cultural Revolution and, by extension, testing their superiors in the Peking and Central Committee apparatus of the Party. Although the results of this test had not yet been made public, they presumably were communicated to mass meetings of Red Guards assembled in Peking in mid-August. Not only had many of the work teams failed the test but also a number of illustrious senior Party leaders, starting with the first secretary of the new Peking municipal committee, Li Hsüeh-feng, and extending up to Secretary-General Teng Hsiao-p'ing and senior Party Vice-Chairman Liu Shao-ch'i. This was the "revisionist leadership"—"those who are in authority within the Party and taking the capitalist road"—which the first contingents of Red Guards in Peking were credited with exposing and subjecting to criticism. To seek out, identify and criticize the counterparts of Li, Teng, and Liu in the provinces was the task which China's Red Guards were now exhorted to accomplish.

The main force of the Cultural Revolution was not directed squarely at the Party apparatus. Whereas all previous rectification-purge campaigns had been carried out against largely pre-selected targets under the control of a highly centralized, disciplined Party machine, the present campaign was for the purpose of "exposing and criticising thoroughly" largely unknown "hidden representatives of the bourgeoisie" and entrusted to a newly formed, loosely organized group of youthful zealots, the Red Guards. It was one thing to stage this drama in Peking where Mao, Lin, and the new Cultural Revolution Group of the Central Committee could provide direct guidance and limit disorder. It was quite another thing, however, to dispatch these youthful fanatics to investigate and test on their own the loyalty of Party leaders at the local level.

An additional cause of difficulty in the Red Guard movement was defective organization. In order to understand the chaotic nature of Mao's Cultural Revolution in the closing months of 1966, it is necessary to realize that imposition of control from above [was] expressly prohibited. As stipulated in the August 8 decision, "the only method" was "for the masses to liberate themselves, and any method of doing things in their behalf must not be used." This meant "the right to parade and demonstrate in the streets, the right to assemble and to form associations, and the right of speech and publication." In this emphasis on "rights" and prohibition against controls, there was an invitation to anarchy.

Although rudimentary in form, the loosely organized, decentralized system devised to supervise the Cultural Revolution was already in existence by the time of the first rally of Red Guards on August 18. At the basic level there were "cultural revolution groups, committees and congresses" to be organized according to the August 8 decision, in "colleges, schools, and government and other organizations . . . [and] generally also in factories, mines, other enterprises, urban districts and villages." The members of these groups (the new revolutionary elite among students, workers and peasants) were to be selected and subject to recall by the "revolutionary masses" in accordance with "a system of general elections like that of the Paris Commune." Although clearly limited in authority, these cultural revolution committees were depicted as providing "general guidance" to Red Guard units when they first appeared in China's schools and universities.

Guidance at the top [was] provided by Mao, his new team of leaders, and especially the Cultural Revolution Group of the Central Committee. An unusual feature of this control system at the top was that, once policy guide-lines were determined, they were then communicated directly and in person by high-ranking leaders to periodic mass meetings of Red Guards in Peking. In this series of meetings Chou En-lai was most prominent, followed by T'ao Chu, Madame Mao and Ch'en Po-ta. By conveying leadership directives directly to the Red Guards, it was possible to by-pass the conventional Party apparatus, itself the object of attack.

Guidance at the intermediate level was provided by a network of cultural revolution groups within the regional bureau, provincial and municipal Party committees. These "groups" constituted an extraordinary *ad hoc* Party apparatus at the local level and presumably received their directives from and were responsible to the Cultural Revolution Group of the Central Committee. Lacking clear-cut directives and limited in authority, the "groups" apparently experienced great difficulty in discharging their assignment of supervising the activities of the Cultural Revolution at the local level.

The charter of the Cultural Revolution was, of course, the August 8 decision of the Central Committee. The ambiguous, contradictory language of the 16 points in this document has proved a basic source of confusion, especially the contradictory provisions identifying those within the Party apparatus to be subjected to attack. In Point Two, the responsibility for initiating the attack is assigned (implicitly) to Red Guards—"the large numbers of revolutionary young people . . . [who] . . . expose and criticize thoroughly, and launch resolute attacks on the open and hidden representatives of the bourgeoisie." In Point Three, however, where Party leaders at different levels are directed to encourage Red Guard criticism of their performance, the authority to determine whether a given Party leader should be dismissed is clearly retained by the Party itself.

A more glaring contradiction was contained in the discussion of methods to be employed in conducting the rectification-purge campaign. In Point Six, the "debate" is to be "conducted by reasoning, not by coercion or force"; but in Point Eight, the prescription for handling "anti-Party, anti-socialist Rightists" is that they "must be fully exposed, hit hard, pulled down and completely discredited and their influence eliminated." Although this contradiction could be reconciled in theory (the first applied to "revolutionary comrades," the second to "class enemies"), the practical difficulty of distinguishing between "friend" and "enemy" remained. For this, the most crucial single issue in any rectification-purge campaign, there was no clear, authoritative guidance.

With this background in mind, the puzzling events of the closing months of 1966 in Communist China become more intelligible. These events, all of which center about the Red Guards, fall into several well-defined phases.

The first phase, extending from the first Red Guard rally of August 18 to mid-September, was one of unrestrained violence. Following a short course in the strategy and tactics of the Cultural Revolution, contingents of Red Guards were sent out to all provinces and major cities to transmit and apply the advanced revolutionary experience of Peking. At this point, the defects of strategy and organization of the Red Guard movement combined to produce a nationwide explosion of violence.

Instead of rebellion on the Peking model, a new pattern of large-scale violence featuring bloody clashes appeared in nearly all the major cities of China. . . . The precipitating factor in nearly all cases was the peremptory demand by Red Guards from Peking on arrival that local Party committees engage in "self-criticism" for their conduct in the initial stages of the Cultural Revolution. When this demand was not met, Red Guard leaders then ordered their detachments to "bombard the headquarters," launching a violent attack against both the premises and leaders of the local Party committees. To defend themselves, local committees then mobilized their own Red Guards, together with workers, peasants and soldiers. The result was a rash of violent "incidents" throughout most of China, in some cases involving thousands of combatants and producing hundreds of casualties, including many dead.

Although the August 8 decision had predicted "relatively great resistance" once the Red Guards were unleashed to attack the Party, the extent and effectiveness of this opposition was clearly beyond expectation. The response of Mao and Lin and the new team of leaders to this crisis was a shift in tactics, a regrouping of forces which would extend throughout September and October. In a series of measures designed to limit the excesses of the Red Guard movement, the first was an explicit and reiterated prohibition against the use of force. Coupled with a demand for greater discipline, this prohibition was now held applicable . . . even to "those in authority who are taking the capitalist road" (i.e., Mao's opponents in the Party apparatus). Moreover, authoritative editorials warned Red Guards not to interfere with production in industry and agriculture, both to safeguard production and remove a major source of friction between Red Guards and workers and peasants.

In addition, a number of organizational measures were taken at this time in an effort to strengthen co-ordination and control. First was the organization of Joint Commands or General Headquarters of Red Guards in the major cities of China, with the aim of coordinating Red Guard activities in a given locality. A special feature of these new Red Guard Corps was the employment of high-ranking PLA officials (military district commanders and political commissars) as "instructors," with the announced objective of turning the Red Guards into a highly organized, disciplined battle force and "strong reserve of the People's Liberation Army." Next was the establishment of Red Guard Control Squads with a limited grant of authority to investigate and punish infractions of the new discipline. Finally, an extensive effort was undertaken at this time to "link up" the local Red Guard Corps on a nationwide basis, achieving co-ordination by sending delegations to "exchange experience." The focal point was Peking, to which in ensuing months literally millions of Red Guards would travel in an unending stream, there to have the psychedelic experience of seeing Chairman Mao and there to receive authoritative instructions on the next phase of the Cultural Revolution.

One of the most significant and revealing of these instructions was contained in a mid-September speech by Chou En-lai to a Red Guard group from Harbin. After admonishing the Harbin Red Guards for publicizing their attack on the Heilungkiang Provincial Party Committee in newspapers and radio broadcasts (a violation of the August 8 directive), Chou then proceeded, according to a wall-poster account, to a general critique of their conduct which applied equally to other Red Guard groups during the initial violent phase of the Cultural Revolution. The basic mistake had been to attack the entire provincial Party leadership, to attach the "black gang" label to the provincial committee as a whole. But, said Chou, "some of the provincial committee comrades are good," and, moreover, "not all Party organizations at all levels are bad." The August 8 decision had clearly specified that "individuals," not "groups," were the main target, and, moreover, "careful investigation" was necessary to determine the identity of these individuals. . . .

The above suggests . . . that the Red Guards had gone too far too fast, the classic definition of "leftist" error. At the same time, and this was a vitally important proviso, it was made abundantly clear that the provincial and municipal Party committees had also erred in resisting the Red Guard attacks. Citing the provision of the August 8 decision that "it is not permitted, whatever the pretext, to incite the masses to struggle against each other," a September 11 *People's Daily* editorial pointed out that "responsible persons in some localities and units openly defied this decision . . . created various pretexts to suppress the mass movement . . . [and] even incited a number of workers and peasants . . . to oppose and antagonize the revolutionary students."

The implications of this editorial were ominous. At the appropriate time, once the Red Guards had been organized into a more effective fighting force, the truce would be lifted and the onslaught against the Party apparatus in the provinces renewed. At that time, the pretext would be at hand for attacking and ultimately purging nearly any leader at the regional bureau, provincial or municipal level whom the Maoists in Peking might select.

The focus now shifted to Peking where, during the months of October and November, Chairman Mao and the new team of leaders would stage bi-weekly rallies until a total of some 11 million Red Guards had passed in review. Photographs of these occasions depict wave upon wave of Red Guards, eyes lifted to Chairman Mao, brandishing their books of Mao's quotations and shouting in unison. A scene of mass hysteria, these rallies were clearly intended to mobilize and motivate the Red Guards to go forth into battle against the "monsters and demons" who continued to oppose Mao's thought. An additional purpose of these rallies, televised and filmed for widespread distribution, may well have been to intimidate these opponents, demonstrating the futility of resistance against such a revered and powerful leader.

There was a marked shift in the strategy of the Cultural Revolution throughout October and November, a shift away from violence and physical coercion toward political pressure and persuasion. The principal weapon employed by the Red Guards during this period was that of political denunciation by means of wall posters. Characterizing the posting of wall posters as a form of "extensive democracy," Lin Piao outlined the purpose and scope of this practice as "fearlessly permitting the broad masses to use the media of free airing of views, big character posters, great debates and extensive contacts, to criticize and supervise the Party and government leading institutions and leaders at all levels." [8] Red Guards, authorized, even encouraged, to criticize, responded by launching wall-poster attacks at one time or another against nearly all of China's top leaders, both in Peking and in the provinces. There were . . . only two exceptions to the application of this rule of "extensive democracy"—Chairman Mao and Lin Piao. Although this wall-poster campaign served diverse purposes, a basic objective was to intimidate the apparently large proportion of Party and government officials who had not yet passed the test of the Cultural Revolution.

Another use of the wall posters was to gradually reveal the fate of those top leaders, principally Liu Shao-ch'i and Teng Hsiao-p'ing, who, to all intents and purposes, had already been purged. . . . The downfall of Liu and Teng occurred at the Eleventh Plenum of the Central Committee in early August. But preparation and revelation of the case against these prestigious veteran "comrades-in-arms" of Chairman Mao was a delicate and time-consuming process, involving the drawing up of a lengthy indictment and the extraction of confessions. What is more, these two were assigned a leading role in the campaign of intimidation waged against those in the Party apparatus who continued to waver or resist. This role was to serve as "negative examples" of "those within the Party who are in authority and are taking the capitalist road," as a warning that a similar fate of total disgrace and purge awaited those who refused to submit.

The strategy of this new plan of attack was spelled out clearly in a major October 31 *Red Flag* editorial entitled "The Victory of the Proletarian Revolutionary Line Represented by Chairman Mao." The victory, which remained to be won, was of course over the "bourgeois reactionary line" which had attempted "to suppress the masses" during the course of the Cultural Revolution. The strategy was to draw a series of distinctions between the "various people who have committed this error of line." On the other hand, there were the small number ("one or two, or just a few") who had "put forward the wrong line" (clearly a reference to Liu Shao-ch'i and Teng Hsiao-p'ing), together with an indeterminate number who had "consciously" implemented it and "persisted in error." On the other hand, there were the "large number" who had "unconsciously" put the wrong line into effect and who were "willing to correct" their error. As opposed to the first group of incorrigibles, the second, much larger group of Party leaders could be rehabilitated. The means whereby these erring Party leaders could redeem themselves was stated explicitly in the *Red Flag* editorial as follows: "A communist who has made an error of line should have the courage to admit and examine his error and, alongside the masses, criticize what he has done wrong." By engaging in self-criticism before the Red Guards and apologizing for previous resistance to Red Guard attacks, Party leaders at the regional bureau, provincial and municipal levels might yet save themselves. Having successfully beaten off the physical attacks launched by Red Guards in late August, local Party leaders were now given the opportunity to surrender peacefully.

The disclosure (by Chou En-lai in an October 31 speech to Red Guards) that China's schools would remain closed "another 10 months" was a good indication that the Party purge was far from over. . . . Despite opposition and setbacks, Mao was determined to carry through this new type of purge from below, employing the Red Guards as a task force to expose, criticize and intimidate his opponents within the Party. . . .

1. *New China News Agency (NCNA)*, June 6, 1966.

2. *The Washington Star*, August 31, 1966.

3. *NCNA*, November 26, 1965.

4. See, for example, the Central-South Bureau directive for this campaign in *Yangcheng Wan-pao* (Canton Evening News), February 1, 1966.

5. Editorial entitled "Thoroughly Criticize and Repudiate the Revisionist Line of Some of the Principal Leading Members of the Former Peking Municipal Party Committee" in *Red Flag*, No. 9, July 3, 1966.

6. *The Washington Post*, September 25, 1966.

7. For a lengthy summary of Madame Liu Shao-ch'i's confession, see *The Washington Post*, December 28, 1966.

8. *NCNA*, November 3, 1966.

MAO'S CULTURAL REVOLUTION IN 1967: THE STRUGGLE TO SEIZE POWER

Philip Bridgham

In January 1967, Communist China's Great Proletarian Cultural Revolution entered a new stage—a stage of violent overthrow of all those in positions of authority in the Party and government who refused to accept Mao Tse-tung's new "revolutionary" order. Erupting in Shanghai under the name of the "January Revolution," this frenzied drive to "seize power" initiated a period of nationwide violence and disorder.

Although implicit in what had gone before, the strident call to seize power transformed the Cultural Revolution from an effort to reform the existing structure of power into an all-out assault against the power structure itself. As originally envisaged by Mao Tse-tung, this revolutionary act of "seizure of power from below" was to have resulted in the creation of a new revolutionary power structure dominated by his "revolutionary Leftist" supporters and modelled after the Paris Commune.[1] As the ultimate expression of Mao's mass-line approach to politics, this undertaking to rely on the "revolutionary masses" to create a viable substitute for a bureaucratic Party and government apparatus was probably doomed from the outset.

Factionalism, more than any other single factor, undermined Mao's grand design to mobilize the forces of the revolutionary Left to seize power from his enemies in 1967. Explaining late in the year why this movement had failed, Premier Chou En-lai pointed to alternating "seizures" and "counter-seizures" of power by contending factions as having produced a situation in which "seizure of power became surrender of power and power could not be retained."[2] Because of factionalism in the ranks of the revolutionary Left, it had been necessary to relinquish the power seized to military control committees set up in nearly all provinces and major cities by the People's Liberation Army.

Although not mentioned by Chou, another important product of Mao's call to seize power from below was to inculcate contempt among Red Guards and revolutionary rebels for authority of any kind, including the authority of new "revolutionary" institutions and even that of

Philip Bridgham, "Mao's Cultural Revolution in 1967: The Struggle to Seize Power," *The China Quarterly*, no. 34 (April–June 1968), pp. 6–37. Reprinted by permission of the publisher.

the Party Center. The net effect of the struggle to seize power in 1967 was to diminish, rather than increase, Mao's power to control developments in Communist China.

The "January Revolution"

Although the August 8, 1966 Central Committee decision on the Cultural Revolution had predicted "relatively great resistance" once the Red Guards were turned loose on society, the extent and effectiveness of this opposition was clearly beyond expectation. . . .

The provincial Party and government apparatus had been able to repulse the first attack by Red Guards in August and September by mobilizing workers and peasants in their defense. To prevent this from happening again, it was necessary for the Maoists to infiltrate and take over these opposition strongholds. This campaign began . . . with the formation of new "revolutionary rebel" organizations in industrial and mining establishments, Party and government organs, and, to a lesser extent, among the peasantry.[3] The expansion of the Cultural Revolution into the government and the economy engendered increasing resistance which, in turn, led to a final test of strength when Mao exhorted his supporters to "seize power" in all those Party, government and economic organizations which continued to resist.

If the expansion of the Cultural Revolution in November and December to cover industry and the countryside was intended primarily to re-establish Mao's control over the provinces, there was a parallel escalation and extension of the revolution at the center encompassing the Party, government and military control apparatus in Peking. In a major speech to a Red Guard rally on December 18, Chiang Ch'ing (deputy head of the Cultural Revolution Group and, of greater importance, Mao Tse-tung's wife) charged that the municipal public security bureau had been largely responsible for recent bloody clashes in Peking. Describing the bureau, along with the Supreme People's Procuratorate and the Supreme People's Court, as bourgeois in nature, she then called upon the Red Guards in her audience to "rise up in rebellion" and "take over" these government organs . . . With this call to the revolutionary Left, the stage was set for the outbreak in Shanghai of what has come to be known as the January Revolution: the Maoist drive to seize power in the Party and government apparatus on a nationwide scale.

The January Revolution in Shanghai resulted in a Pyrrhic victory. Instead of winning over Shanghai's million-odd workers, it antagonized a large proportion of them, precipitating a large-scale strike which for a time crippled the economy of Shanghai. This in turn resulted in the complete paralysis and breakdown of local government and necessitated a premature, disorderly seizure of power in Shanghai for which Mao's revolutionary rebels were ill-prepared.

It is important to understand the nature of the opposition generated in Shanghai at this time, for it was to be duplicated in nearly all major cities and provinces, becoming so widespread and tenacious that the "seize power" movement in China soon ground to a halt. Although depicted in every case as the product of "base and sinister tricks" played by the "handful" of Mao's enemies, the actions of the "opposition" at this time were in most cases taken by organizations and groups who considered themselves to be loyal supporters of Mao and the Cultural Revolution. . . .

Strikes in Shanghai and elsewhere at this time were motivated by economic grievances. But instead of being provoked by "reactionary elements," these strikes were the direct result of exhortations by Madame Mao (together with Ch'en Po-ta and other members of the Cultural Revolution Group) to large numbers of contract workers, temporary workers and apprentice workers to rise up against the "political oppression and economic exploitation" to which they had been subjected by Liu Shao-ch'i and Teng Hsiao-p'ing and all others responsible for foisting these revisionist, capitalist systems on China's working class. . . . But when they rose in revolt, demanding an end to the low-wage policy which was a common feature of all these systems, they were then told that they had been hoodwinked into following the "evil road of economism" and were "pursuing only personal and short-term interests."

Another form of economism (defined as "the conspiracy of issuing the 'sugar-coated bullets' of economic benefits . . . to corrupt the masses' revolutionary will") at this time in Shanghai and elsewhere was the payment of year-end bonuses and of travel allowances to enable large numbers of revolutionary workers to go to Peking to engage in the "large-scale exchange of revolutionary experience," as the student Red Guards had done before them. The responsibility for this unexpected development must also be borne in large part by the Maoists themselves. On the one hand, Party and government cadres in the industrial (also agricultural) sector were accused of "exploiting" and suppressing the workers. On the other hand, the workers were invited to rise up in rebellion against these revisionist, capitalist systems of exploitation and, if need be, to carry their grievances to higher authorities. Having effectively undermined the authority of the local cadres (who quickly succumbed to worker demands for travel funds and economic benefits), the Maoists then accused them of engaging in a "big plot to pass the burden of all kinds of contradictions [i.e., problems] up to us." [4]

The Maoists were confronted with a number of serious problems as they took stock of the Cultural Revolution in mid-January 1967. First, more than a million workers had descended on Peking to protest against their "exploitation" by local Party and government cadres. Next, there were reports of widespread disorder and bloody clashes in a number of cities and provinces where revolutionary rebels were rising up to seize power in response to Mao's call to emulate the example of Shanghai. Also, the preliminary results of the "new stage" of extending the Cultural Revolution into factories and mines were at hand, results which showed that both revolution and production in the industrial sector had been adversely affected by sending in revolutionary students without adequate preparation.

Finally, reports on the progress of the seize power movement in Shanghai revealed growing chaos following the breakdown of Party and government controls in that city. What had been hailed just a few days previously as a "brilliant example" was now repudiated as a model for general emulation. Addressing a workers' rally on January 15, both Chou En-lai and Ch'en Po-ta stressed that "seizure and control of everything . . . as has been done in Shanghai" was "not good" and was not to be repeated in Peking. . . . Rather than the formula of "seizure and control," Chou and Ch'en advocated the "supervision formula" as "much better and more practical"—that is, keeping Party and government cadres on the job under supervision by the revolutionary rebels.[5]

Another of the difficulties involved in taking over power in Shanghai was the inability of "revolutionary workers, peasants and intellectuals" to achieve unity. Indeed, the failure of the revolutionary Left to achieve "great unity" was denounced in a series of statements at this time, not only by Chou and Ch'en Po-ta but also by Madame Mao and even by Mao himself. . . .[6] Having succeeded in the destructive task of overthrowing the Party and government control apparatus, the revolutionary rebels had failed in the constructive task of establishing a "new revolutionary order."

Efforts to Restore Order (Early 1967)

The havoc created by Mao's revolutionary rebels in their frenzied drive to seize power during the January Revolution required immediate and drastic counter-measures. The first of these was the decision of January 23 ordering the People's Liberation Army to intervene in the Cultural Revolution, directed to support the outnumbered and disorganized forces of the revolutionary Left. The second was a shift in policy towards Party cadres, emphasizing more humane treatment and rehabilitation to make use of their administrative skills. The third was an effort to overcome the pronounced tendency towards "anarchism" which had characterized the behavior of the revolutionary Left during the January Revolution, an effort to reorganize, retrench and rectify the ranks of the revolutionary rebels.

Finally, the decision was taken by Mao personally to jettison the Shanghai example in favor of a new model for emulation in the seize power movement throughout China: that provided by the formation of a "three-way alliance to seize power" in the province of Heilung-kiang.[7] Whereas the revolutionary rebels had played the dominant role in Shanghai, they were now to share their power (in fact, the greater part of their power) with two new allies, the People's Liberation Army and "revolutionary Party cadres."

The new, dominant role of the military in the government and administration of China was revealed in discussions of the course of the seize power movement in February. Although at first the fiction was maintained that revolutionary rebels were leading the way in forming the new three-way alliance to seize power, this pretence was dropped in a February 23 *Red Flag* article describing the seizure of power in Shansi province.[8] Here it was made clear that the PLA had taken the initiative throughout, dictating its will and imposing the cadres it had selected upon the representatives of the revolutionary Left. In those provinces (the great majority) where for various reasons the seize power movement had bogged down, the PLA was directed to establish military control commissions charged with maintaining law and order. As the only remaining nationwide organization still intact, the PLA perforce had to step in to replace the now largely defunct Party and government control apparatus.

For the same reason, the PLA was soon deeply involved in administering China's economy. On February 22, the army was directed to restore order in the countryside by supervising the organization of peasants and rural cadres to carry out spring planting. A month later the Central Committee directed workers and cadres in factories and mines to "cooperate effectively with the comrades from the PLA" who were being sent to "support their work in industrial production." The further disclosure in March that PLA personnel had been sent in large numbers to conduct military and ideological training in universities and schools showed the extent of influence and control exercised by the military in China in the early months of 1967. . . .[9]

The most serious problem facing the Maoists in the wake of the January Revolution was that it had succeeded too well, destroying the Party and government control apparatus without providing an effective substitute. The end result, as régime spokesmen emphasized, was "anarchy," a situation aggravated by rivalry and clashes between revolutionary mass organizations acting like "a host of dragons without a leader." [10]

To deal with this alarming situation, the régime instituted what was subsequently referred to as Mao's "mild cadre policy." Reaffirming the original line taken in the Central Committee decision of August 8 on the Cultural Revolution, this policy called first of all for correct treatment and support of "revolutionary leading cadres," defined as "those leading cadres who follow the proletarian revolutionary line represented by Chairman Mao." . . . Described as "more mature politically . . . , more experienced in struggle . . . , and having greater organizational skill" than the "young revolutionary fighters," these revolutionary cadres were "to act as the core of leadership" both in the seizure of power and in the exercise of this power by the new revolutionary committees.[11]

Indeed, the time had come for the young militants of the revolutionary Left (the third component of the "three-way alliance") to be blamed for the chaos of the January Revolution which they had been incited to carry out. They were attacked and criticized from all directions, not just by the relative moderates (like Chou En-lai) but also by the zealots in the Cultural Revolution Group and even by Mao himself. Among the criticisms levelled by Mao at his "little revolutionary generals" were (1) that they were being corrupted by "money" and "cars"; (2) that they "called for criticism after criticism and took part in too many rallies"; and (3) that they had been guilty of "sectarianism" and "splittism" and must endeavour to achieve unity even with those who held "contrary opinions."

In addition to these verbal attacks, a number of measures were instituted at this time in a concerted effort to retrench, reorganize and rectify the unruly ranks of the revolutionary Left. First of all, a February 3 Central Committee directive ordered Red Guards on "revolutionary liaison" throughout the country to return to their schools,[12] a directive expanded on February 21 to encompass all "revolutionary organizations" engaged in liaison. Although justified on grounds of health and economy, the primary reason for these directives was to curtail political and economic instability by reorganizing the seize power movement on the basis of individual localities and units. Next, reorganization of the Red Guards was effected in Peking by merging the three formerly independent Red Guard headquarters into a single Red Guard Congress. Speeches at the rally proclaiming this Congress, moreover, suggested an intent to establish similar congresses in all major cities and provinces, with the ultimate goal of forming a national organization.[13]

Finally, it was announced that Red Guards on returning to their schools would have to undergo rectification—"a painful process of protracted ideological struggle"—in order to overcome their "tendencies of departmentalism, small group mentality, ultra-democracy, individualism and anarchism. . . ."[14] With the disclosure that the PLA would supervise this rectification campaign in schools and universities, it was clear that the revolutionary Left was being disciplined for the excesses it had committed during the January Revolution.

As a result of the urgent need to restore order and maintain production, the seize power movement at the end of February was in a state of suspended animation. Only Shanghai and the four provinces of Heilungkiang, Kweichow, Shansi and Shantung had succeeded in setting up revolutionary committees approved by the central leadership as fulfilling the requirements of a genuine tripartite alliance of revolutionaries, Party cadres and the army. In a major summing-up of the progress of the Cultural Revolution, a March 9 editorial in *Red Flag* entitled "On the Revolutionary Three-in-One Combination" revealed what these requirements were. . . .[15]

The dominant theme of the editorial was that all three components of the alliance (the leaders of revolutionary mass organizations, representatives of the PLA, and revolutionary leading cadres) were essential, as expressed in the injunction not "to overlook or underestimate the role of any one of them." . . . Reiterating the policy on Party cadres laid down the preceding month, the editorial stressed the importance of the role of the revolutionary cadres (that of providing "the nucleus and backbone" of the new revolutionary committees). . . .

The editorial's discussion of the PLA revealed that it too was experiencing difficulties in playing its "extremely important role" in the struggle to seize power. Admitting the existence of "dissension between the revolutionary masses and the PLA," the editorial attempted once again to blame this on the "intrigues" of class enemies. More to the point, it revealed that the PLA was having a hard time carrying out the ambiguous directive by Chairman Mao "to actively support the revolutionary Leftists," conceding that "some comrades in the local army units may commit temporary mistakes in giving their support because of the intricate and complex conditions of the class struggle."

The Resurgence of the Left (Spring 1967)

In the same editorial's allusion to mounting opposition lies the explanation, it is believed, for the next phase of the Cultural Revolution which extended through March and much of April. The principal characteristic of the new phase was the resurgence of the revolutionary Left, incited once again to criticize and attack the opposition and thus maintain revolutionary momentum. In Mao's view, the pendulum had swung too far in the direction of order and stability imposed by the PLA and Party cadres from above, and it was necessary once again to stress the role of the revolutionary masses.

The first target of attack by militant Red Guards and revolutionary rebels, unleashed again in early March, was what was termed the "adverse current of counter-revolutionary restoration" in central government organs. This referred to the practice of "false power seizure" whereby senior Party cadres or revived Party committees had exploited, so it was charged, Mao's "mild cadre policy" to reinstate all or most of the old officials and systems of control, at the same time ignoring and suppressing the opinions of the revolutionary Left.[16] The ringleader of the new "counter-revolutionary current" was Vice Premier T'an Chen-lin, charged with perpetrating sham seizures in agricultural departments, but heavy criticism was also levelled at three more vice premiers—Ch'en Yi, Li Fu-ch'un and Li Hsien-nien, specialists in foreign affairs, economics, and finance respectively. Although defending the last three of his vice premiers against these charges, Chou En-lai . . . also attacked this "tendency of rehabilitating all cadres, disregarding their previous offenses," characterizing it as an "extremely grave" mistake and as the "main danger" at that time. Chou also revealed . . . that this phenomenon of "false power seizures" had appeared not only in central offices but in the provinces as well.[17]

The fact that these "false power seizures" had been widespread, occurring in the great majority of China's provinces, constituted a serious indictment of the army's performance since ordered to intervene in late January to support the Left. . . . What had happened was that [in certain provinces] the revolutionary Left, instead of forming a "great alliance," had split into two factions. When the first of these had seized power and been recognized and supported by the local military command, the other faction had then attempted a counter-seizure, attacking not only the newly established régime but the PLA as well. Reacting to this attack, the local military commander had opened fire in self-defense and suppressed the attacking faction as a "counter-revolutionary organization." To prevent this from happening again, an April 6 Military Affairs Committee directive . . . stripped the army of all real authority in dealing with the revolutionary Left, forbidding it to open fire on mass organizations, to label these organizations counter-revolutionary, to make mass arrests, or in general to "take any important action" towards these organizations without first receiving instructions from Peking.

At the same time that its power was being sharply curtailed, the PLA was ordered to establish military control committees and thereby assume responsibility for exercising "the provincial leadership power" until such time as new revolutionary committees approved by the Center (*i.e.,* genuine power seizures) could be created. Regional and provincial military commands were also directed at this time to "rectify immediately" all of their previous errors in dealing with the Left, releasing all those previously arrested, rehabilitating all those previously labelled counter-revolutionary and, in general, seeking the forgiveness of the revolutionary masses for their wrong conduct. The net effect of this series of decisions in late March and early April was to place an almost intolerable burden on the PLA, subjecting it to severe pressure and strain at the very moment it was being ordered to take over the responsibility for governing the country and administering the economy.

A key ingredient in this new revolutionary upsurge, as in earlier ones, was to escalate the attack against Liu Shao-ch'i, to launch "a powerful general offensive against the number one Party person in authority taking the capitalist road." New features of this intensified campaign in early April were (1) public humiliation at a struggle rally where, nevertheless, Liu continued to deny his guilt as a criminal or counter-revolutionary; (2) wall-poster demands that Liu be put to death for his "betrayal and collusion with a foreign power"; and (3) a barrage of criticism of Liu's leading theoretical work "How To Be a Good Communist," condemned by Mao, Lin Piao, Chou En-lai and other top leaders at this time as "anti-Marxist." [18]

The basic purpose of this general offensive against Liu Shao-ch'i was an attempt once again to form a great alliance of the revolutionary Left (which had split into rival factions in the disorderly struggle to seize power in January) and, following this, an attempt once again to form genuine three-way alliances (which had been dominated by the army and old-line cadres at the expense of the revolutionary Left in February and March). The first objective of "great unity" was to be achieved by inciting the revolutionary masses to undertake "great criticism and great struggle" not only against Liu but also against the "handful" of Mao's enemies in "each area, department and unit" throughout the country, depicted as the supporters of Liu who had to be overthrown in order to bring him down.[19] The second objective was to be achieved by leashing the army and exerting new pressure on Party cadres to step forward in support of the campaign, both by offering a way out for repentant cadres (by joining in the attack against Liu Shao-ch'i and his alleged supporters) and by threatening dire consequences should they refuse. Political and ideological struggle against a common target would serve, it was thought, to unify and strengthen the ranks of Mao's proletarian revolutionaries.

Instead, the result of leashing the PLA while unleashing the revolutionary Left was renewed violence and disorder. Serious, large-scale clashes were soon reported not only in the provinces but in Peking as well. . . . In brief, what happened was that the Red Guards and revolutionary rebels utilized their new freedom of action to attack one another and, for good measure, the PLA as well. . . . Instances of worker revolutionary rebels defying and even seizing PLA representatives were also reported at this time. As a result, leaders of the Cultural Revolution Group headed by Madame Mao convened a series of meetings in mid-April between feuding Red Guard and revolutionary rebel groups to chastise them for attacking the PLA and for engaging in "unprincipled civil wars." . . .[20]

New Calls for Order (May–June 1967)

The disclosure in a May 12 *People's Daily* editorial that the People's Liberation Army was "resolutely carrying out the five tasks of supporting the Left, supporting industry, supporting agriculture, exercising military control, and helping in military and political training" merely confirmed what had already become abundantly clear: that the army was now governing most of China in place of the discredited, largely defunct Party and government apparatus. In its Party role, military control committees at all levels were charged with leading the Cultural Revolution, held responsible for the creation of "true proletarian revolutionary great alliances" and of "revolutionary three-way alliances." This was a delicate political task for which, lacking guidance from Peking, it was singularly ill-prepared. In its government role, the army was responsible for administering the economy and for maintaining order, the latter task rendered virtually impossible by the April 6 Military Affairs Committee directive prohibiting the use of force.

As spelled out in the April 6 directive, the army in dealing with the revolutionary masses was "to learn to do mass work, trust the masses, rely on them and consult with them on important matters . . . to adopt skillful means of persuasion and education instead of adopting simple and crude means of issuing orders." For their part, the proletarian revolutionaries were also enjoined not to use force against the army. . . .[21]

Instead of mutual trust and co-operation, however, the principal characteristic of the Cultural Revolution in the months which followed was increased antagonism and hostility between the army and the revolutionary Left. . . . Instead of increased strength through greater unity, there was a further splitting of the revolutionary ranks, a split brought on (according to Hsieh Fu-chih in a May 7 speech) by those demanding "a great shakeup, great differentiation and great reorganization inside the Left wing." Instead of supporting army commanders, revolutionary mass organizations in the provinces and major cities launched bitter attacks against local military control committees, both for having suppressed them in the past and for failure to support them in the present. For their part, local military district commands continued to experience great difficulty, as Lin Piao had admitted earlier, in "finding out the difference between Left and Right" in their dealings with mass organizations.

Mao's solution to this problem . . . was typical. On May 7, the Chairman directed Lin Piao to carry out an intensive two-week rectification campaign in the army. . . .[22] Central to this campaign was the demand that local military commanders atone for their past errors by engaging publicly in self-criticism, thereby securing the forgiveness and winning the trust of those proletarian revolutionaries whom they had previously wronged. . . .

As a guide for the prevention of new mistakes by the army, the Tsinghai military district commander, Liu Hsien-ch'üan, published a lengthy article in the *People's Daily* in early June summarizing his successful experience in identifying and supporting the Left in Tsinghai province.[23] Although admitting that there had been "complicated struggle" and "all sorts of factions," Liu asserted that there were basically only "two kinds of factions" which could be clearly differentiated —a "Leftist" faction which "wants to revolt" and a "conservative" faction which "wants to conserve." . . .

Liu's account of developments in Tsinghai omitted one important fact—that his predecessor in command of the Tsinghai Provincial Military District . . . had "carried out savage, armed repression of revolutionary mass organizations." [24] That it was dangerous for a provincial military commander to decide on his own which mass organizations were "Leftist" was the most important lesson of the Tsinghai experience, a lesson confirmed in the provision of the April 6 directive prohibiting "taking any important action . . . toward large mass organizations" until a report had been "made to the Central Cultural Revolution Group and the All PLA Cultural Revolution Group and their advice sought." The net effect of this lesson and this prohibition was to suspend the PLA's "work in support of the Left" until such time as the Party Center had made its own investigation and determination of the revolutionary Left on a province-by-province basis.

Related to this was the disclosure in early May that fighting between rival mass organizations had entered a new stage of "armed struggle." The extent of the new disorder in Peking was revealed by Hsieh Fu-chih in a speech on May 14. . . . In the first 10 days of May, according to Hsieh, there had been 133 armed struggles and bloody incidents involving more than 63,000 people of which a "two-figure" number were killed. In addition, cases of beating, destroying, looting, searching houses and illegal arrest had been common and were increasing.

Not long before, on May 5, Hsieh Fu-chih had revealed in a speech to students at Peking University that "armed struggles at factories, schools and various organs" were taking place not only in Peking but in many provinces as well. Despite the fact that "conservative factions" (the opposition) had not yet been defeated in various provinces, the "Leftists" there (as in Peking) had begun to "break up" by fighting among themselves. . . .

Hsieh's pessimistic view of conditions in the provinces was confirmed by wall posters reporting violent clashes and serious disorder in many parts of China throughout May, even to the point of disrupting service on several major rail lines. So serious was this disorder that it was necessary for the Central Committee, State Council, Military Affairs Committee and Cultural Revolution Group to issue a joint circular on June 6 forbidding armed struggle, assaults, destruction, pillage, house-raids and unauthorized arrests and calling on all revolutionary organizations to comply.[25] Although assigning general responsibility to the PLA for implementing this circular, it did not authorize the use of force against these contending revolutionary organizations. Lacking this authority, the army remained powerless to restore order and disorder continued to spread unchecked throughout much of China.

The contradictory elements in the prescription issued by Mao at this time for dealing with a situation of spreading violence and disorder stood out in sharp contrast. On the one hand, he warned that "disregard of discipline and trends toward anarchism existent in many places must be overcome without fail." . . .[26] In accordance with this pronouncement, the principal manifestation of "anarchism"—"conducting struggle by force, such as assault, wrecking, robbery, search and arrest"—was condemned repeatedly in June and July. On the other hand, the one instrument capable of restoring order, the PLA, was still forbidden to use force, reminded once again that the only proper response to criticism and attack by the masses was "to do political and ideological work patiently among them." [27]

As viewed from Peking, the status of the Cultural Revolution in mid-1967 was far from encouraging. Since February, only one new area, Peking, had been "liberated" by Mao's revolutionaries. . . . Since Mao's directives governing the development of the Cultural Revolution were by definition correct, the failure of the campaign to proceed according to plan could only result from faulty execution of these directives. Given the premise of Mao's infallibility, the principal issue over which differences of opinion would arise within the central leadership at this time, then, was whether to assign primary responsibility for this adverse development to the People's Liberation Army (its failure to identify and provide adequate support to the Leftists) or to the revolutionary Left (its refusal to unite and observe revolutionary discipline as manifested in continuing factionalism and anarchism).

The disclosure that differences of opinion had arisen within the central leadership was made in wall-poster reports at this time of "heated discussions" occurring within the Central Committee. Although these reports did not reveal the substance of the discussions nor identify the participants, it is a fair inference . . . that these differences concerned the conflicting claims of restoring order and maintaining revolutionary momentum, with one group (*i.e.,* Chou En-lai, representing the government and presumably spokesmen for the military) arguing the need to restore order and another group (*i.e.,* such leading members of the Cultural Revolution Group as Madame Mao, Ch'en Po-ta and K'ang Sheng) advocating a more militant policy in support of the revolutionary Left.

One outcome of this debate was the decision to send a number of high-level government and military delegations to investigate and provide guidance on the conduct of the Cultural Revolution in the provinces. A major objective of the delegations sent out at this time was to put an end to the armed struggle which had broken out between contending factions and between these factions and local military commands. The means for achieving this objective was a six-point formula advanced by the Central Committee under which representatives of both factions agreed (1) to stop breaking into military organs, assaulting army officials, stealing weapons, and attacking each other; and (2) by means of rectification and self-criticism to form "great revolutionary alliances." [28] When agreements to this effect were negotiated in Yunnan and Anhwei in late June and early July, it appeared that Mao's Cultural Revolution had once again entered a more moderate phase, marked by a concerted effort to damp down violent struggle and reduce the antagonism which had arisen between army commanders in the provinces and the revolutionary Left.

The Wuhan Incident (July–August 1967)

The significance of what has come to be known as the "Wuhan Incident" is that it sharply reversed this trend towards moderation, precipitating a short-lived "ultra-Leftist" phase of the Cultural Revolution extending from late July through most of August. The Wuhan Incident afforded extremist elements in the central leadership an opportunity, which they were quick to exploit, to focus once again on the "mistakes" of the People's Liberation Army as the primary cause of failures and setbacks. It was seized upon as a pretext for launching another great revolutionary upsurge from below, for exhorting the Red Guards and revolutionary rebels to rise up against their oppressors wherever encountered, whether in the military, the new revolutionary committees, or in the central government. The end result of this ill-advised venture was near anarchy and a further discrediting and weakening of the forces of the revolutionary Left.

In bare outline, the story of the Wuhan Incident which unfolded during a seven-day period in mid-July concerns the failure of a high-level mission, headed by Hsieh Fu-chih and Wang Li, to persuade the two factions in this large central China city to stop fighting and accept the six-point formula for achieving unity recently issued by the Central Committee. As applied in Wuhan, however, this formula called for the preferment of one faction (designated an authentic "revolutionary rebel" organization) over the other (labelled a "conservative" organization) and, in so doing, reversed an earlier decision made by the local military. What is more, the leaders of the Wuhan Military Region Command were then ordered to make a public confession of error and conduct self-criticism before the revolutionary masses. Reportedly infuriated, some leaders of this command then encouraged (or at least did nothing to prevent) a demonstration by the much larger "conservative" faction (which included troops from the local military garrison) to protest against this decision, in the course of which the two leaders from Peking were seized and roughed up. Although this demonstration appeared intended primarily as a form of political protest, the response in Peking was one of outrage, coupled with prompt and effective measures to secure the release of Mao's emissaries and to call the offending military commanders to the capital for denunciation and dismissal.[29]

As noted above, the extremist elements in the Cultural Revolution Group of the Central Committee appeared determined to exploit this incident to further their own goals. . . . On July 21, K'ang Sheng attacked the Wuhan Military Region for having committed a "mutinous act." . . .[30] In an even more inflammatory speech on the same occasion, Madam Mao exhorted her audience of "young revolutionary fighters" not "to be naïve," as their comrades in Wuhan had been, but rather "to take up arms to defend yourselves" when attacked by the "handful" using "pistols, rifles, spears or swords." . . .[31] Throughout the following week Mao's propagandists mounted a series of editorial attacks on "capitalist roaders" in the People's Liberation Army, culminating in the shrill call in the July 31 *Red Flag* editorial to "bring down" and "sweep the handful of Party and military persons in authority taking the capitalist road completely and totally into the junkyard."

Reflecting this tough line towards dissident or potentially dissident military commanders in the provinces, Lin Piao delivered a major policy speech on August 9 to a gathering of top political and military leaders (both central and regional) in Peking.[32] As he had on earlier occasions, Lin defended chaos or "upheaval" as essential to achieve the objectives of the Cultural Revolution . . . and counselled those present, even when unjustly attacked, "to stand up to it and restrain your anger." Lin's speech was directed primarily, however, at those who, through lack of understanding of the Cultural Revolution, had made "mistakes" in various military regions, reacting to attacks on their military district commands by "suppressing the masses." The remedy, as Lin reiterated for emphasis, was for these local military leaders quickly to admit their "mistakes" by carrying out public self-criticism . . . "so that the revolutionary rebels may be their teachers and their own mistakes their teaching materials." If not, the fate of these military leaders would be . . . "to have their pigtails grabbed."

Additional evidence of what might be called the over-reaction of the central leadership to the Wuhan Incident was the decision in early August to arm selected Red Guard and revolutionary rebel units, both in Peking and the provinces, to assist in safeguarding property, maintaining order and "assuring the smooth development of the Cultural Revolution." Authorization for this potentially explosive move was attributed to Mao Tse-tung himself.[33] When combined with Madame Mao's earlier call to Red Guards "to take up arms" under the slogan "attack by reason, defend by force," the stage was set for a new form of "revolutionary rebellion" directed towards a second seizure of power, this time from the military commanders and newly established revolutionary committees in several provinces. Mao's Cultural Revolution was about to enter an "ultra-Leftist" phase, as it was called after the violence and anarchy it unleashed necessitated a hasty retreat.

The rationale for this attempt to seize military power was, given the premises of the Cultural Revolution, quite logical. . . . The main contradiction was no longer one with "the handful in the Party" (who had been "dragged out" in the preceding year) but with "the handful in the Army." Aided by Red Guards sent out from Peking, local revolutionary rebels were, according to one plan, "to unite with the broad masses of People's Liberation Army cadres and fighters, drag out these executioners and recapture the military power usurped by them." [34]

Paralleling this drive in the provinces, revolutionary rebels in the Ministry of Foreign Affairs were also incited by extremist members of the Cultural Revolution Group to seize a greater share of power over the conduct of China's foreign relations. In part a function of the continuing attack against Foreign Minister Ch'en Yi, this struggle within the Foreign Ministry also reflected pressures exerted by militants to inject a new "revolutionary" content into China's diplomatic relations, to convert Foreign Ministry and foreign service officials into "red diplomatic fighters." . . .

The results of this sharp turn to the left were nearly catastrophic. In foreign policy, a reign of terror directed at foreign diplomats was instituted in Peking, culminating in the ransacking and burning of the British Chancery and the manhandling of the British Chargé on August 22. In domestic policy, although no single incident served to dramatize the damaging effects of the new militance of the revolutionary Left, the consequences were more serious. . . . The discovery that, at a time of mounting violence and economic disorder, factionalism had spread from the Red Guards and revolutionary rebels into the army was most alarming of all. There was no choice in late August but to apply the brakes, pull back, assess the damage, and initiate a trend towards moderation in the Cultural Revolution which lasted throughout the remainder of 1967.

Renewed Moderation (September–December 1967)

The unfolding of Mao's Cultural Revolution had brought China by the end of August to the brink of anarchy, featuring pitched battles by heavily armed factions in nearly all of China's provinces. Recognizing the gravity of the situation, Mao's new leadership team in Peking sought to achieve two separate but related objectives in the remaining months of 1967: (1) to carry out a series of measures designed to restore minimum levels of public order and production; and (2) to dissociate Mao and his Cultural Revolution from responsibility for the violence and lawlessness endemic in China by finding new scapegoats. The gravity of the crisis was such that for the first time it was necessary to sacrifice a number of prominent members of the Cultural Revolution

Group, holding them, rather than the policies they were administering, responsible for the nationwide disturbance in China.

The vehicle for announcing the sharp reversal in policy was a September 5 speech by Madame Mao in Peking which was subsequently disseminated for study to all revolutionary committees, military control committees and revolutionary mass organizations throughout the country. As a confirmed extremist and a confidante of Mao, Chiang Ch'ing was no doubt selected as a spokesman whose pronouncements would be accepted as authoritative by the revolutionary Left; the more so since most of the policies she now criticized in this speech were ones with which she was formerly associated. . . .

The bulk of Madame Mao's speech was devoted to repudiating the "armed struggle" by Red Guards and "revolutionary rebels" incited by the slogans "seize a small handful in the Army" and "attack by words, defend by force" (which she herself had advanced in a speech of July 22). . . . Although praising the forbearance of the military under this assault, Madame Mao made clear that there were limits to this forbearance, warning repeatedly of the danger of "creating chaos" in "our field armies." And to ensure that these attacks would cease, she stressed that it was no longer permitted for Red Guards to travel about the country "kindling the fire of revolution and exchanging revolutionary experience" as they had done a year earlier.[35]

On the same day as Madame Mao's speech, the Central Committee issued a directive "forbidding seizure of arms, equipment and other military supplies from the PLA" and ordering, in addition, that all such arms and equipment that had been seized "must be put under seal and stored and a time limit set for their return." And for the first time since the Military Affairs Committee directive of April 6, the PLA was authorized to "hit back in self-defense" (*i.e.*, open fire), but only when attacked by "mass organizations or individuals" attempting "to seize their weapons." . . .[36] As stressed in a *Liberation Army Daily* editorial of September 7, these steps were necessary in order to carry out "Chairman Mao's great strategic plan." [37]

This plan was expounded in a series of "supreme instructions" issued by Mao Tse-tung during the course of an extended tour in September through North, Central-South and East China. . . . Most of the principles outlined in these instructions were not new, having been enunciated in earlier stages of the revolution. What had produced the recent nationwide disturbance was not the principles themselves, but rather, as Mao took great pains to demonstrate, that these principles had been misunderstood and mistakenly applied. In fact, the principal lesson which Mao appeared to derive from his September review of developments in the Cultural Revolution was that all three components of the new revolutionary organs of power (the PLA, the revolutionary cadres, and the revolutionary rebels) had made mistakes and would therefore once again have to undergo rectification and ideological education. The most pressing problem was "educating" the Red Guards and revolutionary rebels in order to prevent, as Mao put it, their "turning to the extreme Left." This, of course, had already occurred, creating what Mao referred to elsewhere as "the chief danger at the moment"— "that some people want to beat down the PLA," to "incite the soldiers to oppose their officers" and to create "chaos in the Army." [38] Another manifestation of this phenomenon of "ultra-Leftism" was factionalism, a problem which had bedevilled the Cultural Revolution from the outset and to which Mao now turned his attention.

First were the Olympian pronouncements, widely publicized, to the effect that "there is no reason whatsoever for the working class to split into two great irreconcilable organizations" and "there is no conflict of fundamental interests in the ranks of the Red Guards and revolutionaries." [39] Next was the admission, made more explicit in speeches by other top leaders at this time, that radical Red Guard organizations in Peking had been responsible for spreading factionalism into the ranks of the workers in July and August. . . .

The solution to this problem appeared in another instruction by Chairman Mao given wide publicity in mid-October—"to build revolutionary great alliances on the basis of trade, profession, department or class in school." [40] It was necessary to break up the mass organizations (consisting of students, workers, peasants and cadres) which had become unmanageable, dissolving these organizations into their separate components which then would become easier to control. A prime objective of this reorganization was to get student Red Guards, carriers of the virus of factionalism, out of the factories and the countryside and return them to the class-room where they would once again undergo rectification and a course of "military-political training" conducted by the PLA. . . .

Although assigned major responsibility for restoring order in the ranks of the revolutionary Left, the PLA was still denied the authority necessary to carry out this assignment. As had been the case ever since the April 6 Military Affairs Committee directive, the PLA was still generally prohibited from using force and in addition was specifically forbidden by Chairman Mao at this time to suppress revolutionary mass organizations. Limited to the instrumentality of ideological and political training, the PLA's authority was further restricted by the requirements that only "a handful of bad persons" in these organizations were to be held responsible for factionalism. . . . [41] Forbidden to use force and unable to secure voluntary compliance, the PLA was powerless to carry out its assigned mission.

Further complicating their task, PLA cadres were informed at this

time that they too would have to undergo "training and education" to
atone for and prevent the repetition of mistakes they had committed in
supporting the Left in the previous stage of the Cultural Revolution.
. . . The most important [problem], according to Mao, was that "Army
cadres have not been educated over a long time and have no experience
in this connection." To help correct this deficiency, training classes for
senior military cadres from the provinces were held in Peking beginning in September and extending through the remainder of the year.[42]

A quicker, more effective remedy for these mistakes committed by the
PLA in supporting the Left (*i.e.*, supporting "conservative" rather than
"revolutionary" mass organizations) was to order the army to disengage
from factional struggles altogether. This order appeared in a September 17 *Liberation Army Daily* editorial in the injunction to army troops
"not to involve themselves in struggles among groups" and, more suc-
cinctly, in the slogan enunciated in speeches the same day by Chou
En-lai and Madame Mao: "support the Left but not any particular
factions." [43] An important ancillary purpose of this directive, of course,
was to prevent the virus of factionalism from spreading further into the
army.

Civilian Party and government cadres—the third component of the
"three-way alliance"—were to be given still another chance "to correct
their mistakes" by taking part in this training program in the fall of
1967. As suggested by another Maoist instruction ("it is necessary to
expand the area of education and diminish the area under attack"),
however, the principal concern of this program was to protect these
cadres from the punitive, wholesale attacks to which they had been
subjected by revolutionary rebels.[44] The time had come to reassert
Mao's "mild cadre policy." . . . As discussed in an authoritative *People's Daily* editorial of October 21, this new policy was based on the
recognition that "correct treatment of cadres" was "the key to realizing
the revolutionary three-way alliance." . . .

The final and perhaps most important instruction conveyed by
Chairman Mao during his September tour was that the process of setting up a new governmental structure (the revolutionary committees)
in all the 29 provinces and major cities of China be speeded up and
completed by the end of January 1968. Whereas only seven of these
had been formed in the first nine months of 1967, it was now intended
to create 22 in the ensuing four-month period in order (in Mao's words)
that "problems of the whole country could be solved basically and the
whole situation put into the normal track before the Spring Festival." [45]
To meet this deadline, it was no longer possible to rely on the long,
drawn-out, cumbrous and generally unsuccessful method of seizure of
power from below. Instead, it was necessary to impose solutions from
above, hammering out agreements in Peking on the basis of Mao's
directive "to solve the problems of various provinces one by one." As

reported by Chou En-lai on September 26, delegations from 12 provinces had come to Peking for just this purpose. . . .[46]

Chou's prediction in this speech that "it is not possible to solve very quickly the problems of the 12 provinces" was an accurate one. . . . The Premier indicated a major stumbling-block which would prevent rapid establishment of these revolutionary committees: that the composition and membership of such committees could not be decreed arbitrarily from above but would have to be approved by all three groups comprising these revolutionary organs of power. This meant that top leaders of the Party Center (notably Chou himself) would be forced to spend night after night in protracted and exhausting negotiating sessions lasting a month or more, during which the two factions from the province concerned wrangled over the degree of representation and share of power to be allotted each. As a result of the delay imposed by this time-consuming and laborious process, only seven additional provinces and major cities had succeeded in proclaiming revolutionary committees by or near the time of the Spring Festival.

Although the trend towards moderation initiated in late August continued, two major components of the effort to restore order had run into difficulty by the end of the year. First, the attempt to restore order from below by "establishing revolutionary great alliances on the basis of trade, profession, department or class in school" was foundering because of the refusal of revolutionary mass organizations in many areas to comply voluntarily with this directive. Forbidden by Mao to use force or to suppress revolutionary mass organizations, the PLA was powerless to cope with the fresh outbreak of factionalism in November and December which threatened once again to plunge large areas of China into "armed struggle" and anarchy.

The undertaking to restore order from above by speeding up the establishment of a new government structure had also fallen far short of the original goal. Here again the principal reason this program had not progressed faster was Mao's insistence that the representatives of revolutionary mass organizations be heard in the negotiating process and receive genuine representation in the new organs of revolutionary power. Despite the reverses encountered in 1967, Mao Tse-tung appeared determined at the close of the year on carrying his Cultural Revolution through to the end.

Prospects

. . . Progress towards the original goals of the Cultural Revolution in 1967 was minimal and achieved only at great cost. The first goal—that of discrediting and overthrowing Mao's major opponents within the Party—was achieved readily enough, but in most cases the power "seized" from these opponents had then to be relinquished to the army. Another important result of Mao's call to seize power from below

had been to inculcate widespread contempt among Red Guards and
revolutionary rebels for authority of any kind, including the authority
of new "revolutionary" institutions and even that of the Party Center.
For these reasons, Mao's power to control developments in China—like
that of other leaders—probably declined in 1967.

Progress towards the second goal—that of identifying and training
trustworthy "revolutionary successors"—was limited and uneven. At
the outset, many youthful Red Guards and revolutionary rebels appeared to be enthusiastic in their support of the revolution. After more
than a year of violence and bloodshed, and especially after their demotion to a position of secondary importance, it is likely that many among
the younger generation in China grew cynical and welcomed the opportunity to resume their studies in a quieter and better ordered society.

Failure to make progress towards the third and final goal—that of
achieving an ideological revolution—was most noticeable of all. Instead of smashing the "four olds" (old ideas, culture, customs and
habits) and creating a new Chinese man devoted to Mao's conception
of the good society (featuring class struggle, heroic poverty and collective enthusiasm), the end result of the Cultural Revolution in 1967 was
to make the "four olds" more prevalent than ever, to revive traditional
relationships and intensify the pursuit of narrow, selfish interests (the
most basic, of course, being personal survival) by both legal and illegal
means. . . .

1. See the editorial "On the Proletarian Revolutionaries' Struggle to Seize Power,"
   Hung Ch'i (Red Flag), No. 3, February 3, 1967, in *Peking Review*, February 3,
   1967, p. 13.
2. "Premier Chou En-lai Gives Important Instructions," in *Kung-nun-ping Chan-
   pao* (Worker-Peasant-Soldier Combat News), *Survey of China Mainland Press*
   (SCMP) (Hong Kong: U. S. Consulate General), No. 4078, p. 4.
3. See the editorial "Welcome the High Tide of the Cultural Revolution in Industrial and Mining Enterprises" in *Jen-min Jih-pao* (People's Daily, December 26,
   1966.
4. For a good analysis of this phenomenon of "economism," see Evelyn Anderson,
   "Shanghai: The Masses Unleashed," *Problems of Communism*, January–February
   1968.
5. *Sankei* (Tokyo), January 17, 1967.
6. See, for example, the speech by Ch'en Po-ta in *Huo-ch'e-t'ou* (Locomotive),
   February 1967, *SCMP*, No. 3898, pp. 5–6.
7. *Asahi Shimbun* (Tokyo), February 18, 1967.
8. Chang Jih-ch'ing, "Steadfastly Support the Proletarian Revolutionaries' Struggle
   to Seize Power," *Red Flag*, No. 4, 1967, in *Selections from China Mainland Magazines* (SCMM), No. 567.
9. *Asahi*, March 18, 1967.

10. *SCMM*, No. 566, p. 3.
11. *Ibid.*
12. *Mainichi Shimbun* (Tokyo), February 8, 1967.
13. *New China News Agency* (NCNA), March 2, 1967.
14. *Ibid.*
15. *SCMM*, No. 568, pp. 1–4.
16. *Mainichi*, March 17, 1967.
17. *Ceteka* (Prague), April 28, 1967.
18. *Yomiuri*, April 15, 1967.
19. See the speech by Vice-Premier Hsieh Fu-chih in *SCMP* No. 3925, pp. 8–9.
20. *Tokyo Shimbun*, April 18, 1967.
21. Editorial entitled "Warmly Respond to the Call to Support the Army and Cherish the People," *Red Flag*, No. 6, May 8, 1967, in *Peking Review*, May 5, 1967, p. 22.
22. *NCNA*, June 15, 1967.
23. Radio Peking Domestic Service, June 8, 1967.
24. *Yomiuri*, April 9, 1967.
25. *Yomiuri*, June 8, 1967.
26. *SCMP*, No. 3969, p. 1.
27. *NCNA*, June 27, 1967.
28. *Sankei*, July 3, 1967.
29. For a good account of the Wuhan Incident by a Japanese correspondent, see *Sankei*, September 29 and 30, 1967.
30. For a summary of this speech, see *SCMP*, No. 4023, pp. 20–21.
31. Canton *Kung-an Chan-pao* (Public Security Combat News), August 1, 1967, p. 4.
32. *SCMP*, No. 4036, pp. 1–6.
33. *Sankei*, August 22, 1967.
34. "On Military Power" in *Hung-se Pao-tung* (Red Riot), August 1, 1967, *SCMP*, No. 4071, pp. 13–17.
35. "Important Speech Given by Comrade Chiang Ch'ing," Peking leaflet, September 18, 1967, in *SCMP*, No. 4069, pp. 1–9.
36. *SCMP*, No. 4026, pp. 1–2.
37. *NCNA*, September 7, 1967.
38. "Chairman Mao's Latest Instructions" in *Wen-ke T'ung-hsün* (Cultural Revolution Bulletin), October 9, 1967, *SCMP*, No. 4060, p. 1.
39. *NCNA*, September 25, 1967.
40. *NCNA*, October 17, 1967.
41. *NCNA*, October 10, 1967.
42. "Chairman Mao's Latest Instructions" in *Hung-chan-pao* (Red Combat News), October 10, 1967, *SCMP*, No. 4072, p. 2.
43. "Premier Chou's Important Speech" in *Chu-ying Tung-fang-hung*, October 1, 1967, *SCMP*, No. 4066, p. 5.
44. "Chairman Mao's Latest Supreme Instructions" in *Cheng-fa Hung-ch'i* (Politics and Law Red Flag), October 17, 1967, *SCMP*, No. 4070, p. 3.
45. *SCMP*, No. 4070, p. 3.
46. "Speeches by Leaders of the Central Committee," Canton pamphlet, October 1967, in *SCMM*, No. 611, p. 8.

CHINA: YEAR OF THE MANGOES

Richard Baum

The end, when it finally came, was distinctly anticlimactic. Liu Shao-ch'i, China's chief of state and former heir apparent to Party Chairman Mao Tse-tung, was at long last (and to no one's surprise) officially revealed to be the "number one Party person in authority taking the capitalist road" and formally expelled from the Chinese Communist Party. Ironically, Liu's downfall came on Halloween night, October 31, 1968—a fitting occasion, it would seem, for exorcising the malevolent spirit of a man who for almost two years had been bitterly reviled as an anti-Party, anti-socialist demon and monster.[1]

More surprising perhaps than the fact of Liu's expulsion from the Party was the manner in which it was secured. Notice of Liu's dismissal was contained in the official press communiqué of the Party Central Committee's 12th (enlarged) Plenum, which met under conditions of near-total secrecy in Peking from October 13 to October 31.[2]

Unlike the previous (11th) plenary session of August 1966, which had been packed with large numbers of exuberant young Red Guards, the 12th Plenum was convened in a relatively restrained and sober atmosphere marked by the total absence of Mao's "revolutionary little generals." In their stead were the "principal responsible comrades of the revolutionary committees of the provinces, municipalities and autonomous regions" and "principal responsible comrades of the Chinese People's Liberation Army." [3] This altered pattern of representation in China's highest policy-making council bore mute testimony to a pronounced trend toward conservatism in cultural revolutionary politics in 1968. . . .

The convocation of the 12th Plenum followed by five weeks the inauguration of the last of China's 29 provincial, municipal and autonomous regional revolutionary committees (see Table I, below). The completion of the tortuous, 18-month process of establishing these new provincial-level power organs constituted a watershed in the development of the Cultural Revolution from the stage of radical, planned destruction to that of reconstruction and consolidation. Even before the last of these committees had been established, however, there were visible signs of an impending turn to the right.

As early as the first week of August there were strong indications that

Richard Baum, "China: Year of the Mangoes," *Asian Survey* 9, no. 1 (January, 1969): 1–17. Reprinted by permission of the publisher.

a major drive to curb the revolutionary excesses of the radically anti-establishmentarian Red Guards and "revolutionary rebels" was in the offing. Beginning with the notorious "mangoes affair" of August 5, discussed below, it became increasingly clear that the fractious young Red Guard fighters were being forcibly subordinated to the leadership of the (relatively) more conservative workers and peasants, who were in turn openly organized, led and supported by local units of the People's Liberation Army (PLA).[4]

By mid-October the implications of this movement to restore social order and discipline in China's schools, factories and farms were clear. Prior to that time the Cultural Revolution had been defined in the Party press as "a great Party rectification movement," a definition which was generally accompanied by emotional exhortations for the Red Guards and revolutionary rebels to play a leading role in exposing and criticizing "bourgeois powerholders" at all levels in the party apparatus.[5] Now, however, the authoritative ideological journal, *Red Flag*, explicitly redefined the Cultural Revolution as "an open Party *consolidation* movement"—a clear indication that the unrestricted hunting license previously issued to Mao's revolutionary minions had been revoked.[6]

The Revolution in Retrospect

Prior to the convocation of the 12th Plenum, the Cultural Revolution witnessed the most extensive purge in the history of the Chinese Communist Party—a purge rivaled in scope and intensity only by the Stalinist *Yezhovshchina* of 1936–1938.

The extent to which the ranks of the CCP's top-level leadership were decimated in the course of the Cultural Revolution is graphically illustrated by the fact that no less than 121 (out of a total of 172) members and alternate members of China's ruling Central Committee were publicly criticized, struggled against, "dragged out," or otherwise vilified by the Mao-inspired masses in the two and one-half years following the formal initiation of the movement in the spring of 1966.[7] Much the same fate befell China's top-ranking provincial Party leaders, 23 of whom (out of 28) were either purged outright or suspended from their duties in the same period.[8] While a certain number of these individuals will undoubtedly be rehabilitated during the forthcoming "Party consolidation" stage of the Cultural Revolution, the damage already done to their prestige—and, more important, to the prestige and authority of the CCP itself—will not be easily repaired.

There can be little doubt that neither the extent of this radical purge of the Party apparatus nor its vicissitudinous course of development were fully anticipated by Mao Tse-tung (or anyone else) when the Cultural Revolution was first tentatively launched in the autumn of 1965. In the first place, many of Mao's original, and presumably hand-picked, cultural revolutionary lieutenants were themselves ultimately devoured in the raging, wind-swept flames of the movement. Thus, for example, four members of the original "Group of Five" placed in charge of the Cultural Revolution in September 1965 quickly fell victim to the forces of extremism generated in the early stages of the movement; similarly, 13 members of the 18-man "Central Cultural Revolution Group" which was set up to replace the original "Group of Five" in the summer of 1966 were purged in the middle stages of the movement.[9]

Second, the convulsive, oscillatory development of the Cultural Revolution strongly suggests that once begun, the movement assumed a dialectical dynamic of its own, quite independent of the original designs or intentions of its principal architect. One need only take note of the radical swings in official policy occasioned by such phenomena as the "work team" debacle of June and July 1966,[10] the February 1967 "adverse currents" of "reversing verdicts" and "sham power seizures," [11] or the anarchistic aftermath of the "Wuhan incident" of July 1967 [12] to appreciate the extent to which the vicissitudes of the Cultural Revolution have been determined by forces beyond the immediate control of the Maoist leadership. Like a runaway train derailed, the Cultural Revolution has responded less to the frantic manipulations of its engineer than to the imperatives of the terrain over which it has traveled.

Finally, there has been the oft-noted tendency toward progressively increasing military involvement in political decision-making at all levels of Chinese society—a tendency reflected in the high proportion of PLA officials appointed to positions of leadership on the all-powerful, provincial-level revolutionary committees. A cardinal tenet of orthodox Maoism holds that "the Party commands the gun, and the gun must never be allowed to command the Party." On the basis of available evidence, however, there is every reason to believe that to an unprecedented degree it is the gun that now commands the Party—or what is left of the Party. It is inconceivable that such a fundamentally non-Maoist development could have been part of any Maoist "master plan" for implementing the Cultural Revolution.[13]

The meteoric political ascendancy of China's regional and provincial military leaders has been the most spectacular byproduct of the virtual destruction of the Party machinery in 1967–1968. This ascendancy is graphically illustrated in Table I, which summarizes the leadership composition of the 29 provincial, municipal and autonomous regional revolutionary committees.

Originally, the revolutionary committees were designed to reflect a tripartite sharing of power (the so-called "three-way alliance") among "revolutionary leading cadres" (*i.e.*, those former Party and government officials whose class backgrounds and political histories had been cleared), "revolutionary masses" (*i.e.*, leaders of Red Guard and revolutionary rebel mass organizations), and representatives of the PLA.[14] By mid-1967, however, it became apparent that local and regional military leaders were beginning to occupy more than their (theoretical) fair share of the all-important committee chairmanships and vice-chairmanships.

Of the 12 chairmen and first vice-chairmen appointed to the six provincial and municipal revolutionary committees formed in the winter and early spring of 1967, 8 (or 67%) were identified primarily as former Party officials. After that time, however, the proportion of former Party cadres dropped noticeably, with a corresponding rise in military representation. Thus, of 46 chairmen and first vice-chairmen appointed to the 23 revolutionary committees established after August 1, 1967, 37 (or 81%) were identified as high-ranking regional or provincial army officers.[15] Significantly, at no time during the Cultural Revolution has a single representative of a revolutionary mass organization been appointed either chairman or first vice-chairman of a provincial or municipal revolutionary committee.

The principal explanation for the rapid rise to power of provincial and regional military figures beginning in mid-1967 lies in the fact that it was the PLA that was called upon to preserve—or rather restore—social order in the face of the violent factional struggles which broke out between rival mass organizations throughout China in the spring and early summer of 1967.[16] In addition, a brief flurry of anti-military activity on the part of the more extremist Red Guards and revolutionary rebels in the summer of 1967 (an aftermath of the Wuhan incident) served greatly to heighten the Maoists' awareness of their dependence upon the PLA as a peace-keeping force. Consequently, the value of the army's political stock rose appreciably, to the point where it now appears that provincial and regional military leaders (who are serving concurrently as leaders of the provincial revolutionary committees) are able to exercise effective veto power over the policy decisions of the central (Maoist) leadership in Peking.

Another striking trend revealed in Table I is the increasingly high proportion of politically moderate and conservative leaders appointed to provincial revolutionary committee chairmanships beginning in February 1968. In part this trend undoubtedly reflects the "natural conservatism" generally assumed to be a universal attribute of the "military mentality"—a conservatism born of the professional soldier's long exposure to martial discipline and his positive orientation toward hierarchical authority relationships.

On the other hand, however, the increasing trend toward conservative revolutionary committee leadership has also accurately reflected the newly altered balance of political power between Peking and the provinces. It is no mere coincidence that the last five provinces and autonomous regions to establish revolutionary committees in August and September of 1968 (Yunnan, Fukien, Kwangsi, Tibet and Sinkiang) are

TABLE I: Leadership Composition of Provincial-Level Revolutionary Committees*

Province or Municipality	Date Established	Chairman	First Vice-Chairman	Backgrounds of Chairman and First Vice-Chairman[1]		Main sources of support for Chairman[2]	Total no. Chairmen and all Vice-Chairmen[2]	Backgrounds of all Chairmen and Vice-Chairmen		
				Chairman	Vice-Chairman			M[3]	P-G[4]	MO[5]
Heilungkiang	31 Jan 67	P'an Fu-sheng	Wang Chia-tao	P-MC**	M	mod-civ-Pek	2	1	1	0
Shanghai	5 Feb 67	Chang Ch'un-ch'iao	Yao Wen-yüan	P-G†	P†	rad-civ-Pek	2	0	2	0
Kweichow	14 Feb 67	Li Tsai-han	Li Li	MC	P-G	rad-mil-reg	7	2	2	3
Shantung	23 Feb 67	Wang Hsiao-yü	Yang Te-chih	P-MC	M-P**	rad-mil-reg	14	11	1	2
Shansi	18 Mar 67	Liu Ko-p'ing	Chang Jih-ch'ing	P-MC**	MC	rad-civ-reg	8	3	3	2
Peking	20 Apr 67	Hsieh Fu-chih	Wu Te	P-MC**	P-G**	mod-civ-Pek	5	2	2	1
Tsinghai	12 Aug 67	Liu Hsien-ch'üan	Chang Chiang-lin	MC-P	M	rad-mil-Pek	7	3	1	3
Inner Mongolia	1 Nov 67	T'eng Hai-ch'ing	Wu T'ao	M	MC	rad-mil-Pek	5	2	1	2
Tientsin	6 Dec 67	Hsieh Hsüeh-kung	Hsiao Szu-ming	P-G	P-G	mod-civ-Pek	4	2	1	1
Kiangsi	5 Jan 68	Ch'eng Shih-ch'ing	Yang Tung-liang	M-MC	M	rad-mil-Pek	6	3	1	2
Kansu	24 Jan 68	Hsien Heng-han	Chang Chung	MC-P	M	mod-mil-reg	5	2	1	2
Honan	27 Jan 68	Liu Chien-hsün	Wang Hsin	P-MC**	M	rad-civ-Pek	5	2	3	0
Hopeh	3 Feb 68	Li Hsüeh-feng	Liu Tzu-hou	M	M-P	mod-mil-Pek	8	4	3	1
Hupeh	5 Feb 68	Tseng Szu-yü	K'ung Shih-ch'üan	P-MC**	P-G**	mod-mil-reg	4	2	1	1
Kwangtung	21 Feb 68	Huang Yung-sheng[6]	Liu Feng	M-P**	MC	mod-mil-Pek	10	6	2	2
Kirin	6 Mar 68	Wang Huai-hsiang	Yüan Po-sheng	MC	P	unknown	5	3	2	0
Kiangsu	23 Mar 68	Hsü Shih-yu	Wu Ta-sheng	M-P**	M	con-mil-reg	8	3	3	2
Chekiang	24 Mar 68	Nan P'ing	Ch'en Li-yün	MC	MC	con-mil-reg	8	3	3	2
Hunan	9 Apr 68	Li Yüan	Lung Shu-chin[7]	M	M	con-mil-Pek	5	4	0	1
Ninghsia	10 Apr 68	K'ang Chien-min	Chang Huai-li	M	M	unknown 6 (mil)	8	5	2	1
Anhwei	18 Apr 68	Li Te-sheng	Liao Ch'eng-mei	M	M-MC	con-mil-reg	8	5	2	1
Shensi	1 May 68	Li Jui-shan	Hu Wei	P	M-MC	mod-mil-Pek	11	3	4	4
Liaoning	10 May 68	Ch'en Hsi-lien	Yang Ch'un-fu	M-P**	P	mod-mil-Pek	16	4	3	9
Szechwan	31 May 68	Chang Kuo-hua	Liang Hsing-ch'u	M-P	P-G	con-mil-Pek	14	4	5	5
Yunnan	13 Aug 68	T'an Fu-jen	Chou Hsing	MC	M	mod-mil-reg	4	3	1	0
Fukien	19 Aug 68	Han Hsien-ch'u	P'i Ting-chün	P-G	M	mod-mil-Pek	12	5	3	4
Kwangsi	26 Aug 68	Wei Kuo-ch'ing	Ou Chih-fu	P-MC**	M	con-mil-reg	13	4	4	5
Tibet	5 Sep 68	Tseng Yung-ya	Jen Jung	M	M-P**	con-mil-reg	14	5	4	5
Sinkiang	5 Sep 68	Lung Shu-chin	Wang En-mao	M-P**	M	mod-mil-Pek	6	4	1	1

Chairman: M = 13 (45%), MC = 6 (21%), P = 10 (34%), G = 0 (00%), N = 29††

First Vice-Chairman: M = 16 (55%), MC = 6 (21%), P = 7 (24%), G = 0 (00%), N = 29

All Chairmen and Vice-Chairmen: M³ 94 (43%), P-G⁴ 57 (26%), MO⁵ 69 (31%), N = 220

* Compiled on the basis of information published in various official mainland Chinese media sources.

** Denotes member or alternate member of CCP 8th Central Committee (1956–1969).

† Denotes member of Cultural Revolution Group under the Central Committee (1966–   ).

†† In those cases where the current Chairman or First Vice-Chairman of a revolutionary committee have held prior posts in more than one major capacity, multiple affiliations are indicated. In all cases where the predominant affiliation (in terms of the individual's location in the status hierarchy associated with his role) is listed first. Thus, a former provincial Party Committee First Secretary who served concurrently as the Political Commissar of his provincial Military District would be identified by the notation P-MC, since his Party role was presumably more important than his military role. In the columns below, P = Party, G = government, M = military commander, MC = PLA political commissar.

2 The support sources summarized in this column represent extrapolations made by the author on the basis of an evaluation of available data, including the known political proclivities of the individual chairmen, the nature and duration of their local ties in the province to which they have been assigned, the nature and sources of any (official or unofficial) criticism directed at them during the Cultural Revolution, their known connections with major central figures, etc. In this column, mod = moderate, rad = radical (leftist), con = conservative (rightist); civ = civilian leadership (including Party and government officials), mil = military leadership, Pek = Peking-based support, reg = regional-based support (including greater military regions, provinces, and/or major municipalities).

3 For tabulation purposes, military commanders and PLA political commissars have been grouped together under the designation M (military).

4 Includes all personnel holding responsible positions in Party or governmental organs prior to the initiation of the Cultural Revolution.

5 Includes known representatives of mass organizations (e.g., Red Guards, "revolutionary rebels," etc.) together with those personnel whose prior backgrounds and organizational affiliations are unknown.

6 Huang Yung-sheng became PLA Chief of Staff in March 1968. In July 1969 his position as Chairman of the Kwangtung provincial revolutionary committee was taken by Liu Hsing-yüan, a PLA political commissar.

7 Lung Shu-chin was transferred to Sinkiang province in the summer of 1968. His position as First Vice-Chairman of the Hunan provincial revolutionary committee has not formally been filled in his absence.

all both geographically remote from Peking and vital to the front-line military defense of China. All, moreover, have been the scene of frequent pitched battles between left-wing mass organizations and conservative military commanders. Despite the fact that the PLA authorities in these (and other) provinces have become increasingly coercive and repressive in their relationships with local rebel groups, the strategic importance of these areas has served effectively to insulate their respective military and political leaders against the possible threat of reprisal from the more radical Maoist leadership in Peking.[17]

Rebels in Retreat: The Year in Review

The year 1968 began on a relatively subdued note in China. The military-inspired, conservative "backlash" which had been apparent since the ill-fated rebel attempt to "turn the spearhead of struggle" against the PLA in July and August 1967 was still very much in evidence at the New Year.

The *People's Daily*, in its annual situational report of January 1, declared (somewhat improbably) that the Cultural Revolution had "won decisive victory in 1967." The editorial went on to give top priority in 1968 to the task of "further developing the great mass movement for the creative study and application of the thought of Mao Tse-tung." This constituted a significant (if tacit) retreat from the more radical tone of that newspaper's New Year's editorial for 1967, which had given top priority to the task of unfolding the Cultural Revolution "on a large scale" in factories and rural areas.[18]

Further evidence that a conciliatory mood prevailed in the official Peking line on the Cultural Revolution at the beginning of 1968 came in the form of renewed warnings against the oppositionist tactics of those who besieged Mao's "proletarian headquarters" from the "extreme left"—a newly refurbished term of derogation denoting those who advocated a radical policy of "casting out everything and striking down everything" and who attempted to challenge the authority of the PLA and of the new-born revolutionary committees.[19]

In line with this conservatism, the months of January and February 1968 witnessed a stepped-up campaign to "support the army" throughout China.[20] In conjunction with this campaign, a frontal assault was launched on such alleged ultra-leftist deviations as "anarchism" and "factionalism" on the part of radical mass organizations.

An important official policy statement issued on January 12 listed "ten crimes of factionalism." [21] Prominent among these were: (1) failure of various rebel organizations to obey the highest directives and "strategic plans" of Chairman Mao; (2) lack of regard for the best interests of the Party, the country, and the broad masses of people; (3) a prevalent attitude that "he who agrees with me is a comrade while he who disagrees with me is an enemy"; (4) undue concern for and contention over such things as status, titles and rank; (5) the tendency to attack factionalism with factionalism—a case of "waving the red flag to oppose the red flag"; and (6) the widespread practice of distorting excerpts from Chairman Mao's quotations to serve particularistic, factional ends.

A growing tendency toward anarchism within the ranks of the revolutionary rebels was similarly denounced in the initial months of 1968. A provincial radio broadcast of early February complained that "in our ranks there are a number of comrades who have been influenced by the anarchistic trend, who do not observe labor discipline and do not obey working orders. . . ." [22] Such complaints proliferated rapidly in many areas of China in the late winter and early spring of 1968.

The twin left-wing phenomena of factional violence and incipient anarchy posed a serious threat to the already precarious economic situation in China. Absenteeism, work stoppages, disruption of transport and communications facilities, and looting of states warehouses by rebel groups were all cited as manifestations of the new ultra-leftist trend, and were all condemned by the regime as unprincipled acts of sabotage.[23] Accordingly, increased official reliance was placed on the PLA as a stabilizing force in Chinese society, and the army was authorized to assume control over such vital functions as rail traffic and public security.[24]

In late January the authoritative *Liberation Army Daily* published an important editorial which called on the army to "support the left, *but not any particular faction*" [25]—a slogan which was widely interpreted to mean, in effect, restore order no matter whose toes have to be trod on in the process. It was in this same editorial that the derogatory term "petit bourgeois factionalism" was coined to describe the phenomenon of widespread internecine strife among rival left-wing student organizations. The significance of the new term lay in the fact that the Red Guards and other student revolutionaries were by definition part of the Chinese intelligentsia, a social stratum which in Maoist doctrine belongs to the ideologically impure petit-bourgeoisie. In calling for the army-wide initiation of an "uncompromising struggle against petit-bourgeois factionalism," the above-mentioned editorial thus clearly implied that the dissension-ridden "little generals" were thenceforth to be subjected to external (military) discipline and control.[26]

One of the more critical manifestations of left-wing factionalism to emerge in the early months of 1968 was a conscious effort on the part of revolutionary rebels to sow dissension within the ranks of the newly formed revolutionary committees. In many areas where the composition of the revolutionary committees was ostensibly weighted against the leftist masses (in favor of more moderate Party cadres and PLA representatives), the rebels had directed heavy criticism against individual committee members in an effort to discredit the moderates and secure their replacement by more sympathetic, rebel-affiliated elements.[27] This "splittist" tendency was officially opposed as being "Left in form but right in essence," and in early February a nationwide press campaign was launched to "cherish and support the new-born revolutionary committees."[28]

The Rebels Rebound

By the end of March there were increasing signs (in Peking and elsewhere) of an active left-wing movement to reverse the recent rightward drift of Cultural Revolution policy. Beginning with the purge of PLA Acting Chief of Staff Yang Ch'eng-wu (who was alleged to have been active in a right-wing plot to discredit Chiang Ch'ing), a new round of anti-rightist criticism unfolded in April and May.[29] The stated purpose of this new campaign was to oppose a second "adverse current of reversing verdicts" which allegedly had been allowed to spread unchecked throughout the provinces in February and March of 1968. A secondary purpose was the desire on the part of militant Maoists in Peking—most notably Lin Piao and Chiang Ch'ing—to strengthen their position vis-à-vis the increasingly influential (and generally conservative) provincial military and civil authorities.[30]

In a series of meetings and receptions held in Peking in late March and early April, various central cultural revolutionary leaders repeatedly warned that the "principal danger" at the present stage of the movement came not from the extreme left, but from the right.[31] Even Chou En-lai, who has generally been regarded by outside observers as a "moderate" throughout the Cultural Revolution, joined in the denunciation of the new "adverse current" and praised Chiang Ch'ing, albeit somewhat unenthusiastically, for her unwavering support of the left:

> From last winter to the present, the extreme left has been criticized and repudiated. Now the right has risen again, the February "adverse current" has made a comeback, and the royalists have tried to emancipate themselves and launch a counter-attack. . . .[32]

> Comrade Chiang Ch'ing has stood firmer than anybody else; her stand has been most unequivocal and she has examined problems with acute insight. . . .[33]

> At the present time, our principal attack is directed at the diehard conservatives on the right. . . .[34]

As the pendulum of the Cultural Revolution thus took a discernible swing to the left in the spring of 1968, provincial and local military and civil authorities found their freedom of action severely circumscribed by Peking's new reluctance to issue a blanket condemnation against the divisive activities of radical mass organizations. Indeed, the left-wing rebel groups received considerable tacit encouragement from Peking when a new official definition of "factionalism" was promulgated in mid-April.

In late January, it will be recalled, "factionalism"—and particularly "petit-bourgeois factionalism"—had been severely criticized; now, however, a new concept of factionalism was articulated which eliminated the category of "petit-bourgeois factionalism" altogether and replaced it with the dichotomous categories of (good) "proletarian factionalism" and (bad) "bourgeois factionalism":

> Chairman Mao teaches us that we should make a class analysis of factionalism. The proletariat and the bourgeoisie are in fact two big factions diametrically opposed to each other. *We must adhere to the factionalism of the proletarian revolutionaries.* This means that we must adhere to . . . the revolutionary spirit of the Left. . . . We must oppose all manifestations of bourgeois factionalism within the revolutionary ranks. . . .[35]

Thus freed from the negative stigma previously associated with the term "petit bourgeois factionalism," left-wing Red Guards and student revolutionaries soon stepped up the pace of their attack against rival (conservative) organizations and against moderate and conservative elements in their respective provincial and local revolutionary committees.[36]

By the end of June, reports of widespread physical violence in the provinces were leaking out of China (via a well-organized underground press) with alarming regularity. Dead bodies, bound and trussed, were photographed floating into Hong Kong harbor, presumably the victims of factional violence in nearby Kwangsi province.[37] Arms and ammunition were openly seized by rebel groups from military arsenals and supply trains bound for Vietnam, subsequently to be used against rival factions.[38] In some extreme instances entire cities or sections of cities were reported to be in flames as a result of rapidly escalating "local civil wars." [39] University campuses, factories, railway depots and farms became the scene of bloody, pitched battles.[40] It was in this situation of increasingly unrestrained civil chaos that Mao Tse-tung was finally compelled to intervene personally on behalf of "law and order."

The Mangoes Affair

The event which served to precipitate Mao's intervention was a renewed outbreak of violence between rival rebel groups at Peking's Tsinghua University in mid-July. On July 28, Mao reportedly presided over a meeting of five student leaders representing the various factions involved in the fighting. With tears in his eyes (according to one unofficial account), Mao addressed the young rebels plaintively: "You have let me down, and what is more you have disappointed the workers, peasants and soldiers of China." [41]

Specific charges leveled by Mao against the student leaders reportedly included complaints about their inability (and/or unwillingness) to unite in common cause, their failure to maintain self-discipline, and

their increasingly frequent resort to physical violence as a means of resolving factional differences. Henceforth, warned Mao, rival student
organizations were to be physically separated and/or subjected to external (worker-peasant-soldier) control.[42] Within 48 hours after Mao
delivered his remarks, the nation's first "Worker-Peasant Thought of
Mao Tse-tung Propaganda Team" was dispatched to Tsinghua University with the primary objective of quelling student violence. Although the majority of the propaganda team's members were said to be
workers, the active leadership and support of the PLA were singled out
as major factors contributing to the success of the team's mission.[43]

A few days later, on August 5, the action of the Tsinghua University
propaganda team in imposing discipline on the fractious student rebels
was memorialized with the presentation of a "treasured gift" of mangoes from Mao Tse-tung to the members of the team.[44] The symbolic
significance of this act was not lost on anyone: in signalling his approval of the work of the propaganda team, Mao had signed the death
warrant of the Red Guards.

From then on it was simply a matter of time before the predomi-
nantly conservative provincial and local military authorities throughout China put into operation a program of organized "re-education"
(read: suppression) of student revolutionaries.[45] In several provinces
Mao's "little generals" were openly condemned as "foul intellectuals,"
"buffoons," "double-dealers" and "petit-bourgeois ambitionists," and
were dealt with accordingly.[46] The "crime" most frequently attributed
to the now-disgraced Red Guards was that of promulgating a so-called
"theory of many centers"—a term used to describe the prevalent situation wherein each rebel organization (or faction thereof) claimed for
itself alone the mantle of proletarian legitimacy.[47] In effect the "theory
of many centers" was held to be a "theory of no center," *i.e.*, a thinly
veiled defense of anarchism.

Under the aegis of the slogan "purify class ranks" (which was raised
in one of Mao's numerous "latest instructions" of mid-summer), provincial and local revolutionary committees in September and October
began the task of eliminating "impure" class elements from their ranks
by "dragging out" and "repudiating" the petit-bourgeois Red Guard
intellectuals.[48] Using Mao's instructions to "streamline organizational
structures" and "send down office personnel to work at the grass-roots
level" as a pretext, the revolutionary committee leadership in many
areas (particularly those areas dominated by military officers and Party
cadres) apparently wasted little time in getting rid of their ambitious
and troublesome Red Guard "allies" by shipping them out to serve
as administrative personnel and/or common workers in basic-level organs. Although such blatant acts of systematic discrimination were
repeatedly condemned in the official media as manifestations of "bourgeois mentality," the very frequency and intensity of these condemna-

tions were indicative of the extent to which the Red Guards (and other intransigent left-wing rebels) were being methodically removed from their newly won positions of influence.[49]

What Price Revolution?

By the time the Central Committee's 12th Plenum met in mid-October, the rout of the revolutionary rebels was in full swing in China's provinces. Although it is still too early to state with any degree of finality that the conservative trends of the past six months have put a decisive end to the Cultural Revolution as an instrument of radical mass mobilization, it nevertheless appears that the flame of revolution is on the verge of being extinguished.

Viewing the events of the year 1968 in retrospect, one is ineluctably drawn to the conclusion that Mao Tse-tung, Lin Piao and company have rid themselves of Liu Shao-ch'i and his fellow "bourgeois power-holders" within the Party apparatus only at the cost of creating a new, regionally based and military-dominated power structure which may ultimately prove even more intractable and difficult to manipulate. Nor have the high social costs of the Cultural Revolution been borne exclusively by China's domestic political institutions. Whether measured in terms of damage to China's international prestige and influence, declining foreign trade, decreasing industrial productivity or the total disruption of the nation's education system, the costs of Mao's "last revolution" have been staggering.[50]

Long ago Mao Tse-tung stated that the aim of periodic Party rectification campaigns in China was "like that of a doctor treating an illness, solely to save the patient and not to doctor him to death." Had the Chairman been acquainted with Molière's venerable physician, however, he might well have profited from the latter's sage observation that "more men die of their remedies than of their illnesses." Therein, perhaps, lies the most appropriate epitaph for the moribund Great Proletarian Cultural Revolution.

1. Liu's fall from power and the attendant campaign of criticism directed against him have been documented elsewhere. See, for example, Richard Baum and Frederick C. Teiwes, "Liu Shao-ch'i and the Cadre Question," *Asian Survey*, Vol. VIII, No. 4 (April 1968), pp. 323-45.

2. With the Party apparatus in a visible shambles after two and one-half years of continuous purges, the convocation of a Central Committee Plenum prior to a reconstitution of that body had been regarded by most outside observers as a highly unlikely occurrence. Since such a reconstitution can only be implemented by the National Party Congress, it had been widely speculated that a new Party Congress would be convened sometime in the latter half of 1968. Such speculation was initially triggered by Party Politburo spokesman Hsieh Fu-chih, who

stated as early as October 1967 that the Ninth Party Congress would be held in the near future. Neither Hsieh nor anyone else, however, had indicated that a Central Committee Plenum might be called prior to a new session of the Party Congress.

3. "Communiqué of the Enlarged 12th Plenary Session of the Eighth Central Committee of the Communist Party of China" (October 31, 1968), in *Peking Review* 44 (supplement), November 1, 1968, p. v.

4. The so-called "Worker-Peasant Thought of Mao Tse-tung Propaganda Teams" which began to enter Chinese schools and universities in August 1968 were a concrete manifestation of the movement to muzzle the Red Guards. These propaganda teams were specifically charged with supervising the "re-education" of the dissention-ridden young intellectuals. See Yao Wen-yüan, "The Working Class Must Exercise Leadership in Everything," in *Peking Review* 35 (August 30, 1968), pp. 3–6.

5. See, for example, the *People's Daily* (Peking) New Year's editorial of January 1, 1968, in *Peking Review* 1 (January 3, 1968), pp. 1–13.

6. See "Absorb Fresh Blood From the Proletariat," *Red Flag* 4 (October 14, 1968), in *Peking Review* 43 (October 25, 1968), pp. 4–7 (emphasis added).

7. For extensive documentation and analysis of the purge of the Party apparatus at the central and provincial levels, see Charles Neuhauser, "The Impact of the Cultural Revolution on the Chinese Communist Party Machine," *Asian Survey*, Vol. VIII, No. 6 (1968), pp. 465–88; also Parris H. Chang, "Mao's Great Purge: A Political Balance Sheet," *Problems of Communism*, Vol. XVIII, No. 2 (March–April 1969), pp. 1–10.

8. Chang, *loc. cit.*

9. The original "Group of Five" comprised Peking Mayor P'eng Chen; Party propaganda chief Lu Ting-yi and his deputy, culture czar Chou Yang; *People's Daily* editor-in-chief Wu Leng-hsi; and Party Politburo member K'ang Sheng. Of this group, only K'ang Sheng survived to play a leading role in the middle and later stages of the Cultural Revolution. The remainder were purged in May 1966 following the disclosure that they had attempted to severely restrict the scope and intensity of the movement in academic and literary circles.

Following the Central Committee's 11th Plenum of August 1966, the "Central Cultural Revolution Group" was set up under the guidance of Mao's long-time personal confidant and *Red Flag* editor-in-chief, Ch'en Po-ta. Members of this new committee included Chiang Ch'ing (Mme. Mao), K'ang Sheng. Shanghai Party and cultural leaders Yao Wen-yüan and Chang Ch'un-ch'iao, the PLA Political Department's Deputy Director Liu Chih-chien, Central-South regional Party boss T'ao Chu, Party Deputy Director of Propaganda Chang P'ing-hua, Hupeh provincial Party boss Wang Jen-chung, *Red Flag* editorial staffers Ch'i Pen-yü, Kuan Feng and Wang Li, *Kuang-ming Daily* editor Mu Hsin, PLA Cultural Affairs Director Hsieh T'ang-ch'ung, Southwest regional Party propaganda chief Liu Wei-chien, Northeast regional Party propaganda chief Cheng Chi-chiao, and Tsinghai provincial Party boss Yang Chih-lin.

In January and February of 1967, T'ao Chu, Liu Chih-chien, Wang Jen-chung, Hsieh T'ang-ch'ung, Liu Wei-chien, Chang P'ing-hua, Cheng Chi-chiao and Yang Chih-lin were dismissed from the group for various (undisclosed) acts of alleged disloyalty to Mao. In August 1967, following the Wuhan incident, Wang Li was implicated in a plot to overthrow Premier Chou En-lai and was dismissed. In September and October 1967, Mu Hsin and Kuan Feng were suspended along with *Red Flag* deputy editor Lin Chieh (who had recently been added to the original group) for their alleged involvement in an utra-leftist "May 16" plot to discredit the leadership of the PLA. Finally, in February 1968, Ch'i Pen-yü was dismissed for his alleged duplicity in covertly backing the "May 16" group.

By the spring of 1968, only five members of the original group of 18 remained in good standing—Ch'en Po-ta, Chiang Ch'ing, K'ang Sheng, Yao Wen-yüan and Chang Ch'un-ch'iao. The combined attrition rate of the 22 members of the original "Group of Five" and its successor, the "Central Cultural Revolution Group," has thus been 17/22, or almost 80%—a figure which argues strongly against the idea that the Cultural Revolution purges unfolded according to a comprehensive "master plan" drawn up in advance.

10. See Baum and Teiwes, *loc. cit.*

11. See Philip Bridgham, "Mao's Cultural Revolution in 1967: The Struggle to Seize Power" [reprinted as selection 11 in the present volume—ED.].

12. *Ibid.*

13. This conclusion is reinforced by the following verbal interchange recorded in China early in 1968: "*Question:* 'Is the Cultural Revolution being directed from the top?' *Answer:* 'To some extent, but not in the sense in which a person [Mao] makes a definite plan and gives out orders. It means arousing the people and then noticing trends that you want to give publicity to . . .'" (Interview with Anna Louise Strong, quoted in *Far Eastern Economic Review*, March 14, 1968). This *ad hoc,* run-it-up-the-flagpole-and-see-who-salutes style of leadership has been evident throughout the Cultural Revolution. This is not meant to imply that Mao has played a negligible role in the movement, or that he has been totally the captive of events beyond his control; rather, it is meant to underline the lack of credibility of any hypothesis which assumes Mao's omnipotence in the face of a manifestly unstable and unpredictable revolutionary environment.

14. The "three-way alliance" form of revolutionary committee leadership was first put into practice on an experimental basis in Heilungkiang province in January 1967. Subsequently, Mao gave the form his personal blessing in one of his numerous "latest instructions" issued in the spring of that year. While no specific numerical ratio of cadres to masses to PLA representatives was ever officially established, it is assumed that the "three-way alliance" was meant to provide roughly equal representation to each of its three constituent elements.

15. In characterizing an individual leader as an "army officer," care should be taken to distinguish between military commanders and PLA political commissars. Only the former actually have troops at their disposal, while the latter are in many respects more similar (particularly in terms of background and political orientation) to regular Party cadres. Only the commander is a "professional soldier"; the commissar is essentially a political propagandist.

16. For documentation and analysis of the events of this period, see Bridgham, *loc. cit.*

17. Of the five provinces mentioned above, Kwangsi has provided the best example of local military commanders openly suppressing radical mass organizations. See, for example, the various (unofficial) Red Guard accounts of military action against the "April 22" rebels in *Survey of the China Mainland Press* (SCMP) 4150, 4202, 4213, 4227, 4230 and 4234. For additional documentation on PLA-Red Guard confrontations, see *Radio Nanchang* (Kiangsi), March 21, 1968; *Radio Hangchow* (Chekiang), July 26 and 31, 1968; also, *SCMP*, 4127, 4150, 4154 and 4181.

18. The 1967 editorial had also been replete with bitter denunciations of "certain muddle-headed persons" who were "afraid to make revolution" and who had been "hoodwinked" into suppressing the revolution by landlords, rich peasants, counter-revolutionaries, "bad elements" and rightists. By contrast, the 1968 editorial dwelt at great length on the need for establishing and consolidating "three-way alliances," opposing "unprincipled factional disputes," and overcoming "small group mentality and sectarianism."

19. See, for example, *Radio Hangchow* (Chekiang), March 13, 1968; also, *Radio Tsinan* (Shantung), February 21, 1968.

20. See *New China News Agency* (NCNA), Peking, January 29, 1968.

21. *Wen Hui Pao* (Shanghai), January 12, 1968.

22. *Radio Chengchow* (Honan), February 8, 1968; also, *Wen Hui Pao*, February 6, 1968.

23. See, for example, the various reports of destructive rebel violence in *SCMP* 4132, 4144, 4153, 4176, 4179, 4201 and 4203. For an evaluation of the damage to China's economy caused by such actions, see "Communist China's Economy at Mid-Year 1968," *Current Scene* (Hong Kong), Vol. VI, No. 12 (July 17, 1968), pp. 1–16.

24. See, for example, the description of the military takeover of Canton's Railway Sub-Bureau, in *SCMP* 4120.

25. *Liberation Army Daily*, January 28, 1968, in *Peking Review* 5 (February 2, 1968), pp. 8–9 (emphasis added).

26. *Ibid*. As early as January 17, Premier Chou En-lai had reportedly revoked the "revolutionary vanguard" status of the Red Guards by stating that "the working class is now to take the lead in the revolution, just as the intellectuals and students did at an earlier stage . . ." (From a Canton Red Guard tabloid, in *SCMP* 4148). It was not until early August, however, that Chou's words were backed up by resolute action with the dispatch of the previously mentioned "Worker-Peasant Thought of Mao Tse-tung Propaganda Teams" to China's schools and universities.

27. See n. 19, above; also, *SCMP* 4115, 4121, 4167, 4174 and 4190.

28. This campaign was first tentatively inaugurated in a *Wen Hui Pao* editorial of February 2, which stated that "under no circumstances should we overthrow [revolutionary committee] comrades just because they have been discovered to have committed a few errors. . . . All revolutionary committees must further strengthen their unity. . . ." Subsequently, it was officially stated that "comrades of the revolutionary committees belong to the Party and not to any individual faction" (*Radio Peking*, February 23, 1968). In a further warning to ambitious rebels, it was affirmed that revolutionary leading cadres formed the "backbone" of the revolutionary committees, while PLA representatives constituted the "bulwark" of the new power organs (*NCNA*, Peking, February 25, 1968). Finally, a *People's Daily* editorial of March 20 warned that "it is necessary to be on guard against plots by the class enemy to subvert the revolutionary committee either from the right or the extreme left."

29. A Red Guard tabloid seen in Hong Kong in July 1968 recounts an incident in which Yang Ch'eng-wu reportedly expressed his lack of affection for Chiang Ch'ing in the following terms: "When the old hen begins to crow at sunrise, the honorable farmyard is in danger." Quoted in *Far Eastern Economic Review*, July 18, 1968, p. 149.

30. Rightist opposition to such inveterate Maoists as Lin and Chiang is inferred from the otherwise inexplicable spate of laudatory propaganda concerning these two leaders which began to appear in the provincial and national mass media in early March. On the glorification of Lin Piao, see *Liberation Army Daily*, March 3, 1968, in *Peking Review* 10 (March 8, 1968), pp. 8, 12. On the genesis of a movement to "learn from comrade Chiang Ch'ing," see *Radio Hofei* (Anhwei), May 29, 1968. Subsequently it was revealed that an active "smash the piano" movement (directed against Chiang Ch'ing's introduction of piano accompaniment to Peking operas in February 1968) had occurred in Shanghai's cultural circles (*Liberation Army Daily*, August 30, 1968). On Yang Ch'eng-wu's alleged anti-Chiang Ch'ing activities, see *SCMP* 4168 and 4172.

31. See, for example, the speeches of Ch'en Po-ta, Chiang Ch'ing and K'ang Sheng, as reported in *SCMP* 4166, 4168, 4189 and 4196.

32. Chou En-lai, speech of March 21, 1968, in *SCMP* 4166.

33. Chou En-lai, statement of March 30, 1968, in *SCMP* 4196.

34. Chou En-lai, speech of April 7, 1968, in *SCMP* 4189.

35. *People's Daily*, April 19, 1968 (emphasis added). A subsequent *People's Daily* editorial of April 27 stated that "we oppose bourgeois factionalism precisely in order to safeguard and strengthen the factionalism of proletarian revolutionaries. . . . The petit-bourgeoisie is an ally of the proletariat and an important force in the revolution. . . ." The full significance of this type of exhortation became apparent when a provincial radio broadcast accused right-wing elements of "using antifactionalism as a pretence . . . to sling mud at the proletarian revolutionaries . . . in a vain attempt to stage a comeback and recover their lost paradise." (*Radio Hofei*, Anhwei, April 24, 1968).

36. See, for example, *Radio Kweiyang* (Kweichow), July 12, 1968; also, *Radio Chengchow* (Honan), May 29, 1968.

37. *Far Eastern Economic Review* 22 (July 6, 1968).

38. *SCMP* 4181, 4215, 4227.

39. *SCMP* 4213, 4234; *Far Eastern Economic Review* 29 (July 18, 1968), pp. 142–43.

40. *SCMP* 4201, 4123, 4219, 4222, 4225, 4245.

41. Quoted in *Far Eastern Economic Review* 35 (August 29, 1968), pp. 377–78.

42. *Ibid.*

43. *Peking Review* 36 (September 6, 1968), pp. 13–14; also, *Kuangming Daily*, August 30, 1968.

44. *Peking Review* 32 (August 9, 1968), pp. 5–6.

45. See the important editorial on the "re-education" of intellectuals in *People's Daily*, September 12, 1968.

46. See, for example, *Radio Changsha* (Hunan), August 15 and September 7, 1968; *Radio Shanghai*, August 17, 1968; and *Radio Chengtu* (Szechwan), August 20, 1968. One of the most favored techniques used by local authorities to rid themselves of the troublesome Red Guards was to send large numbers of student "volunteers" to the countryside to participate in productive labor for "several years." See, for example, *Radio Kweiyang* (Kweichow), September 27, 1968; and *NCNA* (Peking), September 25, 1968.

47. The first official attack against the "theory of many centers" appeared in *People's Daily*, August 5, 1968. See also Yao Wen-yüan's important article, "The Working Class Must Exercise Leadership in Everything," *loc. cit.*

48. See *Radio Chengtu* (Szechwan), October 31, 1968; *Radio Sian* (Shensi), October 31, 1968; and *Radio Kweiyang* (Kweichow), September 8, 1968.

49. In many cases, the "downward transfer" of the leaders of left-wing mass organizations was accompanied by a movement to rehabilitate previously disgraced Party and government cadres. See, for example, *Radio Kweiyang* (Kweichow), September 8, 1968.

50. It has been estimated that China's industrial production declined on the order of 15% in 1967. Peking's foreign trade also reportedly fell off by over $100 million in 1967. See "Communist China's Economy at Mid-Year 1968," *loc. cit.* There is no reason to assume that similar declines were not experienced in 1968, although only scattered and unsystematic data are available at the present time. In international affairs, Peking suffered a noticeable decline of prestige in 1968. Her opposition to the peace overtures of North Vietnam estranged her from that country,

as did her bitter denunciation of the Soviet Union's invasion of Czechoslovakia. In the annual struggle in the United Nations over the question of Chinese representation, the People's Republic of China suffered a further loss of support as compared with 1966 and 1967. A rough indication of Peking's present isolation in international affairs may be deduced from the fact that only three sovereign governments (Albania, Pakistan and North Vietnam) sent official delegations to China's National Day festivities in Peking on October 1, 1968.

THE PARTY, THE GOVERNMENT
AND THE GUN

Ralph L. Powell

Although the organizational structure of the Communist Party of
China was a major victim of the Cultural Revolution, Mao Tse-tung
never seriously planned to abolish the Party. The thought of Mao does
not visualize a communist system without "a party of the proletariat."
Furthermore, in China, as in other communist countries, the control of
the Party will be a crucial factor in the future domination of the state.
What Mao sought to do during the Cultural Revolution was to purge,
revitalize and reorganize the Party. He had sought to make it subject to
his will. . . .

During the Cultural Revolution the structure of the Communist
Party was first shattered by attacks from non-Party organizations—Red
Guards and the revolutionary rebels. Then the Party began its reorganization largely under the auspices of another non-Party organization—
the revolutionary committees. . . . Party-soldiers, augmented by old
Party cadres, dominated the revolutionary committees. Also, Party committees of the PLA played a very important role in reorganizing the
civil Communist Party. . . .

The extensive role of the armed forces in the reconstruction of the
Communist Party has been partially camouflaged. The PLA's Party
committees or "support the left" personnel have usually been referred
to as "helping" the revolutionary committees or other groups involved
in the reorganization of the Party. Yet, it is often apparent that the
military personnel have provided the leadership or taken the initiative.
. . . PLA units have helped to launch mass Party rectification movements. They have encouraged the study of Mao's teachings regarding
Party organization and have pushed Party members into undergoing
the "tempering of violent class struggle." [1] Military officers . . . have
presided at political work conferences and have spoken at Party functions.[2] Military representatives have "helped" revolutionary committees
to choose new Party members and to select "vigorous" Party members
for leadership posts.[3] PLA groups have also helped to eliminate "renegades, spies and counter-revolutionary elements." [4] . . .

In any struggle to control the Party machinery in the revolutionary

Ralph L. Powell, "The Party, the Government and the Gun," *Asian Survey* 10,
no. 6 (June, 1970): 441–71. Reprinted by permission of the publisher.

committees the Party-soldiers have several advantages. The officers command military power; they control the "gun" and they still have inside the PLA the only extensive, functioning, nation-wide Party structure. Also, in the past the armed services already contained an unusually high percentage of Party members and the PLA continued to recruit new members during the Cultural Revolution, while the civilian Party was disrupted. . . .[5]

Despite the campaign of Party reorganization, during the National Day ceremonies on October 1, 1968 the Party was not honored by place or tributes. Instead, representatives of the revolutionary committees and military men were given places of honor. Senior officers of the PLA were far more in evidence than were Party leaders.[6] In an important address Lin Piao emphasized the task of developing and consolidating the revolutionary committees more than the problem of Party reconstruction.[7] However, during the Twelfth Plenum [October 13–31, 1968 —Ed.] there was a new upsurge of articles devoted to Party rectification. This drive was sparked by a "vivid analogy," attributed to Mao. This concept maintained that a proletarian Party, like the human circulatory system, must eliminate waste and let in fresh oxygen in order to be vigorous. It was claimed that this analogy contained "profound dialectics." The *Red Flag* editorial announcing this dialectical gem stressed selecting "advanced elements from among the industrial workers," as well as peasants and soldiers as new Party members. The Red Guards were not mentioned. The "waste" to be eliminated include the usual "renegades," "counter-revolutionaries" and other "degenerated elements," including the senile. . . .[8]

Preparation for the Ninth Party Congress

After the Twelfth Plenum, preparations for the Ninth Party Congress were stepped up and led to activities in several important fields. Numerous congresses of Party members of revolutionary committees and of military commands were held; delegates were selected; the draft constitution was discussed, and propaganda campaigns were carried out. The joint 1969 New Year's Day editorial of the *People's Daily, Liberation Army Daily* and *Red Flag* listed the National Party Congress as the number one task of the year. There are reports of provincial congresses in ten provinces and in the major municipalities of Canton and Shanghai.[9] It is likely that such meetings were held in most, if not all provinces, but the others were not reported. Similar meetings were held by several military region or district commands. Some of the congresses were limited to Party members of the provincial revolutionary committees, others included Party representatives from county level committees and above. This system obviously excluded from the congresses all the "revolutionary" members of the committees who did not belong to the Party, while the military would be almost completely represented, as would the civilian Party cadres. . . .

The congresses and forums of Party members of revolutionary committees studied the unpublished speeches of Mao and Lin at the Twelfth Plenum, pledged themselves to implement the policies enunciated in the communiqué of the Plenum and condemned Liu Shao-ch'i and his allies. . . .

A most significant aspect of preparations for the National Party Congress was the selection of delegates, a subject on which there is very little concrete evidence. According to the first press communiqué of the Ninth Congress, "The delegates to the congress were unanimously chosen . . . through full democratic consultation by Party organizations at various levels and after seeking the opinions of the broad masses." [10] The "Party organizations" referred to were actually the existing ones inside the PLA and the Party members of the revolutionary committees. There was no indication in the press or radio reports of a campaign to seek the opinion of the masses. Apparently the delegates had been "chosen" by "Party leadership groups." . . . It is possible that a list of acceptable delegates was sent down from Peking, but it is more likely that in keeping with the principle of "democratic centralism" candidates were first selected at the conferences of Party members of provincial revolutionary committees and military headquarters. Then the lists were screened by the Mao-Lin headquarters which must have had some veto power to assure a loyal majority at the congress. Certainly there was bargaining and compromises between the provincial leaders and the Maoist regime in Peking and between the various factions of Maoists in the capital. In the end it was claimed of the members of the Ninth Congress that they had "high spirit and strong fighting will" for they had been "tempered" in the Cultural Revolution. . . .[11]

Another form of preparations for the Congress consisted of a number of propaganda and indoctrination campaigns seeking further to establish "Marxism-Leninism—Mao Tse-tung's thought" as the sole orthodoxy and standard of political legitimacy. Major campaigns included an on-going policy of rewriting the history of the "two lines" in the Party—the "proletarian revolutionary line" of Chairman Mao and the "bourgeois reactionary line" of the voiceless Liu Shao-ch'i.[12] Related themes included the continuing class struggle, the need for "inner Party struggle" and the campaign to "purify class ranks." [13] Another campaign urged that all policies be taken seriously and "thoroughly implemented," [14] which indicated that there was opposition and foot dragging.

The draft of a new Party constitution was drawn up at the suggestion of Mao and was reported to have been worked on by the Shanghai revolutionary leaders and members of the Cultural Revolution Group, Chang Ch'un-ch'iao and Yao Wen-yüan. The draft was discussed at the Twelfth Plenum of the Central Committee and then distributed to the "whole Party." Revolutionary committees and Party committees of the PLA at all levels were to "lead" the masses in discussions of the draft. Then the Party Center was to revise it on the basis of the recommendations rendered.[15] There was no overt campaign to publicize the draft constitution, but it must have been discussed fairly widely in military and revolutionary committee circles. Multiple copies of the document reached foreign observers, and there were only a few significant changes between the unofficial drafts and the final version adopted by the Ninth Congress.

In comparison to the 1956 Party Constitution the draft was a relatively short, sometimes vague, radical and authoritarian document. Where the former constitution took "Marxism-Leninism as its guide," the draft stated that the Party takes "Marxism-Leninism-Mao Tse-tung Thought as the theoretical basis guiding its thinking." Also the draft gave more prominence to Party organizations in the PLA than had the previous constitution. . . . With regard to the military, the document took the unprecedented step of naming Lin Piao to be Mao's successor. Revolutionary servicemen were specifically mentioned as being eligible for membership in the Party. . . . Furthermore, all primary Party organizations were called on to carry out the political four-first program and the three-eight work style of the PLA. These were policies that had been promoted by Lin Piao. Finally, there was no specific mention that the armed forces must accept the leadership of the Party.[16]

The Ninth Party Congress

The National Party Congress finally opened formally on April 1, 1968. . . . The opening of the Congress was greeted by great fanfare and massive organized rejoicing. The Maoist objectives of the National Congress were to legitimatize the unique leadership of Mao Tse-tung and the official appointment of Lin Piao as his successor, to establish the thought of Mao, now known as "Marxism-Leninism-Mao Tse-tung Thought" as the sole orthodox ideology and guide to action, and to vindicate the Cultural Revolution and the domestic and foreign policies associated with it. The regime sought national unity on the basis of these objectives. The Party Congress did not officially end the Cultural Revolution; Mao believes in permanent revolution and the political report of the congress maintained that "final victory" involves "decades" and "the victory of the world revolution. . . ."[17] Yet the Ninth Party Congress certainly marked the close of a major phase of Mao's continuing revolution and it is very unlikely that events of the next few years will repeat the actions of the recent past. . . .

The Party Congress was attended by 1,512 "chosen" delegates. It was claimed that no previous congress had ever had so many industrial workers, peasants or women among its members. Actually the group with the highest percentage of representatives was the Party-soldiers and the PLA was praised for making "outstanding contributions" during the Cultural Revolution. When 176 members were named to a Presidium, Mao was made the Chairman, Lin Piao was Vice-chairman and Chou En-lai was Secretary General.[18] Although no official mention was made of the number of military delegates, 67 (or 37%) of the Presidium members were known to be from the PLA. At least 53 of these had been generals before ranks were officially abolished in 1965. Even Mme. Mao (Chiang Ch'ing) and Mme. Lin (Yeh Ch'un) wore PLA uniforms to the Congress. It is estimated that there were 48 to 51 civilian cadres from Party, government, scientific and cultural circles on the Presidium, but only a dozen were from the government offices in Peking. There were probably at least fifty "proletarian revolutionaries"—workers, peasants, a very few Red Guards, and other representatives of "mass organizations." [19] A number of the members of the Presidium were previously unknown. Most of these were probably "revolutionaries," but some of them may have been soldiers.

The agenda of the Ninth Party Congress consisted of only three items: first, the political report presented by Marshal Lin Piao; second, revision of the Constitution of the Communist Party on the basis of the circulated draft, and third, the "election" of the new Central Committee of the Party. Mao, looking old but active, presided at the first session and made an "important speech," which was not officially published.[20] Then a rather frail and unhealthy appearing Lin Piao presented the three hour political report, which in Maoist terms "summed up the basic experience of the Great Proletarian Cultural Revolution, analyzed the domestic and international situation and put forward the fighting tasks of the Party." [21] Actually Lin rewrote the history of the Party, defended the need for the Cultural Revolution and repeated the slogans and propaganda themes of the recent past. There was no blueprint for the future and even little guidance regarding future policies. Instead stress was placed on the need for carrying out continuing policies "to the letter." The report borrowed from Mao's revolutionary strategy in calling for a united front of the largest possible majority, based on the tactic of "win over the many, oppose the few and crush our enemies one by one. . . ." [22]

In his speech, Marshal Lin devoted only one paragraph directly to the armed forces, but he declared that the PLA is "the mighty pillar of the dictatorship of the proletariat" and cited Mao as saying that it is "the main component of the state." Although it was maintained that the PLA is "an army of the proletariat," Lin did not mention Mao's maxim that "the Party must control the gun." In listing the "great historic feats" of the PLA, Lin did mention the Korean War, dropping the pretense that the Chinese forces in Korea had been volunteers. After praising the extremely diverse roles and the ideological revolutionization of the armed forces during the Cultural Revolution, Lin made the dubious claim that these nonmilitary activities of the PLA were "the best preparation against war. . . ." [23]

Lin Piao's political report was presented on April 1 and adopted, along with the revised Constitution, on the 14th, but only after having been discussed "sentence by sentence." Despite glowing praise for the report, the delegates had made "many good proposals for additions to and modifications of the report." Then the Congress decided to send both Lin's report and the Constitution to the Secretariat of the Presidium for publication, "after making modifications in wording." [24] The report was not actually published until the 27th and the publicizing of modifications was a reflection on Lin and an indication of differences of view even within the carefully selected Congress. Chiang Ch'ing did not speak at the Congress and hence did not publicly support Lin's report. An aging and apparently tired Chou En-lai did speak and praised Lin's speech, as did the Cultural Revolution Group leaders, Ch'en Po-ta and K'ang Sheng. [25]

The constitution finally adopted by the Ninth Congress is so similar to the drafts circulated abroad that the latter certainly were not forgeries, yet there were several significant changes made by the Congress that affect the PLA. Militancy was maintained. In Chapter I it was added that the Party had long been tempered for the "seizure and consolidation of state power by armed force." Yet, in Chapter III traditional policy was reaffirmed; the PLA was formally added to the list of organs that "must all accept the leadership of the Party." In Chapter VI the statement that primary Party organs must "persevere in the four firsts, and foster the three-eight working style in a big way" was dropped, [26] as was a section which had actually called on the Party to learn from the political work style of the PLA. This reflected unfavorably on Marshal Lin, as these were well-known to be his political work policies. Nevertheless Lin was named as Mao's legal heir by the same constitution. Mao and Lin are still the principal figures in the power structure, but it is obvious that despite Mao's support there is influential opposition to Lin even in the reorganized Party leadership.

Given the great strength demonstrated by the Party-soldiers in the selection of the new Central Committee and Politburo, constitutional action that again legally placed the PLA under Party control must have been approved by the military leaders. In part, these modifications may have been another example of the tendency to camouflage the extremely influential, often dominant, political role of the military. More important, the senior officers are old Party members. They were trained under the basic concept that, "the Party must control the gun." It is

judged that most of them would not object to or would even support
the concept of Party leadership, so long as the Party-soldiers continued
to play a leading or dominant role in the Party as individuals or as
factions.

The Central Committee and the Politburo

The communiqué that announced the conclusion of the Party Congress also presented the names of a surprisingly large new Central Committee, consisting of 170 regular members and 109 alternates. These
had been "elected" by a complex system utilizing "democratic centralism," [27] but the fact that the process required ten days of meetings indicates extensive bargaining and sparring for advantage. Unlike the past,
the members of the Committee, except for Mao and Lin, were listed
in stroke order, the Chinese equivalent of alphabetical order. Even
Chou En-lai, who had long been number three in the Party, was not
listed separately. This form of listing could indicate both conflicts
over seniority and a desire to present an appearance of unity and
democracy. The large size of the new Central Committee probably represented an attempt by Mao and Lin to seek a favorable majority, to
placate powerful provincial forces and yet to provide representation to
Maoist revolutionaries.

In actuality the membership of the Central Committee roughly represented the balance of political forces in Communist China, and
demonstrated the greatly increased political power of the military.
Owing to a number of obscure individuals, especially among the alternate members of the Central Committee, estimates of the numerical
strength of various groups vary somewhat. Party-soldiers from Marshal
Lin down to combat heroes numbered 123 to 127 (or 44% of the total).
. . . Some 70 members held both military and revolutionary committee
posts. . . . The senior officers of the PLA had obviously become far
more powerful than Mao had originally intended. However, they were
partially counterbalanced by civil officials and "revolutionaries," but
more so by factionalism within the officers' corps. As for civil officials,
roughly 28% of the total Central Committee and 33½% of the regular
members were Party or government cadres, including about 30 ministers and officials of the central government. Some 24% have been
classed as "revolutionaries" or representatives of mass organs. More
than a dozen were unknown.[28] Only 52 members of the previous Eighth
Central Committee were reelected. This indicates a heavy purge and a
high percentage of new blood in the committee. Yet except for the
majority of the "revolutionaries" and the few unknowns, most of the
new members were already fairly senior military or civil officials. Like
the Cultural Revolution itself, the Party Congress did not represent a
revolution from below. It was neither a sergeant's revolt nor a proletarian revolution.

The composition of the new Central Committee did mark a significant decentralization of political power. The military regions demonstrated great political strength. The eleven known commanders of military regions were elected. . . . At least 53 "general" officers from the military regions, excluding officers from military districts or units under district command were also elected as regular or alternate members of the Central Committee. . . .

The chairmen of all twenty-nine provincial level revolutionary committees, the large majority of whom are military men, were elected to the Ninth Central Committee. Most of them are regular members, but the chairmen of the Hunan, Kweichow, Ninghsia and Tibet committees—all of whom are military men—are only alternate members. There were about 125 members of revolutionary committees named to the Party's Central Committee: of these some 70 were military men. Certain provincial level revolutionary committees were strongly represented by vice chairmen or standing committee members. . . .

Although military representation on the Central Committee both expanded and shifted toward the regions and provinces, the headquarters of the armed forces and the staff departments of the PLA were also strongly represented on the Central Committee. The Ministry of Defense and military headquarters in Peking gained a total of at least 34 representatives, 12% of the total. The General Staff Department has seven or eight representatives, the Air Force Headquarters has at least eight, and the Navy six. The Ministry of Defense has five members and most of the special arms and services have one each.

The powerful Politburo, which was "elected" by the new Central Committee at its first plenary session on April 28, 1969, consists of 21 members and four alternates.[29] It tends to counterbalance the Central Committee for it is heavily weighed in favor of central officials. Mao Tse-tung is the Chairman and Lin Piao is the Vice Chairman. A strong majority of the Politburo are active supporters of Mao or Lin, but the Bureau is even more heavily burdened with military members than is the Central Committee. Yet, there is only one Party-soldier on the five-man Standing Committee of the Politburo, Marshal Lin Piao. Beside Mao, the other members are the Premier, Chou En-lai, and two members of the Cultural Revolution Group, Ch'en Po-ta and K'ang Sheng. But of the 21 regular members of the Politburo, eleven are Party-soldiers. . . . It was in the selection of new members that the military demonstrated their increased strength. Of ten new members six were generals and a seventh is a camp follower, Lin Piao's wife, Yeh Ch'un. One of the four alternate members is also a Party-soldier. . . .

The next largest group consists of Maoist "radicals," the five members of the Cultural Revolution Group, Chiang Ch'ing, Ch'en Po-ta, K'ang Sheng, Chang Ch'un-ch'iao and Yao Wen-yüan. . . . The radicals preserved more strength than some had expected, but the administrators lost influence. This small group now consists of only Chou En-lai, Vice-Premier Li Hsien-nien and possibly Hsieh Fu-chih. Chou En-lai has effectively supported Mao and Lin during the Cultural Revolution, but he is a very flexible politician who has never supported a loser in a Party power struggle. Four Vice Premiers, including the Foreign Minister, Ch'en Yi, were not reelected to the Politburo, but were retained on the Central Committee. . . .

The influential Military Affairs Committee, serving under the Politburo, has been expanded and is believed to consist of at least 17 senior Party-soldiers, most of whom are members of the new Politburo. Thus half of the Party's highest policy making body also sit on the Party's military planning and supervision organ. . . .

The Post-Congress Period

The Ninth Party Congress and the election of a new Central Committee and Politburo failed to create unity or even speed up the work of Party reconstruction at lower levels. The reorganization of the Party has continued to be a slow and strife-ridden process. There have apparently been conflicts of interest within the Party leadership, in the PLA and between revolutionary committees and the new Party organs which threaten their authority. Mao's concept of selecting political activists and of involving the masses in an "open door" assessment of Party members have clashed with the power of the military and the need for the administrative skills of the old Party cadres. The Maoist leaders have sought to purge the Party along "class lines," which means primarily in accordance with attitudes regarding the thought of Mao.[30] Denied a major voice in most of the revolutionary committees, the leftist revolutionaries, who were once the vanguard of the Cultural Revolution, have incessantly clamored for greater representation in the new Party organs and have criticized the old members. Yet the "rebel" representatives of mass organizations are still often themselves divided by factionalism. Frequently the civil cadres have allied with the military officers to oppose revolutionaries and to send many of them down to the factories and farms to labor. Still, there are some indications of natural resentment on the part of civil officials against the new influence of the armed forces.[31] The civilian cadres have not, however, been in a position effectively to challenge the military. Thousands of cadres have been sent down to cadre schools to do manual labor and confess their political sins. Many of the much abused cadres, quite understandably, now suffer from "overcautiousness." [32]

As a result of multiple conflicts and frictions, by the end of 1969 the only regional and provincial Party committees in existence were still the PLA committees in the military headquarters. In the fall a new drive was launched to speed up civil Party rebuilding. Although a considerable number of local committees were established in factories,

mines, schools and production brigades, often with the "help" of PLA
representatives, the first mid-level *hsien* (county) committee was not
organized until mid-November.[33]

After the Ninth Party Congress, it first appeared that the ultra-leftists
had considerable official support in their demands for a leading role
in the Party. There was a revival of mass organizations and some reinstatement of Red Guards. These actions, combined with the rehabilitation of "veteran cadres," would only be carried out at the expense of
the excessively powerful PLA officers.[34] Hence, late in the year the
military led a press attack against the "revolutionaries," especially the
representatives of the "mass organizations," accusing them of anarchism, lack of discipline, bourgeois factionalism and petit bourgeois
thought.[35] The argument that the "rebels" should automatically be
admitted to the Party because of their services during the Cultural
Revolution was rejected.[36]

Joint editorials published for the 48th anniversary of the Chinese
Communist Party on July 1 proclaimed the leadership role of the Party
and stated that the "organs of state power of the dictatorship of the
proletariat," including the PLA, must accept the "leadership of the
Party." But major stress was placed on subordination to the Central
Committee, headed by Chairman Mao and Vice-chairman Lin. That
committee was declared to be the "sole center of leadership for the
whole Party, the whole army and the people of the whole country." [37]
Occasional articles have continued to call for the leadership of the
Party over the PLA, but usually in terms of the central role of Mao and
Lin.[38] Official articles have also maintained that revolutionary committees must obey their Party committees or "core groups." Yet frequently the leading members of the two committees have been virtually
identical and the military have controlled both. . . . In toto, it appears that the military have been seeking to consolidate their great
new political power by controlling a reconstructed Communist Party.[39]

The PLA and the Central Government

The presence of the military in Peking during the Cultural Revolution was highly visible and until 1969 was openly flaunted by the official press and radio. The major role taken by the PLA leaders in the
revised Party structure and in the revolutionary committees has been
well documented. Reams of material exists regarding the extensive
activities of the armed forces in the economy, in schools and in police
organs. Nevertheless, during most of the Cultural Revolution, a veil of
official secrecy covered the relationships between the PLA and the State
Council and the lesser machinery of the central government. . . .

In the Spring of 1966 Premier Chou En-lai's State Council consisted
of some fifty ministries and commissions, with more than 350 ministers
and vice-ministers, chairmen and vice-chairmen. The State Council was

the center of administrative expertise and as was the case with provincial civil and military officials, there had been a fairly high degree of continuity among the senior personnel of the council.[40] Then the purges of the Cultural Revolution and the many attacks of the Red Guards and revolutionary rebels against the government bureaucracy seriously disrupted the ministries and their operations. Numerous senior officials were criticized, "dragged out" or otherwise humiliated. Still, despite the deep purges, the government machinery was not as massively damaged as was the Party apparatus. The government was a less important focus of power than the Party; it did not challenge Mao's authority and many of its operations were specialized and vital to the functioning of the state. Furthermore, Chou En-lai cast his lot with Mao and Lin and was able to protect some of his bureaucratic subordinates.[41]

Still, eight of the fifteen vice-premiers were purged. One of the remaining seven is Lin Piao, who is no longer subordinate to the Premier. Through mid-February 1968, when the high level purges had largely subsided, 182 of 366 ministers and vice-ministers were known to have been criticized. . . . Available data indicated that approximately half of the ministers and vice-ministers had been missing from view since the spring of 1966. Cultural and educational institutions had been especially hard hit by purges. Almost half of the ministries were believed to be without active ministers. A half dozen ministries appeared to be defunct and another dozen largely inoperative. The organizational structure of the State Council is also reported to have been simplified. From a positive standpoint, the available information indicates that more than half of the top officials were still active in about 65% of the ministries. Those in the defense related offices had fared somewhat better than the average. The small minority of non-Party ministers and vice-ministers had the best record and largely escaped the purge.[42] They did not constitute a political challenge. . . .

Despite numerous attacks against individual ministers and ministries, Premier Chou En-lai retained and probably actually gained influence during the Cultural Revolution. Also the State Council as an institution retained considerable prestige. Most important directives and policy statements were issued in the joint names of the Central Committee, the State Council, the Military Affairs Committee and the Cultural Revolution Group.[43] These formed a quadruple revolutionary alliance aimed at giving authority and prestige to policy statements.

At the time of the Ninth Party Congress, the State Council was only a large skeleton of its former self, but the remaining members did fairly well. About thirty officials of the central government were elected to the Central Committee. Three of the vice-premiers, Lin Piao, Hsieh Fu-chih and Li Hsien-nien were placed on the Politburo and the other four are members of the Central Committee; yet all four of these had previously been members of the Politburo. Eight other ministers and a dozen vice-ministers were also elected to the Central Committee.[44] However, the Ministry of Defense with five senior military officers on the Central Committee and the Ministry of Internal Security with three members, provided a disproportionate share of the ministers and vice-ministers. Furthermore the military had seriously penetrated the other institutions of the State Council.

During the Cultural Revolution, with the threatened collapse of ministries and commissions that were vital to the national security and economy, the PLA moved into an unknown number of government departments. Military control committees were established in the Ministry of Railways and the General Bureau of Civil Aviation.[45] They may also have been formed in other ministries dealing with communications and defense.[46] . . . Some analysts believe that during the Cultural Revolution the armed forces moved in to supervise the majority or all of the ministries and commissions of the State Council, especially the economic, arms industries and communications ministries. Military officers were transferred to the State Council to carry out the PLA's new missions.[47] As in the better publicized military control of factories and schools, it is believed that the PLA representatives have not attempted to manage and direct the specialized activities of the various ministries. They do not have the necessary administrative skills. Rather, as in complex industrial plants, the armed forces have probably propagated the thought of Mao Tse-tung, while attempting to assure the continuation of essential functions, reduce factionalism, and organize functioning supervisory alliances consisting of military officers, cadres and "revolutionaries." . . .

The Future

During the Cultural Revolution the power of the military increased greatly. This was especially true of regional and provincial leaders. The major roles of the Party-soldiers in the reviving Party and government structures are buttressed by their leading positions in the revolutionary committees of the provinces and by their other military and nonmilitary roles. Still, the military leaders have not become independent elements of power. They are not warlords. They are still operating within a system, a system which they are helping to reshape. . . .

Nevertheless, the military leaders have their hands on many levers of power. If the situation were sufficiently stable, they would probably gladly withdraw their forces from the agricultural brigades, schools, nonstrategic industries and public security offices. These functions tend to be thankless and overextend the armed forces during a period of intensified conflict with the Soviet Union. Yet it is judged that as a group the officers will not voluntarily retire from their new positions of political power and prestige. The leaders of the PLA are senior members of the Communist Party, as well as being the military officials of a Chinese state and of a developing nation. The history of modern China, of the world communist movement and of developing nations indicates that Party leaders and generals do not normally withdraw gracefully from power.

If the aged Mao passes from the scene before a stable, disciplined and essentially united Party and government can be reestablished, and this is very likely, then almost *ipso facto* we will be confronted by a new political phenomenon—a communist military régime. Marshal Lin Piao, Mao's legal heir, is a military man, but even if he does not succeed Mao, military men are now in a position to dominate the Party and the state after Mao dies. . . . Civil officials are already working for the military in numerous revolutionary committees and in many other institutions in which the PLA is playing the dominant role. The Chinese Party-soldiers are already extremely influential and they may very well become more so after Mao passes from the scene. Conditions are weighed in their favor. Hence, we may be confronted by a situation in which a reorganized Party still controls the gun, but only because the generals control the Party.

1. *Wen Hui Pao*, Oct. 19, 1968, in *Survey of the China Mainland Press* (SCMP) No. 4299.

2. Canton Provincial Radio in Cantonese, March 12, 1968; Radio Hunan, Oct. 20, 1968.

3. Hangchow Provincial Radio in Mandarin, June 24, 1968; Changsha Provincial Radio in Mandarin, Oct. 19, 1968.

4. *China News Analysis* (Hong Kong), No. 732 (November 8, 1968), pp. 4–5 (hereafter cited as *CNA*).

5. See Kao Hsueh-shih (PLA instructor), "Getting Fresh Blood Through Class Struggle," *People's Daily*, Oct. 21, 1968, in *SCMP*, No. 4289, p. 3.

6. *New China News Agency* (NCNA), Peking, in English, October 2, 1968; *Washington Post*, October 6, 1968, p. A25.

7. *New York Times*, Oct. 14, 1968, p. 3.

8. *Red Flag*, edit., 4th Issue, 1968, by Peking *NCNA* in English, Oct. 15, 1968.

9. This section on provincial and municipal Party congresses is based on data from, "Provincial Party Congresses," *CNA*, No. 746 (Feb. 28, 1969), pp. 3–5.

10. *Peking Review*, No. 18 (April 30, 1969), p. 41.

11. *Peking Review*, No. 18 (April 30, 1969), p. 41.

12. For examples, Shanghai City Service in Mandarin, Nov. 27, 1968; Urumchi Regional in Mandarin, Dec. 13, 1968.

13. For examples, Shanghai City Service in Mandarin, Nov. 15 and Nov. 20, 1968; Peking *NCNA* in English, Nov. 30, 1968; Huhehot Regional in Mandarin, Dec. 27, 1968.

14. Foochow Provincial in Mandarin, Dec. 17, 1968; Tsinan Provincial in Mandarin, Feb. 26, 1969; Changsha Provincial in Mandarin, March 1, 1969.

15. Lin Piao, "Report To The Ninth National Congress" [see selection 14, below— ED.]

16. For translations of very similar unofficial versions of the draft constitution, see *New York Times*, Jan. 8, 1969, p. 6; *SCMP*, No. 4334 (Jan. 9, 1969), pp. 1–5; also portions in *Yomiuri Shimbun*, Jan. 7, 1969.

17. Lin Piao, "Report to the Ninth National Congress," *loc. cit.*

18. *Peking Review*, No. 14 (April 4, 1969), pp. 7–9.

19. *CNA*, No. 754 (April 25, 1969), p. 4; "Report on Mainland China," Chinese Information Service, May 20, 1969, pp. 7 and 8; *Facts and Features* (Taipei), April 16, 1969, p. 3, gives the figure of 65 military men on the Presidium of the Congress.

20. *Peking Review*, No. 14 (April 4, 1969), p. 7.

21. *Ibid.*, pp. 7–8.

22. Lin Piao, "Report to the Ninth National Congress," *loc. cit.*

23. *Ibid.*

24. "Press Communiqué of the Ninth National Congress," April 14, 1969, *Peking Review*, No. 16 (April 18, 1969), pp. 8–9.

25. *Ibid.*, p. 9.

26. Cf. "Constitution of the Communist Party of China," *Peking Review*, No. 18 (April 30, 1969), pp. 36, 38 and 39 with "Draft of Proposed Constitution . . . ," *New York Times*, Jan. 8, 1969, p. 6.

27. Text in *Peking Review*, No. 18 (April 30, 1969), pp. 45–48.

28. Cf. "An Analysis of the CCP Ninth Central Committee," *Facts and Features*, May 14, 1969, pp. 10–12; *K.D.K. Information* (Tokyo), No. 5/69, May 1, 1969, p. 4.

29. "Press Communiqué of the First Plenary Session of the Ninth Central Committee . . . ," *Peking Review*, No. 18 (April 30, 1969), pp. 48–49.

30. "Rely on the Masses to Carry Out an Open-door Party Consolidation Campaign," *People's Daily*, Oct. 12, 1969; "A Party Branch Maintains Close Ties with the Masses," *Peking Review*, No. 3 (Jan. 16, 1970), pp. 10–12; Richard Solomon, "On Activism and Activists," *China Quarterly*, No. 39 (July–Sept. 1969), pp. 103–114.

31. Stanley Karnow, "Rifts Hurt Party Rebuilding in China," *Washington Post*, Dec. 18, 1969, p. A32.

32. Harbin Provincial in Mandarin, Oct. 5, 1968; Peking Domestic in Mandarin, Nov. 19, 1969; *CNA* No. 790 (Feb. 6, 1970), pp. 1–2.

33. Tillman Durdin, "Peking Asks Masses to Assess and Criticize Members of Party," *New York Times*, Oct. 13, 1969, p. 6; Changsha Provincial in Mandarin, Dec. 30, 1969.

34. *New York Times*, July 13, 1969, p. 3 and Oct. 13, 1969, p. 6; Philip Bridgham, "Mao's Cultural Revolution: "The Struggle to Consolidate Power," *China Quarterly*, No. 41 (Jan.–March, 1970), p. 21.

35. Peking *NCNA* in Chinese, Jan. 7, 1970; *CNA*, No. 790 (Feb. 6, 1970), pp. 3–4.

36. "Peking Rebuffs Extreme Leftists on Building Party," *New York Times*, Jan. 7, 1970, p. 4.

37. *Peking Review*, No. 27 (July 4, 1969), p. 8.

38. Harbin Provincial in Mandarin, Sept. 9, 1969; Shanghai City Service in Mandarin, Feb. 4, 1970.

39. Stanley Karnow, in *Washington Post*, Dec. 18, 1969, p. A32.

40. Donald W. Klein, "The State Council and the Cultural Revolution," *China Quarterly*, No. 35 (July–Sept. 1968), pp. 78–80.

41. Tang Tsou, "The Cultural Revolution and the Chinese Political System," (see selection 15, below—ed.).

42. Klein, *op. cit.*, pp. 80–87; See also Tillman Durdin, "Leadership Gaps Persist in China," *New York Times*, May 3, 1969, p. 6; and Fang Chun-kuei, "An Analysis of the Current Status of Chinese Communist Party and Government Organs," *Issues and Studies*, Jan. 1970, pp. 52–54.

43. For early examples, see *Peking Review*, No. 4 (Jan. 20, 1967), p. 5, and No. 5 (Jan. 27, 1967), p. 14.

44. "List of the 279 Members and Alternate Members of the Ninth Central Committee . . . ," *Peking Review*, No. 18 (April 30, 1969), pp. 47–48.

45. Chengtu Provincial in Mandarin, Nov. 13, 1967; Peking NCNA in Chinese, Aug. 24, 1967; Tientsin Provincial in Mandarin, June 20, 1968; *New York Times*, Feb. 11, 1967, p. 1.

46. Charles Neuhauser, "The Impact of the Cultural Revolution on the Chinese Communist Party Machine," *Asian Survey*, Vol. VIII, No. 6 (June 1968), p. 475.

47. See *China Reporting Service* (USIS, Hong Kong), No. 3, Feb. 25, 1969, p. 1; Parris H. Chang, "Mao's Great Purge," *Problems of Communism*, March–April 1969, p. 10.

PART FOUR

The Cultural Revolution in Retrospect

The play is done. The final curtain has descended on the profound political drama that was China's Great Proletarian Cultural Revolution. It now remains for the critics—philosophers, historians, and social scientists—to piece together the many disparate threads of the drama, evaluate them, and render their verdict. In this section, three such critics—one participant and two outside observers—seek to assess the overall impact of the Cultural Revolution: its successes and failures, its long-range implications for China's social and political development, and its lessons for the outside world. Not surprisingly, there is considerable room for disagreement on these points. The three selections included in Part IV have been chosen for the uniqueness of their respective approaches to the problem of evaluation.

Lin Piao was a principal actor—a "leading man"—in the cultural revolutionary drama. His recreation and assessment of the events and trends of the movement (pp. 178–90) presents us with an "inside look" at the aspirations, motivations, and expectations of at least one group of participants. His perspective is, of course, influenced by the nature of his role as a leading spokesman for the Maoists; and his review of the revolutionary endeavor is therefore somewhat one-sided, tending toward uncritical acclaim of the "great achievements" of the movement. As an apologist for the Cultural Revolution, Lin argues that the upheavals of 1966–68 were necessary in order to rid China of "bourgeois influences" in the political and ideological superstructure. Quoting Chairman Mao at every turn, he lauds the vitality and courage of the "revolutionary masses" in their drive to criticize and remove "capitalist roaders" from positions of power in China. And he states that the recently concluded Great Proletarian Cultural Revolution was but the first stage of a new "permanent revolution" in Chinese society—a revolution aimed at the total remolding of man to eliminate all vestiges of privatism, self-interest, and elitism from human behavior. Despite Lin's obvious vested interest in defending the Cultural Revolution against its critics, his analysis of the events and implications of the movement should not be dismissed out of hand. For he gives us a glimpse of what has been termed the "living thought of Mao Tse-tung"—the ideals and aspirations that have inspired one of the truly important revolutionists of the twentieth century.

In rather stark contrast to Lin Piao's unbridled optimism, Tang Tsou (pp. 191–204) views the events of 1966–68 as having inflicted serious—perhaps irreparable—damage to the structure of political authority in China. He argues that in virtually destroying the CCP as a legitimate ruling body, the Cultural Revolution not only undercut the consensual basis of leader-follower relationships, but also—and equally damaging—"destroyed the very institution which was . . . able to accommodate the material interests of various social groups and the needs for differentiation and specialization in a rapidly developing nation." Tracing the source of this destruction to Mao's utopian preoccupation with the problem of reducing (if not eliminating) the political gap between leaders and led, between domination and subjection, he stresses the disintegrative by-products of the Cultural Revolution, arguing in effect that the revolutionary baby was thrown out with the bath-water. He concludes that the political damage caused by the Cultural Revolution, measured by the widespread demoralization, resentment, cynicism, and loss of self-confidence on the part of Party officials and "the masses" alike, may be vastly more difficult to repair than the economic disasters which followed in the wake of the earlier Great Leap Forward.

In the final selection of Part IV, Richard Pfeffer (pp. 205–27) presents an analysis of the Cultural Revolution that diverges appreciably in many respects from those of both Lin Piao and Tang Tsou. Arguing that the Cultural Revolution was "too complex and too diffuse a configuration of phenomena to be 'explained' within the confines of any single perspective," Pfeffer walks the thin line between the roles of apologist and critic. Like Lin, he takes the Cultural Revolution *qua* revolution seriously; like Tsou, he views the movement as being in some sense "anti-historical." He attempts to reconcile these two ostensibly contradictory perspectives with the observation that the Cultural Revolution was virtually a unique phenomenon in history—"a revolution that continued to place the same high ideal and practical value on egalitarianism and mass participation [after] the mobilization and destructive phases of the [original] revolution were completed." It is this latter quality—Mao's unwavering devotion to the idea of "permanent revolution"—that Pfeffer views as the principal virtue of the Cultural Revolution: a virtue because never before has a revolutionary leader "substantially maintained his radical purity after being in power for over a generation." Yet Pfeffer is not altogether uncritical of the Cultural Revolution. For he notes a fundamental paradox underlying Mao's alternating use of Red Guards (to attack China's political establishment) and the PLA (to curb Red Guard excesses) during successive stages of the movement. The paradox was a profound one, and one that may well prevent Mao from ever realizing his ideal of "permanent revolution." For while the Maoists "needed an organization to wage permanent revolution," they soon found that "organizations tend, at some point in the process of institutionalization, to become counterrevolutionary."

The Cultural Revolution was indeed an unprecedented phenomenon in modern world history: an assault by the founder and leader of a national political establishment upon the very foundations—the values, institutions, and elite personnel—of that establishment. Clearly, Mao's assault did not succeed in totally eliminating privatism, self-interest, and elitism from Chinese society; nor has the Chairman succeeded in establishing the Chinese worker-peasant masses as "masters of their own house." In this sense, the Cultural Revolution was a failure. But should Mao be condemned for trying? This question poses a central dilemma not just for China, but for the rest of mankind as well.

REPORT TO THE NINTH NATIONAL CONGRESS OF THE COMMUNIST PARTY OF CHINA, Part 2

Lin Piao

Comrades!

The Ninth National Congress of the Communist Party of China will be a Congress with a far-reaching influence in the history of our Party.

Our present Congress is convened at a time when great victory has been won in the Great Proletarian Cultural Revolution personally initiated and led by Chairman Mao. This great revolutionary storm has shattered the bourgeois headquarters headed by the renegade, hidden traitor, and scab Liu Shao-ch'i, exposed the handful of rene-gades, enemy agents, and absolutely unrepentant persons in power taking the capitalist road within the Party, with Liu Shao-ch'i as their arch-representative, and smashed their plot to restore capitalism; it has tremendously strengthened our Party and thus prepared ample conditions for this Congress politically, ideologically, and organizationally. . . .

On the Course of the Great Proletarian Cultural Revolution

The Great Proletarian Cultural Revolution is a great political Revolution personally initiated and led by our great leader Chairman Mao under the conditions of the dictatorship of the proletariat, a great revolution in the realm of the superstructure. Our aim is to smash revisionism, seize back that portion of power usurped by the bourgeoisie, exercise all-round dictatorship of the proletariat in the superstructure, including all spheres of culture, and strengthen and consolidate the economic base of socialism so as to ensure that our country continues to advance in giant strides along the road of socialism. . . .

Chairman Mao has always attached major importance to the struggle in ideology. After the liberation of our country, he initiated on different occasions the criticism of the film *The Life of Wu Hsun,* the Hu Feng counter-revolutionary clique, *Studies of "The Dream of the Red Chamber,"* etc. And this time it was Chairman Mao again who led the

From Lin Piao, "Report to the Ninth National Congress of the Communist Party of China," *Peking Review,* no. 18 (April 30, 1969), 16–35. Part 1 of Lin Piao's speech is reproduced above, pp. 12–16.

whole Party in launching the offensive on the bourgeois positions occupied by Liu Shao-ch'i and his gang. . . . At the call of Chairman Mao, the proletariat first launched a revolution in the spheres of Peking Opera, the ballet and symphonic music, spheres that had been regarded as sacred and inviolable by the landlord and capitalist classes. It was a fight at close quarters. Despite every possible kind of resistance and sabotage by Liu Shao-ch'i and his gang, the proletariat finally scored important successes after arduous struggles. A number of splendid model revolutionary theatrical works came into being and the heroic images of the workers, peasants and soldiers finally rose aloft on the stage. After that, Chairman Mao initiated the criticism of *Hai Jui Dismissed from Office* and other poisonous weeds, focusing the attack right on the den of the revisionist clique—that impenetrable and watertight "independent kingdom" under Liu Shao-ch'i's control, the old Peking Municipal Party Committee. . . .

Under the guidance of Chairman Mao's proletarian revolutionary line, the broad revolutionary masses plunged into the fight. In Peking University a big-character poster was written in response to the call of the Central Committee. And soon big-character posters criticizing reactionary bourgeois ideas mushroomed all over the country. Then Red Guards rose and came forward in large numbers and revolutionary young people became courageous and daring pathbreakers. Thrown into a panic, the Liu Shao-ch'i clique hastily hurled forth the bourgeois reactionary line, cruelly suppressing the revolutionary movement of the student youth. However, this did not win them much time in their death-bed struggle. Chairman Mao called and presided over the Eleventh Plenary Session of the Eighth Central Committee of the Party. The Plenary Session adopted the programmatic document, *Decision of the Central Committee of the Chinese Communist Party Concerning the Great Proletarian Cultural Revolution (i.e., the 16-Point Decision)*. Chairman Mao put up his big-character poster *Bombard the Headquarters*, thus taking the lid off Liu Shao-ch'i's bourgeois headquarters. In his letter to the Red Guards, Chairman Mao said that the revolutionary actions of the Red Guards

> express your wrath against and your denunciation of the landlord class, the bourgeoisie, the imperialists, the revisionists, and their running dogs, all of whom exploit and oppress the workers, peasants, revolutionary intellectuals and revolutionary parties and groups. They show that it is right to rebel against reactionaries. I warmly support you.

Afterwards, Chairman Mao received 13 million Red Guards and other revolutionary masses from all parts of the country on eight occasions at T'ien An Men in the capital, which heightened the revolutionary fighting will of the people of the whole country. The revolutionary movements of the workers, peasants and revolutionary functionaries developed rapidly. Increasing numbers of big-character posters spread like raging prairie fires and roared like guns; the slogan "It is right to rebel against reactionaries" resounded throughout the land. And the battle of the hundreds of millions of the people to bombard Liu Shao-ch'i's bourgeois headquarters developed vigorously.

No reactionary class will ever step down from the stage of history of its own accord. When the revolution touched that portion of power usurped by the bourgeoisie, the class struggle became all the more acute. After Liu Shao-ch'i's downfall, his revisionist clique and his agents in various places changed their tactics time and again, putting forward slogans which were "Left" in form but Right in essence such as "suspect all" and "overthrow all," in a futile attempt to go on hitting hard at the many and protecting their own handful. Moreover, they created splits among the revolutionary masses and manipulated and hoodwinked a section of the masses so as to protect themselves. When these schemes were shattered by the proletarian revolutionaries, they launched another frenzied counter-attack, and that is the adverse current lasting from the winter of 1966 to the spring of 1967.

This adverse current was directed against the proletarian headquarters headed by Chairman Mao. Its general program boiled down to this: to overthrow the decisions adopted by the Eleventh Plenary Session of the Eighth Central Committee of the Party, reversing the verdict on the overthrown bourgeois headquarters headed by Liu Shao-ch'i, reversing the verdict on the bourgeois reactionary line, which had already been thoroughly repudiated and discredited by the broad masses, and repressing and retaliating on the revolutionary mass movement. However, this adverse current was seriously criticized by Chairman Mao and resisted by the broad revolutionary masses; it could not prevent the main current of the revolutionary mass movement from surging forward.

The twists and reversals in the revolutionary movement further brought home to the broad masses the importance of political power: the main reason why Liu Shao-ch'i and his gang could do evil was that they had usurped the power of the proletariat in many units and localities and the main reason why the revolutionary masses were repressed was that power was not in the hands of the proletariat in those places. . . . Especially when the capitalist-roaders in power whipped up the evil counter-revolutionary wind of economism after failing in their scheme to suppress the revolution on the pretext of "grasping production," the broad masses came to understand still better that only by recapturing the lost power was it possible for them to defeat the capitalist roaders in power completely. Under the leadership and with the support of Chairman Mao and the proletarian headquarters headed by him, the working class in Shanghai . . . uniting with the broad revolutionary masses and revolutionary cadres, seized power from below in January 1967 from the capitalist roaders in power in the former Municipal Party Committees and Municipal People's Council.

Chairman Mao summed up in good time the experience of the January storm of revolution in Shanghai and issued his call to the whole nation: *"Proletarian revolutionaries, unite and seize power from the handful of Party persons in power taking the capitalist road!"* Following that, Chairman Mao gave the instruction: *"The People's Liberation Army should support the broad masses of the Left."* He went on to sum up the experiences of Heilungkiang Province and other provinces and municipalities and laid down the principles and policies for the establishment of the revolutionary committee which embraces representatives of the revolutionary cadres, representatives of the People's Liberation Army, and representatives of the revolutionary masses, constituting a revolutionary three-in-one combination, thus pushing forward the nationwide struggle for the seizure of power.

The struggle between the proletariat and the bourgeoisie for the seizure and counter-seizure of power was a life-and-death struggle. During the one year and nine months from Shanghai's January storm of revolution in 1967 to the establishment of the revolutionary committees of Tibet and Sinkiang in September 1968, repeated trials of political strength took place between the two classes and the two lines, fierce struggles went on between proletarian and non-proletarian ideas, and an extremely complicated situation emerged. As Chairman Mao has said:

> In the past, we fought north and south; it was easy to fight such wars. For the enemy was obvious. The present Great Proletarian Cultural Revolution is much more difficult than that kind of war.

> The problem is that those who commit ideological errors are mixed up with those whose contradiction with us is one between ourselves and the enemy, and for a time it is hard to sort them out.

Nevertheless, relying on the wise leadership of Chairman Mao, we finally overcame this difficulty. In the summer of 1967, Chairman Mao made an inspection tour north and south of the Yangtze River and issued extremely important instructions, guiding the broad revolutionary masses to distinguish gradually the contradictions between ourselves and the enemy from those among the people and to further bring about the revolutionary great alliance and the revolutionary three-in-one combination and guiding people with petit-bourgeois ideas onto the path of the proletarian revolution. Consequently, it was only the enemy who was thrown into disorder while the broad masses were steeled in the course of the struggle.

The handful of renegades, enemy agents, unreformed landlords, rich peasants, counter-revolutionaries, bad elements and rightists, active counter-revolutionaries, bourgeois careerists and double-dealers who had hidden themselves among the masses would not reveal their colors until the climate suited them. In the summer of 1967 and the spring of 1968, they again fanned up a reactionary evil wind to reverse correct verdicts both from the Right and the extreme "Left." They directed their spearhead against the proletarian headquarters headed by Chairman Mao, against the People's Liberation Army and against the newborn revolutionary committees. In the meantime, they incited the masses to struggle against each other and organized counter-revolutionary conspiratorial cliques in a vain attempt to stage a counter-seizure of power from the proletariat. However, like their chieftain Liu Shao-ch'i, this handful of bad people was finally exposed. This was an important victory for the Great Proletarian Cultural Revolution.

On Carrying Out the Tasks of Struggle-Criticism-Transformation Conscientiously

As in all other revolutions, the fundamental question in the current great revolution in the realm of the superstructure is the question of political power, a question of which class holds leadership. The establishment of revolutionary committees in all provinces, municipalities and autonomous regions throughout the country (with the exception of Taiwan Province) marks the great, decisive victory achieved by this revolution. However, the revolution is not yet over. The proletariat must continue to advance . . . and carry the socialist revolution in the realm of the superstructure through to the end.

Chairman Mao says:

> Struggle-criticism-transformation, . . . on the whole, goes through the following stages: Establishing a three-in-one revolutionary committee; carrying out mass criticism and repudiation; purifying the class ranks; consolidating the Party organization; and simplifying the administrative structure, changing irrational rules and regulations and sending office workers to the workshops.

We must act on Chairman Mao's instruction and fulfill these tasks in every single factory, every single school, every single commune and every single unit in a deep-going, meticulous, down-to-earth and appropriate way.

Confronted with a thousand and one tasks, a revolutionary committee must grasp the fundamental: it must put the living study and application of Mao Tse-tung's Thought above all work and place Mao Tse-tung's Thought in command of everything. . . .

All revolutionary comrades must be clearly aware that class struggle will by no means cease in the ideological and political spheres. The struggle between the proletariat and the bourgeoisie by no means dies out with our seizure of power. We must continue to hold high the banner of revolutionary mass criticism and use Mao Tse-tung's Thought to criticize the bourgeoisie, to criticize revisionism and all kinds of Right or extreme "Left" erroneous ideas which run counter to Chairman Mao's proletarian revolutionary line, and to criticize bourgeois individualism and the theory of "many centers," that is, the theory of "no center." We must continue to criticize thoroughly and discredit completely the stuff of the renegade, hidden traitor and scab Liu Shao-ch'i . . . so as to ensure that our cause will continue to advance in the direction indicated by Chairman Mao.

Chairman Mao points out:

> The revolutionary committee should exercise unified leadership, eliminate duplication in the administrative structure, follow the policy of "better troops and simpler administration" and organize itself into a revolutionized leading group which maintains close ties with the masses.

This is a basic principle which enables the superstructure to serve its socialist economic base still better. A duplicate administrative structure divorced from the masses, scholasticism which suppresses and binds their revolutionary initiative, and a landlord and bourgeois style of formality and ostentation—all these are destructive to the socialist economic base, advantageous to capitalism and disadvantageous to socialism. In accordance with Chairman Mao's instructions, organs of state power at all levels and other organizations must keep close ties with the masses, first of all with the basic masses—the working class and the poor and lower-middle peasants. Cadres, old and new, must constantly sweep away the dust of bureaucracy and must not catch the bad habit of "acting as bureaucrats and overlords." They must keep on practicing frugality in carrying out revolution, run all socialist undertakings industriously and thriftily, oppose extravagance and waste and guard against the bourgeois attacks with sugar-coated bullets. They must maintain the system of cadre participation in collective productive labor. They must be concerned with the well-being of the masses. . . . They must make criticism and self-criticism regularly, and in line with the five requirements for the successors to the revolution as set forth by Chairman Mao, *"fight self, criticize revisionism"* and conscientiously remold their world outlook.

The People's Liberation Army is the mighty pillar of the dictatorship of the proletariat. Chairman Mao has pointed out many times: from the Marxist point of view the main component of the state is the army. The Chinese People's Liberation Army personally founded and led by Chairman Mao is an army of the workers and peasants, an army of the proletariat. It has performed great historic feats in the struggle for overthrowing the three big mountains of imperialism, feudalism and bureaucrat-capitalism, and in the struggles for defending the motherland, for resisting U.S. aggression and aiding Korea, and for smashing aggression by imperialism, revisionism, and the reactionaries. In the

Great Proletarian Cultural Revolution, large numbers of commanders
and fighters have taken part in the work of "three supports and two
militaries" (i.e., support industry, support agriculture, support the
broad masses of the Left, military control, political and military training) and representatives of the army have taken part in the three-in-one
combination; they have tempered themselves in the class struggle,
strengthened their ties with the masses, promoted the ideological revolutionization of the army, and made new contributions to the people.
And this is also the best preparation against war. . . . For the past
three years, it is precisely because the people have supported the army
and the army has protected the people that renegades, enemy agents,
absolutely unrepentant persons in power taking the capitalist road
and counter-revolutionaries have failed in their attempts to undermine
this great people's army of ours.

Departments of culture, art, education, the press, health, etc., occupy
an extremely important position in the realm of the superstructure.
The line *"We must whole-heartedly rely on the working class"* was decided upon at the Second Plenary Session of the Seventh Central Committee. And now, at Chairman Mao's call that *"The working class must
exercise leadership in everything,"* the working class, which is the main
force in the proletarian revolution, and its staunch ally the poor and
lower-middle peasants have mounted the political stage of struggle-
criticism-transformation in the superstructure. From July 27, 1968,
mighty contingents of the working class marched to places long dominated by the persons in power taking the capitalist road and to all
places where intellectuals were predominant in number. It was a great
revolutionary action. Whether the proletariat is able to take firm root
in the position of culture and education and transform them with Mao
Tse-tung's Thought is the key question in carrying the Great Proletarian Cultural Revolution through to the end. . . .

On the Policies of the Great Proletarian Cultural Revolution

In order to continue the revolution in the realm of the superstructure, it is imperative to carry out conscientiously all Chairman Mao's
proletarian policies.

Policies for the Great Proletarian Cultural Revolution were early
explicitly stipulated in the . . . *16-Point Decision* of August 1966.
The series of Chairman Mao's latest instructions have further specified
the various policies.

The main question at present is to carry them out to the letter.

The Party's policies, including those towards the intellectuals, the
cadres, . . . the mass organizations, the struggle against the enemy and
the economic policy—all these policies come under the general subject
of the correct handling of the two different types of contradictions,
those between ourselves and the enemy and those among the people.

The majority or the vast majority of the intellectuals trained in the old type of schools and colleges are able or willing to integrate themselves with the workers, peasants and soldiers. They should be "re-educated" by the workers, peasants, and soldiers under the guidance of Chairman Mao's correct line, and encouragement should be given to those who have done well in the integration and to the Red Guards and educated young people who are active in going to the countryside or mountainous areas. . . .

With regard to people who have made mistakes, stress must be laid on giving them education and re-education, doing patient and careful ideological and political work. . . . With regard to good people who committed the errors characteristic of the capitalist-roader in power but have now raised their political consciousness and gained the understanding of the masses, they should be promptly "liberated," assigned to suitable work, and encouraged to go among the masses of the workers and peasants to remold their world outlook. As for those who have made a little progress and become to some extent awakened, we should continue to help them, proceeding from the viewpoint of unity. . . .

In the struggle against the enemy, we must implement Chairman Mao's policies of *"Leniency towards those who confess their crimes and severe punishment of those who refuse to do so"* and of *"giving a way out."* We rely mainly on the broad masses of the people in exercising dictatorship over the enemy. As for bad people or suspects ferreted out through investigation in the movement for purifying the class ranks, the policy of *"killing none and not arresting most"* should be applied to all except the active counter-revolutionaries against whom there is conclusive evidence of crimes such as murder, arson or poisoning, and who should be dealt with in accordance with the law.

As for the bourgeois reactionary academic authorities, we should . . . criticize them and provide them with a proper livelihood. In short, we should criticize their ideology and at the same time give them a way out. To handle this part of the contradiction between ourselves and the enemy in the manner of handling contradictions among the people is beneficial to the consolidation of the dictatorship of the proletariat and to the disintegration of the enemy ranks.

In carrying out the policies of the Party, it is necessary to study the specific conditions of the unit concerned. In places where the revolutionary great alliance has not yet been sufficiently consolidated, it is necessary to help the revolutionary masses bring about, in accordance with revolutionary principles, the revolutionary great alliance on the basis of different fields of work, trades and school classes so that they will become united against the enemy. In units where the work of purifying the class ranks has not yet started or has only just started, it is imperative to grasp the work firmly and do it well in accordance with the Party's policies. In units where the purification of the class ranks is by and large completed, it is necessary to take firm hold of other tasks in keeping with Chairman Mao's instructions concerning the various stages of struggle-criticism-transformation. At the same time, it is necessary to pay close attention to new trends in the class struggle. What if the bad people go wild again? . . . If the class enemies stir up trouble again, just arouse the masses and strike them down again.

As the *16-Point Decision* indicates, *"The Great Proletarian Cultural Revolution is a powerful motive force for the development of the social productive forces in our country."* Our country has seen good harvests in agricultural production for years running and there is also a thriving situation in industrial production and science and technology. The enthusiasm of the broad masses of the working people both in revolution and production has soared to unprecedented heights. Many factories, mines and other enterprises have time and again topped their production records, creating all-time highs in production. The technical revolution is making constant progress. The market is flourishing and prices are stable. By the end of 1968 we had redeemed all the national bonds. Our country is now a socialist country with neither internal nor external debts. . . .

Chairman Mao always teaches us: *"Political work is the life-blood of all economic work."* . . . Politics is the concentrated expression of economics. If we fail to make revolution in the superstructure, fail to arouse the broad masses of the workers and peasants, fail to criticize the revisionist line, fail to expose the handful of renegades, enemy agents, capitalist-roaders in power and counter-revolutionaries, and fail to consolidate the leadership of the proletariat, how can we further consolidate the socialist economic base and further develop the socialist productive forces?

We must bring the revolutionary initiative and creativeness of the people of all nationalities into full play, firmly grasp revolution and energetically promote production and fulfill and overfulfill our plans for developing the national economy. It is certain that the great victory of the Great Proletarian Cultural Revolution will continue to bring about new leaps forward on the economic front and in our cause of socialist construction as a whole.

On the Final Victory of the Revolution in Our Country

The victory of the Great Proletarian Cultural Revolution of our country is very great indeed. But we must in no way think that we may sit back and relax. . . . There will be reversals in the class struggle. We must never forget class struggle, and never forget the dictatorship of the proletariat. In the course of carrying out our policies at present, there still exists the struggle between the two lines and there is interference from the "Left" or the Right. It still calls for much effort to accomplish the tasks for all the stages of struggle-criticism-transformation. We must closely follow Chairman Mao and steadfastly rely on the broad revolutionary masses to surmount the difficulties and twists and turns on our way forward and seize still greater victories in the cause of socialism.

On the Consolidation and Building of the Party

The victory of the Great Proletarian Cultural Revolution has provided us with valuable experience on how we should build the Party under the conditions of the dictatorship of the proletariat. . . .

The Communist Party of China owes all its achievement to the wise leadership of Chairman Mao and these achievements constitute victories for Mao Tse-tung Thought. For half a century now, in leading the great struggle of the people of all the nationalities of China for accomplishing the new-democratic revolution, in leading China's great struggle for socialist revolution and socialist construction and in the great struggle of the contemporary international communist movement against imperialism, modern revisionism and reactionaries of various countries, Chairman Mao has integrated the universal truth of Marxism-Leninism with the concrete practice of revolution . . . and has brought Marxism-Leninism to a higher and completely new stage. Mao Tse-tung Thought is Marxism-Leninism of the era in which imperialism is heading for total collapse and socialism is advancing to worldwide victory. The entire history of our Party has borne out this truth: departing from the leadership of Chairman Mao and Mao Tse-tung Thought, our Party will suffer setbacks and defeats; following Chairman Mao closely and acting on Mao Tse-tung Thought, our Party will advance and triumph. We must forever remember this lesson. Whoever opposes Chairman Mao, whoever opposes Mao Tse-tung Thought, at any time or under any circumstances, will be condemned and punished by the whole Party and the whole nation. . . .

Opposition and struggle between the two lines within the Party are a reflection inside the Party of contradictions between classes and between the new and the old in society. If there were no contradictions in the Party and no struggles to resolve them, and if the Party did not get rid of the stale and take in the fresh, the Party's life would come to an end. Chairman Mao's theory on inner-Party contradiction is and will be the fundamental guiding thinking for the consolidation and building of the Party. . . .

Liu Shao-ch'i's revisionist line on Party building betrayed the very essence of the Marxist-Leninist teaching on the dictatorship of the proletariat and of the Marxist-Leninist theory on Party building. At the crucial moment when China's socialist revolution was deepening and the class struggle was extraordinarily acute, Liu Shao-ch'i . . . spread such reactionary fallacies as the theory of "the dying out of class struggle," the theory of "docile tools," the theory that "the masses are backward," the theory of "joining the Party in order to climb up," the theory of "inner-Party peace" and the theory of "merging private and public interests" (i.e., "losing a little to gain much"), in a vain attempt to corrupt or disintegrate our Party, so that the more the Party members "cultivated" themselves, the more revisionist they would become and so that the Marxist-Leninist Party would "evolve peacefully" into a revisionist Party and the dictatorship of the proletariat into the dictatorship of the bourgeoisie. We should carry on revolutionary mass criticism and repudiation and thoroughly eliminate the pernicious influence of Liu Shao-ch'i's reactionary fallacies.

The Great Proletarian Cultural Revolution is the most broad and deep-going movement for Party consolidation in the history of our Party. The Party organizations at various levels and the broad masses of Communists have experienced the acute struggle between the two lines, gone through the test in the large-scale class struggle, and undergone examination by the revolutionary masses both inside and outside the Party. In this way, the Party members and cadres have faced the world and braved the storm and have raised their class consciousness and their consciousness of the struggle between the two lines. . . .

The study and spread of the basic experience of the Great Proletarian Cultural Revolution, the study and spread of the history of the struggle between the two lines, and the study and spread of Chairman Mao's theory of continuing the revolution under the dictatorship of the proletariat must be conducted not just once but should be repeated every year, every month, every day. Only thus will it be possible for the masses of Party members and the people to criticize and resist erroneous lines and tendencies the moment they emerge, and will it be possible to guarantee that our Party will always forge ahead victoriously along the correct course charted by Chairman Mao.

The revision of the Party Constitution is an important item on the agenda of the Ninth National Congress of the Party. The Central Committee has submitted the draft Party Constitution to the Congress for discussion. This draft was worked out jointly by the whole Party and the revolutionary masses throughout the country. Since November 1967 when Chairman Mao proposed that basic Party organizations take part in the revision of the Party Constitution, the Central Committee has received several thousand drafts. On this basis the Enlarged Twelfth Plenary Session of the Eighth Central Committee of the Party drew up the draft Party Constitution, upon which the whole Party, the whole army, and the revolutionary masses throughout the country once again held enthusiastic and earnest discussions. . . . Especially important is the fact that the draft Party Constitution has clearly reaffirmed that Marxism-Leninism-Mao Tse-tung's Thought is the theoretical basis guiding the Party's thinking. This is a great victory for the Great

Proletarian Cultural Revolution in smashing Liu Shao-ch'i's revisionist line on Party building, a great victory for Marxism-Leninism-Mao Tse-tung's Thought. The Central Committee is convinced that, after the discussion and adoption of the new Party Constitution by the Congress, our Party will, in accordance with its provisions, surely be built into a still greater, still more glorious and still more correct Party. . . .

The Whole Party, the Whole Nation Unite to Win Still Greater Victories

The Ninth National Congress of the Party is being held at an important moment in the historical development of our Party, at an important moment in the consolidation and development of the dictatorship of the proletariat in our country and at an important moment in the development of the international communist movement and world revolution. Among the delegates to the Congress are proletarian revolutionaries of the older generation and also a large number of fresh blood. . . . The fact that so many delegates have come to Peking from all corners of the country and gathered around the great leader Chairman Mao to discuss and decide on the affairs of the Party and state signifies that our Congress is a Congress full of vitality, a Congress of unity and a Congress of victory. . . .

Through the Great Proletarian Cultural Revolution our motherland has become unprecedentedly unified and our people have achieved a great revolutionary unity on an extremely broad scale under the great red banner of Mao Tse-tung's Thought. This great unity is under the leadership of the proletariat and is based on the worker-peasant alliance; it embraces all the fraternal nationalities, the patriotic democrats who for a long time have done useful work for the cause of the revolution and construction of our motherland, the vast numbers of patriotic overseas Chinese, . . . our patriotic compatriots in Taiwan who are oppressed and exploited by the U.S.-Chiang reactionaries, and all those who support socialism and love our socialist motherland. We are convinced that after the present National Congress of our Party, the people of all the nationalities of our country will certainly unite still more closely under the leadership of the great leader Chairman Mao and win still greater victories in the struggle against our common enemy and in the cause of building our powerful socialist motherland.

Let the whole Party unite, let the whole nation unite, hold high the great red banner of Mao Tse-tung's Thought, be resolute, fear no sacrifice and surmount every difficulty to win victory!

Long live the great victory of the Great Proletarian Cultural Revolution!

Long live the dictatorship of the proletariat!

Long live the Ninth National Congress of the Party!

Long live the great, glorious and correct Communist Party of China!
Long live great Marxism-Leninism-Mao Tse-tung's Thought!
Long live our great leader Chairman Mao! A long, long life to Chairman Mao!

THE CULTURAL REVOLUTION AND THE CHINESE POLITICAL SYSTEM

Tang Tsou

One of the most extraordinary and puzzling events of the twentieth century is surely the Great Proletarian Cultural Revolution in China. This most profound crisis in the history of the Peking regime provides us with the best available opportunity to study the Chinese political system. For it is during a crisis that the nature, the strength, and the vulnerabilities of a political system fully reveal themselves. Furthermore, we can attempt not only to note the unique features of this extraordinary event, and of Chinese politics itself, but also to see whether the seemingly unique Chinese experience does not reveal some universal dilemma of the human condition and fundamental problems of the socio-political order in a magnified and easily recognizable form.

It is my belief that the Chinese political system prior to the Cultural Revolution is one of the purest forms found in human experience of a type of association in which there is a clear-cut separation between the elite and the masses. If one follows Ralf Dahrendorf in asserting that in every social organization there is a differential distribution of power and authority, a division involving domination and subjection,[1] the Chinese political system can be taken as one of the polar examples of all social organizations, showing clearly their possibilities and limitations, their problems and dilemmas. From this perspective, the Maoist vision as it has revealed itself in its extreme form during the . . . Cultural Revolution can be considered a critique of this type of political organization. It represents an attempt to minimize the consequences arising from the division between domination and subjection by changing the pattern of participation of the dominated in the political process within every single organization, by redefining the role of those in positions of authority, and by changing their attitudes and values so that the line between domination and subjection is blurred and a new type of relationship between the two groups will be obtained. . . .

Obviously, the establishment and the successful functioning of the Maoist political system requires a concomitant change in public and private morality and indeed in what we call human nature. Marx has

Tang Tsou, "The Cultural Revolution and the Chinese Political System," *The China Quarterly*, no. 38 (April–June 1969), pp. 63–91. Reprinted by permission of the publisher.

written that "the whole of history is nothing but a continual transformation of human nature." [2] Whereas Marx seems, as Robert Tucker
puts it, to "look at the future Communist revolution as the source of a
radical transformation of man or 'change of self,' " Mao in effect has
attempted to make a series of revolutions to bring Communist society
into existence by a radical transformation of man. From this general
perspective, let me now discuss . . . the course of the Cultural Revolution so that I can give concrete meaning to these abstract generaliza-
tions. . . .

The Disruption of the Political System During the
Cultural Revolution

Chou En-lai told the revolutionary rebels on January 25, 1967 that
the "form of mobilization in the early phase" of the Cultural Revolution was "not entirely the same" as that in all other mass movements in
the past in Communist China. He explained that whereas these other
mass movements were conducted both "from the top to the bottom"
and "from the bottom to the top," the unprecedented Cultural Revolution was "essentially" a movement "from the bottom to the top." He
then added immediately that "of course, we cannot detach ourselves
from the supreme leadership, the leadership of Chairman Mao and the
Party Center." . . .[3] Viewed in the light of the course of the Cultural
Revolution, these statements suggest that the Cultural Revolution is a
rebellion of the dominated against the establishment in most spheres of
Chinese society—a rebellion inspired and manipulated by the supreme
leader. The emphasis on "from the bottom to the top," as the essential
form, implies that a measure of spontaneity and autonomy on the part
of the masses and their own leaders was permitted and encouraged
during the early stages of the Cultural Revolution. It indicates that this
was so much greater than that permitted in the mass movements in the
past as to make the Cultural Revolution qualitatively different and
thus unprecedented. Indeed, the masses, i.e., the Red Guards and the
revolutionary rebels, constituted Mao's main instrument of attack in
the first 18 months.

Even with the Red Guards and the army as his instruments, Mao was
confronted with the very difficult problem of justifying his revolution
and legitimizing his attack on the Party organization. For the Party
and the Party organizations in various units had become symbols of
authority, and the policies pursued by the Party organization were
eminently successful when measured in terms of practical results. What
Mao did essentially was to use personal, moral, and ideological appeals
to override pragmatic standards. Immediately before and during the
Cultural Revolution, the Maoists elevated the position of Mao's
thought to a new peak. Lin Piao made the following statement in May
1966: "Chairman Mao's experience in passing through many events is

more profound than that of Marx, Engels, and Lenin. No one can surpass Chairman Mao in his rich revolutionary experience." . . .[4] This cult of Mao and his thought served a definite political purpose. It set a new standard of legitimacy and correctness with which the actions and opinions of many top leaders were to be judged.

This apotheosis of Mao was accompanied by a further radicalization of his thought by pushing to their extremes its constituent elements: the idea of conflict, the tendency toward polarization, the concept of centrality of man, the controlling importance of politics, and finally, the importance of ideas and revolutionary morality. To exploit the conflict between those in positions of superordination and those in positions of subordination in order to smash a well-entrenched establishment, the Maoists revived and incessantly used a hitherto neglected assertion made in 1939 by Mao in a speech celebrating Stalin's sixtieth birthday: "In the last analysis, all the myriad principles of Marxism can be summed up in one sentence: 'To rebel is justified.' " The destructive purpose of conflict was blatantly extolled: "Without destruction there cannot be construction, and destruction must come before construction."

Mao and the Maoists drew the picture of a Party which was polarized into two groups reaching up to the very top. The class struggle became the struggle between the bourgeois and the proletarian lines within the Party. Mao personally called on his followers to bombard the headquarters, i.e., the headquarters of the bourgeoisie within the Party. . . . Polarization gives rise to double standards. The Red Guards solemnly announced that "we are permitting only the Left to rebel, not the Right." The Chinese people were urged not to obey the orders of their superiors blindly. But at the same time, they were told to carry out Mao's instructions and follow his great strategic plans even if they did not understand these for the time being. . . .

To mobilize the masses to rebel, the role of man, not man as an individual but man as a member of the masses, was glorified. A *Red Flag* editorial of January, 1967, stated that "the masses are reasonable and they are able to distinguish the people from the enemy." Repeatedly, the Maoists declared, "Let the masses liberate themselves and educate themselves." "Trust the masses, rely on them, and respect their initiative." . . . Glorifying the creative role of the masses in history also serves the purpose of downgrading the importance of the experts and of refuting the pragmatists' view that material conditions impose a limit on rapid changes.

Likewise, the controlling importance of politics has been pushed a step further. The Maoists consistently pointed out that so long as the general political orientation of individuals or groups is correct—that is to say, so long as they directed their attack against Liu Shao-ch'i and his followers—their mistakes should be overlooked. The Maoists explained that in a period of great upheaval, great division, and great realignment the only thing that counted was the general political orientation, and that mistakes were inevitable, and disturbances, disruptions, and disorder must not be feared. In effect, this meant that laws and traditions, customary standards and humane considerations could be violated with impunity.

Finally, correct ideology and revolutionary morality must override everything else including such long-established principles of democratic centralism as the minority obeying the majority. Many Western observers doubt whether Mao had majority support within the Party council. According to a Red Guard newspaper, Mao said in one of his "latest instructions" that he had the support of just a little over the majority at the Eleventh Plenum which gave full Party sanction to the Cultural Revolution.[5] Whatever the case may have been at the Eleventh Plenum, there is no doubt that the Red Guards constituted a minority in the various universities, schools, and units for a long period of time. Thus Chiang Ch'ing, the wife of Mao Tse-tung, justified the right of the majority on the ground that "one could not talk about a 'minority' or 'majority' independent of class viewpoint." [6] In effect, this meant that the thoughts of Mao and Mao himself were placed above the Party as the ultimate source of authority and standard of right and wrong.[7] Practical results achieved by Party and government bureaucrats were considered to be contaminated by their appeal to the self-interests of the individuals. Complete devotion to public interests and standards of revolutionary virtues as defined by Mao have been used to judge the actual performance and the motives of the Party leaders and cadres. The Red Guards attempted to set up puritanical rules of behavior and enforce them on everyone. The new revolutionary committees set up to replace the government administration and Party committees on the provincial level and below adopted stringent regulations on improving their style of work. These regulations were aimed at maintaining collective leadership, preserving the anonymity of the individual members, ensuring constant contact between the officials and the masses, and eliminating the outward differences between the leaders and the led. In turn, these proclaimed virtues were used to justify the revolution and the new revolutionary order. Thus, the Maoist vision is both a long-term goal and an immediately available means to destroy the opposition.

The strategy adopted by Mao in launching and making the revolution bears on the problem of legitimizing his actions. The Maoists have made it clear that the criticism of "academic authorities" and the intellectuals had the purpose of preparing public opinion for the so-called seizure of power which took place after January 1967 in many units below the top level. The Maoists captured the control of the propaganda agencies and mass media of communication before they attempted to seize power from the Party committees.

At first, P'eng Chen and later Liu Shao-ch'i were left in charge of the Cultural Revolution. Harry Gelman and Philip Bridgham,[8] two leading U.S. Government analysts in the field of Chinese Communist internal affairs, have developed the theory that Mao put his erstwhile lieutenants through tests to determine their loyalty and purged them when they failed. This interpretation is correct as far as it goes. But Mao's strategy also served the purpose of legitimizing his removal of top Party leaders and mobilizing the masses to attack them.

The intellectuals in a totalitarian society, because of their role as the seekers of truth and critics of society, are the most vulnerable targets of attack by the ideologues. Their published writings are indestructible proof of guilt, once a policy of liberalization is replaced by a drive to re-impose strict ideological control. Wu Han and other intellectuals fell victim to this process. There is no question that they also criticized Mao by historical analogy or in Aesopian language. After the cult of Mao and his thought had been pushed to a new peak, their veiled criticism could be made into the most serious political offense. When P'eng Chen tried to protect them, he could be charged with protecting "freaks and monsters." Similarly, when the work teams endeavored to restore control over the revolutionary students, a sharp conflict occurred between the establishment and those outside it. The resentment of revolutionary students against the work teams was transferred to Liu Shao-ch'i and other Party leaders responsible for sending them.

By adopting the principle of letting the masses liberate themselves, trusting the masses, and relying on them, the time-honored method of using work teams became an error in orientation and an error of line. After Mao had criticized the dispatch of work teams, top leaders like Liu Shao-ch'i and Teng Hsiao-p'ing could only defend their decision by saying that they were old revolutionaries who encountered new problems, they had no understanding of new things, and that their failure of understanding stemmed from their lack of a firm grasp of Mao's thought. Once Mao had succeeded in making a case out of a specific mistake, he then generalized his criticism by linking this error with the past and present policies, proposals, and actions of the other leaders and traced them to basic ideological sources. In this process, Mao and the Maoists perverted history and departed from the standards of fair play, which notion they specifically repudiated. But in this way they attempted to present a plausible case for their sweeping purge.

There is still another aspect of Mao's strategy which should be noted. Mao is a revolutionary romantic with a radical vision, but he is also a cautious man in his strategy and tactics. Generally speaking, he tends to try out less radical measures first before he resorts to more radical ones. The events from September 1962 to March 1967 suggest that he followed the same rule. The resistance of the Party organization made it necessary for him to escalate his conflict with the Party organization until he purged its top leaders.

During the Cultural Revolution, the resistance put up by the Party organization was a matter of self-protection and survival. It has brought out several interesting points about the Chinese political system. In the first period of 50 days, most of the work teams were able to gain ready acceptance of their authority and received adequate support from the students, even though they took fairly stern disciplinary actions against some of the cadres on the one hand and repressive measures against the Red Guards on the other. They succeeded in keeping the Maoist students under control until Mao returned to Peking, criticized the work teams and ordered their withdrawal. Although both persuasion and coercion were extensively used by the work teams, it is also true that they enjoyed genuine authority and obtained obedience to their orders without too much difficulty, so long as they were considered the embodiment of the Party. "To oppose the work team is to oppose the Party" was one of the most effective slogans at this time.[9] During the early autumn of 1966, most of the workers and peasants also obeyed the orders of Party committees in various units when some of them were instigated here and there by the Party committees to attack the Red Guards. This shows that the rule of the Party was accepted as legitimate and that a true relationship of authority existed between those in command and those in subordination. It is precisely because obedience to the orders of the Party organizations had become quite habitual, and because this obedience was based at least partly on the internalization of those values and norms justified in and propagated by Liu Shao-ch'i's many writings, that the Maoists had to launch an attack on "the slave mentality advocated by China's Khrushchev."

Another significant but not surprising point about the Party committees was their amazing tactical skill and their cohesiveness. In the first seven months, revolutionary committees were established in only six out of 29 units at the provincial level. Leaving aside Shanghai and Peking as special cases, all the four provinces in which revolutionary committees were successfully set up were those in which one or several Party leaders of fairly high rank came out at a fairly early stage to support Mao. In the rest, the Party committees maintained their solidarity. In some places, they staged what was called sham seizure of power by handing over the office building and the official seals to Red Guard units organized by them or at least sympathetic to them. One of the reasons why revolutionary committees could not be as rapidly set up as Peking wanted was that most of the top Party and government leaders refused to break with their colleagues and join the Maoists.[10] Hence,

Peking's repeated call for the cadres to "stand out," and its constant emphasis that correct treatment of the cadres, by forgiving their former mistakes and supporting them in their work, was an indispensible condition for successfully establishing the revolutionary committees.

But the tactical skills and the cohesiveness of the local Party committees stand in contrast to another phenomenon. I have uncovered no evidence that Liu Shao-ch'i, other non-Maoist Party leaders, and the various Party committees, ever had a nationwide strategic plan to oppose Mao publicly and to take offensive action against him. The opposition to Mao was essentially a case of the Party organization trying to defend itself under the major premises and the rules of the game as laid down by Mao. All the organizations pledged allegiance to Mao and his thought. All of them said that they supported the Cultural Revolution. Mao's prestige, Lin Piao's control over the army, the narrow majority obtained by Mao at the Eleventh Plenum by rather irregular means, are three obvious explanations. But still another explanation is, I suspect, Mao's success in making his thought the sole legitimate criterion of right and wrong, whether one actually agrees with it or not. The disability of the Party organization shows the significance of political ideology and the difficulty of challenging an established doctrine and evolving a new one in a totalitarian system.[11]

Another major target of the attack launched by Red Guards and revolutionary rebels was the government bureaucracy. The disruption of the government bureaucracy has received less publicity in the American press than the fighting and conflicts in the provinces. But a perusal of Red Guard publications shows its seriousness. Still, the government bureaucracy survived the Cultural Revolution in much better shape than the Party. With notable exceptions, like Chiang Nan-hsiang, the Minister of Higher Education, and Po I-po, the Chairman of the State Economic Commission, many of the top government leaders are still at their posts. In contrast to Liu Shao-ch'i, Premier Chou En-lai's influence and power increased during the Cultural Revolution. No doubt, Chou's personality and skills in political maneuver and his ability to protect his subordinates constitutes one explanation. Another, and perhaps more basic, reason is that although the government administration, like the Party organization, is also a huge bureaucracy with its tendency towards conservatism and routinization, the Party bureaucracy and the government bureaucracy in the Chinese political system differ from each other in their respective relationship with the supreme leader. First, the Party is the locus of power, whereas the government bureaucracy is one step removed from the center of authority. When actual conflicts occur over policies, they are inevitably linked up with issues of power, and the Party organization becomes the focus of conflict with the leader. Secondly, ideological matters are one of the main concerns of the Party organization. The innate tendencies of the organization and the attitudes and views of its members would sooner or later find expression in ideological writings or statements. These incipient ideological intrusions into the eminent domain of the supreme leader, and these doctrinal deviations, however slight, can easily be viewed as a challenge to the authority of the leader. Thirdly, in the government bureaucracy each of the various vertical systems has some specialized function. They are usually not the immediate source of generalized political power. In contrast, the core of the Party organization is its system of Party committees and secretaries at the regional, provincial, and local levels, having generalized political authority over most activities. These can more easily become "independent kingdoms." Finally, the tasks performed by the government bureaus are of greater practical use to the supreme leader than the control functions performed by the Party organization.[12]

The army has also behaved in an interesting manner during the Cultural Revolution. Its behavior stems from its dual, ambiguous role in its relation to Mao and within the Chinese political system. Under Lin Piao, it has been Mao's main basis of power. It has been highly indoctrinated with the thought of Mao Tse-tung. But it is an organization which has its own professional standards and expertise. It was also a part of the establishment. The ties between the military leaders in various military regions and districts and the Party leaders on the regional and provincial levels were particularly close. Thus, while the army has been one of Mao's two chief instruments during the Cultural Revolution, it has also become a conservative force in the Maoist coalition, frequently resisting the more extreme measures advocated or undertaken by the Cultural Revolution Group and the Red Guards, particularly after Liu Shao-ch'i had been effectively pushed aside. While it has dutifully carried out what it believed to be Mao's instructions, it has also tended to interpret these orders with a bias toward preserving law and order and limiting the extent of the political purge.[13] This role offers an explanation for the relative compliance of the army until its integrity as a whole was threatened in August 1967, when Wang Li and other radicals in the Cultural Revolution Group raised the slogans of "dragging out a small handful in the army." The dismissal of the Acting Chief of Staff Yang Ch'eng-wu, in March 1968, suggests that despite the growing power of the People's Liberation Army, China is still not under army dictatorship. Mao remains the pivotal figure who welds together a coalition of forces and maintains a balance among them by throwing his influence on one side or the other. His purpose has been to keep the Cultural Revolution going without plunging China into intolerable political chaos or a civil war.

While Mao's ultimate source of power was the army, the spearhead of Mao's Cultural Revolution was the Red Guards and the revolutionary rebels. The reasons why Mao had to use them as his offensive forces are obvious. Such a momentous undertaking as the Cultural Revolution must be justified on the ground that it is demanded and supported by the masses. Mao and his followers had no direct control over the mass organizations and thus could not use them as their instruments. Strictly speaking, the Maoists cannot be said to have been an organized faction prior to the Cultural Revolution. They had no organization of any kind under their direct control, with the exception of the army. If the difficulty confronting Liu Shao-ch'i was Mao's success in making his ideology the only source of legitimacy, the problem confronting Mao was Liu Shao-ch'i's control over all the organizations with the exception just mentioned. Yet Liu Shao-ch'i and the numerous persons purged by Mao cannot be called a faction in the strict sense of the term. If there had been a Liu-Teng faction, this must have had almost complete direct control over the Party apparatus. This is now shown by the fact that 90 per cent of the work teams were accused of having committed errors in the 50 days in June and July of 1966. Almost all the Regional Bureaus and Party committees at the provincial and municipal levels resisted the Cultural Revolution. Operationally speaking, such a faction would be almost identical with the whole Party organization.[14]

Mao's shrewd sense of politics led him to see the potential conflict between the establishment and those outside the establishment, and he set out to exploit the repressed resentment against the establishment to attack the leaders of the Party organization. Furthermore, the students, unlike Party leaders engaged in practical work, had no real knowledge of the actual consequences of the thought of Mao and his disastrous policies. Instead, they had been exposed in the communication media to nothing but the praise of Mao, his thought, and his achievements. The Party organization's practice of "waving the red flag to oppose the red flag" may have been a necessary expedient, but it also played a part in promoting the cult of Mao among the masses. Brought up under a relatively stable regime and without any personal experience of the social dislocation and ideological confusion of pre-1949 China, the students knew only one set of legitimate values and had a remarkable sense of moral certitude. Thus Mao permitted and indeed encouraged, during the early stages, the Red Guards to take spontaneous action, and granted them a large measure of autonomy. Not only were their mistakes overlooked, but the blame for any conflict between them and those in authority was placed on the latter. Vice-Premier Hsieh Fu-chih told the students that Chairman Mao had said:

> Where outside cadres assume leadership responsibility, if their relationship with local cadres is bad, then the outside cadres should bear the main responsibility for it. . . . Where army cadres are actually in leadership positions, under normal circumstances, if their relationship with local cadres is unsatisfactory, the main responsibility should be placed on the

army cadres. . . . Where veteran cadres assume the main responsibility of
leadership, if the relationship between the old and new cadres is poor,
then the former should bear the responsibility.[15]

Then the Vice-Premier added as his own opinion that in regard to the
contradictions between the majority and minority factions, the former
must bear greater responsibility. After the work teams were withdrawn,
every political leader including Ch'en Po-ta and Chiang Ch'ing assumed, at least for a brief period, the posture of learning from the
students in talking to them.[16]

The students and rebels organized themselves into numerous small
units with all sorts of strange names. To form or join a Red Guard unit
became an absolutely essential means of self-protection and of obtain-
ing power and prestige. Power soon drifted into the hands of Red
Guard units sponsored by Maoists like Nieh Yüan-tzu of Peking University and Kuai Ta-fu of Tsinghua University, and these units maintained close contact with the Cultural Revolution Group. Probably,
most of the members of these units were not members of the Party or
the League and the majority of them were children of workers, peasants
and soldiers.

The exploits of the Red Guards have been reported extensively in
the press. But there are several interesting points which ought to be
made. Not all the students took an active part in the Revolution. In a
remark reminiscent of Karl Marx's description of the Communist
utopia, a Red Guard newspaper reported that "in the high schools the
students read Mao's *Selected Works* in the morning, took a rest in the
afternoon, and learned to swim after four o'clock." [17] The active Red
Guards, however, waged their struggle on many fronts. They carried
their quarrels and their factionalism everywhere they went. Not long
after the Red Guards were sent to the factories to promote the Cultural
Revolution, Ch'en Po-ta found it necessary to scold them for bringing
to the workers the bourgeois and petit bourgeois ideas of small-group
mentality and factionalism instead of proletarian influences.[18] Several
months later, he bluntly told a group of workers not to be misled by
the factionalism of the students into adopting a wrong orientation. The
fragmentation of the Red Guard movement reveals one of the general
consequences of the breakdown of political authority. It also forcefully
demonstrates the impotence of ideology which is not supported by an
organization. For ideology and general directives cannot create unity
and produce united action unless there is a hierarchy of organizations
to give them authoritative interpretation, to translate them into specific decisions, and to enforce them in various units.

The movement to seize power did nothing to improve matters. In a
speech in January 1967, Ch'en Po-ta said:

> In some units the seizure of power is like this: you want to seize power
> and I also want to seize power. Instead of seizing power from power hold-

ers taking the capitalist road, some small groups struggle with one another for power to see who can seize power first. Those groups which did not seize power before now also want to seize power. Thus, internal struggles are created.

He asked: "If, for instance, a small group of yours cannot represent the great majority of a school but still want to take over a nationwide unit, whom can you ask to recognize your seizure of power?" He concluded: "Now, the 'small-group mentality' has become a national problem." [19]

To counter this development, Mao adopted the policy of making the formation of a great alliance among various small units a condition for recognizing their seizure of power in various schools, universities, departments, units and localities. But new problems immediately emerged. The Red Guards and revolutionary rebels in power were more concerned with personal prestige and position than with the interests of the whole. What the Maoists call "bourgeois and petit bourgeois ideas" turn out to be simply human tendencies of those in positions of power.

In waging their struggle against the Party leaders, the Red Guards resorted to methods not approved by the Maoist leaders. In a speech to the Red Guards in February 1967, Ch'en Po-ta pointed out that such slogans as "Smashing So and So's Dog Head" and such actions as putting a dunce cap on a person and forcing him to kneel down were not advocated by the Cultural Revolution Group. Some of the difficulties confronting the Maoist leaders arose from the amazing organizational and tactical skill of the Red Guard units. In December 1966, Chou En-lai noted that the Red Guards arrested P'eng Chen, the former mayor of Peking, in an action lasting only seven minutes, keeping even the Peking Garrison Command in the dark.[20] Even more serious was the Red Guards' attack on the army and the revolutionary committees and their refusal to obey orders. On September 17, 1967 Chou pointed out to the Red Guards that when students went to other localities, they always supported those opposing the established leadership. But he told them that times had changed and they should not act in the same way as they acted in 1966.

Ch'en Po-ta is partly correct when he characterized some of the excesses committed by the Red Guards as "the shortcomings of the methods of struggle spontaneously created by the masses." It was also probable that many of the extreme actions taken by the Red Guards were encouraged or backed by a radical faction within the Cultural Revolution Group. But Mao must ultimately bear the responsibility because he explicitly permitted the masses to commit "minor" mistakes so long as their general orientation was correct; and because he praised similar methods of struggle in his famous [1927] report on the Hunan Peasant Movement. Furthermore, the Maoists' ideological pronouncements, used at the beginning of the Cultural Revolution to mobilize the students to attack the Party leaders, also served as justification for their excessive acts. It is also apparent that the Red Guards had absorbed the strategic thinking of Mao without accepting his idealistic values. For example, Mao has written that political power grows out of a gun. The Red Guards have raised the slogan that "political power grows out of strength" and used it to justify their self-serving actions. Repeatedly, the Maoist leaders told them to smash self-interest and establish public interest, but to no avail. Thus, the Red Guards had ultimately to be brought under control by the workers' teams in mid-1968.

Conclusion

The foregoing analysis of the Cultural Revolution shows that it has not only destroyed the Party organization and badly disrupted the government bureaucracy, but has also inflicted serious damage on the relationship of authority which had been established in Communist China. This damage will be vastly more difficult to repair than the economic disaster produced by the Great Leap. For the rebuilding of a new set of stable political relationships in the aftermath of the demoralization, resentment, cynicism, and frustrated hopes stirred up by the upheaval is a much more complex and intricate task than economic recovery and adjustment of institutions in the economic sphere. The loss of confidence on the part of the Chinese Communist leaders in their own political institutions and their own political wisdom must have been profound. For some time to come, they will be preoccupied with the problems of rebuilding the political system.

The Cultural Revolution had its roots in the increasing divergence between Mao's ideology and the changing social reality. Yet the Cultural Revolution has destroyed the very institution in China which was more able than Mao to accommodate the material interests of the various social groups and the needs for differentiation and specialization in a rapidly developing nation. In classical revolutions, the alienated intellectuals together with the rising expectations of the people played crucial roles in bringing about the upheaval. In the Cultural Revolution, the intellectuals who were alienated by Mao but supported by the Party organization became its first victims, and the rising expectations of most social groups were denounced as morally wrong. In the long run, many aspects of the Cultural Revolution and many elements in Mao's thought will probably be implicitly or explicitly repudiated.

But one must also not forget that in making the Cultural Revolution Mao has also been motivated by a noble vision. It is a vision of a society in which the division involving domination and subjection will be blurred, the leaders will be less distinguishable from the led in status and privileges, and the led will take part more directly in the policy-making process. The full realization of this vision is an impossibility.

But it is just possible that somehow the Cultural Revolution will leave as a legacy a higher degree of political participation and economic equality, even if the former means merely a wider sharing of the high political risks and the latter is nothing more than an equality in poverty.

1. Ralf Dahrendorf, *Class and Class Conflict in Industrial Society* (Stanford, California: Stanford University Press, 1959), pp. 165, 169.

2. Karl Marx, *The Poverty of Philosophy*, p. 160, quoted in Robert C. Tucker, "The Marxian Revolutionary Idea," in Carl J. Friedrich (ed.), *Revolution* (New York: Atherton Press, 1967), p. 219.

3. Premier Chou En-lai's important talk on January 25, 1966 to a rally of more than 20,000 revolutionary rebels on "the scientific and technological fronts" as reported in *K'o-chi chan-pao* (Science and Technology Battle Bulletin) (Peking, No. 2, February 1, 1967), p. 3.

4. Lin Piao's talk at an enlarged session of the meeting of the Political Bureau in May 1966, quoted in *Chingkangshan*, Nos. 13–14 (February 1, 1967), p. 6. It is clear that the cult of Mao was used to overcome the resistance to Mao's thought and policies. Mao himself said in 1967 that at the time when he presided over the drafting of the May 16, 1966 circular, a large group of persons considered his views outmoded and that, at times, only he himself agreed with his own views. *Wu-ch'an-che chih sheng* (The Voice of the Proletariat) (Wuchow, Kwangsi), No. 10 (January 1, 1968), p. 1.

5. "A great strategic disposition—Chairman Mao's Latest Instruction," reproduced in *Wu-ch'an-che chih sheng, loc. cit.*

6. *Peking Review*, December 9, 1968, p. 1.

7. For example, Ch'en Po-ta told students at Peking University, on June 26, 1966, that "this leadership of the Party is the leadership of Mao Tse-tung's thought and the leadership of the Party Central Committee." On August 21, 1966, T'ao Chu said that "now the only correct leadership is that of Chairman Mao and the Central Committee under his leadership." *Hung-se tsao-fan pao*, December 26, 1966, p. 4, translated in *Joint Research Publication Service* (JPRS), No. 40, 349 (March 1967), pp. 76–77.

8. Harry Gelman, "The New Revolution," *Problems of Communism*, November–December 1966, pp. 2–14. Philip Bridgham, "Mao's Cultural Revolution: Origin and Development" [Reprinted in selections 2 and 11 of the present volume—ED.].

9. The Maoists had to counteract the tendency to obey Party committees in various units by constantly reiterating the point that not every Party organization or individual Party member represents leadership by the Party. Ch'i Pen-yü told the Red Guards on November 12, 1966: "Leadership by the Party is mainly political and ideological leadership and leadership by Mao Tse-tung's thought. It is not specifically the leadership of a certain person or a certain organization."

10. As we shall note later, another reason was that Mao made the establishment of a "great alliance" among the revolutionary rebel groups a condition for the establishment of revolutionary committees and their recognition by Peking.

11. Tang Tsou, "Cultural Revolution: Causes and Effects," *Proceedings of the Symposium on China*, January 13, 1968 (Berkeley, California: Chinese Students Association and the Center for Chinese Studies, 1968), pp. 34–41.

12. In outlining the steps to be taken in the seizure of power, Chou En-lai told the Red Guards on January 23, 1967 that as a first step they should merely supervise the business operations of the various agencies. But if the agencies concerned "do not have business operations as in the case of the departments and units within the Party, a thorough-going revolution can be made by the Red Guards." *Yu-tien feng-lei* (Thunderstorm in the Postal and Telecommunications Services), No. 5 (February 10, 1967), p. 3.

13. The worst offender against the Maoist line of supporting the Left was Chao Yung-fu, Deputy Commander of the Tsinghai provincial military district. See "Order of the Military Commission of the Central Committee," April 6, 1966, in *CCP Documents of the Great Proletarian Cultural Revolution* (Hong Kong: Union Research Institute, 1968), pp. 409–412.

14. Tsou, "Cultural Revolution: Causes and Effects," pp. 34–41.

15. "Vice-Premier Hsieh Fu-chih's Seven Viewpoints," in *JPRS*, No. 40,391 (March 24, 1967), p. 7.

16. From the minutes of a forum held by the revolutionary teachers and students of the College of International Relations under the auspices of Teng Hsiao-p'ing and Li Fu-ch'un. See also *Current Background*, No. 819 (March 10, 1967), p. 72.

17. *Wu-ch'an chieh-chi wen-hua ta-ko-ming ta-shih chi: 1965.9–1966.12* (Record of Major Events in the Great Proletarian Cultural Revolution: September 1965 to December 1966), in *JPRS*, No. 42,349 (August 25, 1967), p. 26.

18. *Yu-tien Feng-lei, loc. cit.*

19. *Ibid;* also *Huo-ch'e-t'ou* (Locomotive), No. 7, February 2, 1967, in *Survey of the China Mainland Press* (SCMP), No. 3898 (March 14, 1967), p. 4.

20. *Tou-cheng Pao* (Struggle News), early January 1967, p. 7.

THE PURSUIT OF PURITY:
MAO'S CULTURAL REVOLUTION

Richard M. Pfeffer

China's Great Proletarian Cultural Revolution is too complex and too diffuse a configuration of phenomena to be "explained" within the confines of any single perspective. It has been described, derisively, as "really three things in one: an enigmatic multiple power struggle, wrapped in a crusade, and superimposed on a scattering of more or less spontaneous, more or less politicized student riots, strikes, peasant uprisings, mutinies, and palace coups." [1] Quite clearly, the Cultural Revolution, unlike Pallas Athena, did not spring full-blown from anyone's brow. While Mao appears to have fathered it, various groupings within the elite, the masses, and the middle levels of power have, for their own reasons, contributed to its development. Individual interpretations of its motive forces, focusing on one or more of its aspects and levels of relevant "facts," vary widely. [2]

We are not yet, and perhaps never shall be, at a stage where we can systemically appreciate all the facets of so momentous a complex of events as the Cultural Revolution. But if it is too early to set down refined theoretical frameworks for understanding the CR as a whole, we can at least begin to formulate tentative approaches toward understanding each of its levels of reality and the nature of the relationships among certain of those levels. This article focuses on what Mao Tsetung has been attempting to accomplish through the CR. The assumptions behind this focus are twofold: (1) Mao's intentions are significant in shaping the events of the CR; and (2) Mao's "intentions" are, in some sense, knowable.

If the assumption that Mao planned the CR in advance and deftly manipulated it to his own taste requires a near-deification of the man, the contrary assumption that Mao simply played events by ear and in fact exercised little influence over their development trivializes one of the great men of the 20th century. The reality doubtless lies somewhere in between. Mao probably had no detailed plan for developing the CR; but, on the basis of his ideology, his personality, his experience as a revolutionary, and the actual course of events as seen in retrospect, it

Richard M. Pfeffer, "The Pursuit of Purity: Mao's Cultural Revolution," *Problems of Communism* 18, no. 6 (November–December 1969): 12–25. Reprinted by permission of the publisher.

seems fair to conclude that Mao had a vision of what he sought to accomplish and an intuitive conception of the means appropriate to those ends. Moreover, although Mao's power to determine events is limited, the CR has reminded the world of the immense power of ideology and of a supreme leader who, to a large degree, can shape ideology, through propaganda, to fit his needs.

Undoubtedly Mao provoked the CR for a variety of reasons: he sought to achieve multiple goals, some minimal, others maximal. The minimal goals might be said to include the purge of particular individuals, the shake-up of the bureaucracy (in the manner of past but less intense campaigns), and even the temporary breakup of the Party machine.[3] The maximal goals seem to have included the training of a successor generation in revolution by allowing and encouraging youth to wage "revolution from below" (i.e., without the disciplined control from above characteristic of past intraparty rectification movements); the creation of a new morality and "superstructure" in China; and, more specifically, the reinstatement in practice of the revolutionary ideals of equality and mass participation, and the transformation of the nature of the Communist Party.

This article concerns itself almost exclusively with Mao's maximal goals, in large part because the dimensions of the CR and Mao's role in it seem hardly intelligible in terms of his more minimal goals.

Viewed from Mao's perspective, the CR may be taken as the latest and most striking manifestation of the historical dialectic involving leader, Party, and masses that is at the heart of Maoism and the Chinese Communist Revolution. It represents part of the continuing search for a Chinese way—more particularly, a Maoist way—to carry on that revolution.

Few analysts to date have begun to take the CR seriously as a revolution.[4] Yet it seems appropriate to understand it as such. For while it is true that the CR is not a comprehensive socio-political revolution in the sense of the earlier Communist Revolution in China, it clearly goes beyond the limits of any lesser category of socio-political change. Through the CR Mao has sought to transform a whole culture and its central legitimating institution. If he has not attempted, in the classical mode of great revolutions, to eliminate physically the members of a ruling class, he appears at least to have tried to prevent members of the post-1959 elite from becoming entrenched to the point where they take on the characteristics of such a class. If he has not attempted a fundamental change in the economic relations of Chinese society, he has tried to an unprecedented degree to delegitimize, on the level of ideals, the individual pursuit of material gain. If, in short, the CR has not embodied several of the core elements of the major social revolutions in history, the reason is simply that the CR is the progeny of such a revolution, and its function is not to repeat the earlier revolution but to revitalize it.

Franz Schurmann, placing the CR in the historical perspective of a continuing Chinese revolution, writes:[5] ". . . for decades now, elite upon elite has been dragged into the mire of discreditation. . . . Today the new elite of the Party is sharing their fate." In this sense, the CR is a testament to the fact that social revolutions which are not permanent revolutions tend to eliminate one mode of inequality—e.g., the inequality of traditional societies—only to establish another mode of inequality. The events in China suggest that Mao, the visionary, is no longer satisfied with such a substitution.

The CR was directed against Communist China's "New Class," to use Djilas' term. Its first-stated aim, "to struggle against and crush those persons in authority who are taking the capitalist road," [6] can be meaningfully understood only in this sense. In Mao's view, the growth of such an "increasingly privileged and powerful social stratum in command of . . . [China's] politico-economic apparatus" [7]—paralleling developments in other socialist countries—posed the threat of death to the Chinese Revolution.[8]

Inextricably related to the growth of this stratum has been a decline in the Chinese popular spirit of revolutionary solidarity and sacrifice. To quote two sympathetic yet perceptive American observers of recent Chinese Communist development,

> . . . life has become "privatized," especially among the youth who tend increasingly to concentrate on their careers and to neglect social responsibilities; admiration for the material achievements and the supposedly freer ways of the affluent capitalist societies has grown; an abyss has opened up between the style of life and modes of thought of the leading stratum on the one hand and the still poor, toiling masses on the other.[9]

Mao and his supporters have increasingly come to believe that these trends, if unrestrained, will sooner or later result in the "restoration of capitalism."

Revolution Against History

But viewed in this light, the CR also seems to be a revolution against history—that is, against what appears to be the inevitable development of a privileged stratum in the process of economic development, or, even more boldly, against modernization itself.[10] Never in history has there been a revolution that has continued to place the same high ideal and practical value on egalitarianism and mass participation once the mobilization and destructive phases of the revolution were completed. As every major social revolution became institutionalized, egalitarianism and mass participation have been substantially sacrificed in favor of other goals such as national power or modernization. It is this historical pattern—again repeating itself in post-1949 China—that Mao has sought to combat through the CR.

It is not clear whether Mao still embraces modernization as a major goal of the Chinese Revolution. If he does, then—in the words of the observers quoted above—"it makes no sense to talk about completely preventing the growth of a privileged stratum" since "that is part of the necessary price of economic development," but "it [still] does make sense to talk about limiting the power of this stratum, keeping its privileges to the necessary minimum, and preventing it from solidifying its position and transforming its vested interests into [the equivalent of] inheritable property right." [11] If this, indeed, has been one of Mao's aims in the CR, his decision to make allies of the very young—particularly those below college age who are neither dominated by traditional mores nor tainted by careerism—is readily understandable. For one of the difficulties of preventing the development of a new ruling class is that many members of the very groups that have the greatest interest in preventing it too frequently "still live under the influence of old moral and religious ideas which sanction and sanctify the privileges of the few and confer legitimacy on their rule." [12] This problem has been compounded in China since 1949 by the elitist and careerist element in the Communist Party. The thinking of Mao and his allies is probably well summarized by Huberman and Sweezy when they point out that the initiative in preventing the emergence of a new ruling class therefore devolved upon

> those, both in the leadership and in the rank and file, who made the revolution and remain uncorrupted by the temptations of actual or potential privilege. It is up to them to lead the struggle and to enlist as much support as possible from the ranks of the underprivileged and the uncorrupted. If those who made the revolution fail in this task, or if they do not understand the necessity . . . then they will have put their country firmly on what the Chinese [i.e., the Maoists] call the capitalist road, and their successors who never had their revolutionary experience and understanding will almost certainly not be able, and in all probability will not want, to divert it from that road.[13]

In the 1950's and 1960's, the Chinese Party leadership, as it turned to the task of reconstruction and economic development, undertook a series of campaigns aimed in part at maintaining the revolutionary élan. The CR, viewed in this perspective, might be understood as a bigger and more ambitious campaign to protect certain revolutionary goals while continuing the drive toward modernization but hoping, through the CR, to minimize the negative social implications of the modernization process. Thus, according to Huberman and Sweezy:

> Mao and his colleagues are realists enough to know that it will be a long . . . time before China can hope to wipe out substantial inequalities. The target [of the CR] is the privileged ones who are misusing their power to

promote special and private interests. . . . The method of dealing with them is not terror [selectively] wielded by a secret police . . . but the mobilization of [certain of] the unprivileged and particularly the youth who have not yet been exposed to the temptations of privilege and power. The [Maoist] . . . leadership evidently believes that if the privileged stratum can be contained and controlled and the young . . . won for the Revolution . . . , then the country can be kept from taking the capitalist road for at least one more generation while economic development brings closer the day when general abundance will make possible the real elimination of inequality and privilege.[14]

But if the CR, in one sense, was just a bigger and better campaign against the regularized abuses of the new privileged stratum, it was also more than that. Besides being an attack on those who abused their privileged positions, it was at the same time an attack on the legitimacy of the institutions and organizations from which privilege in Communist China arose. And it also appears to have entailed the relegation of modernization as a national goal to a lower priority. Seen in this broader context, the CR seems to have been an extremely radical attempt to establish what might be called counter-institutions capable both of limiting the drift towards hierarchy and privilege and of reasserting the revolutionary goals of egalitarianism and mass participation. The three central counter-institutions—none of which requires a high degree of disciplined organization, and all of which are therefore relatively free at least of the inflexibilities toward which organizations are prone—are: (1) the supreme leader; (2) the Thought of Mao Tsetung; and (3) "the masses" as participants (the role of the masses being legitimized, in part, in much the same way as peasant rebellions were legitimized in China's traditional political system by the concept of the passing of the mandate of heaven).[15]

Leader, Party and Masses

The Chinese Communist political system since the mid-1930's has been characterized by a dialectical process involving leader, masses, and organization, a process that can be personified partially in the historical relation between Mao and Liu. In that relationship, Mao functioned primarily as the radical initiator, the leader who set general directions, stimulated the release of mass energies, and worked to prevent the ossification of institutions. Liu on the other hand, functioned more in the role of coordinator and consolidator of gains, the relatively conservative "organization man," the implementer on the ground.[16] Generally speaking, the mutuality and tension between the two roles has been healthy for the ongoing revolution.

Mao, the great leader, has been consistently ambivalent about large-scale bureaucratic organizations. In part, this may simply reflect his personal and historical awareness, as a 20th-century Chinese, of China's two major pre-Communist examples of such organizations. Born in 1893, at the end of the Ch'ing dynasty, Mao grew up while the traditional Chinese bureaucracy disintegrated. He also saw at first hand the efforts of the Kuomintang to build its own bureaucracy in Republican China, and he observed its rapid corruption. Thus, Ezra F. Vogel is probably right in observing that "Chinese Maoists are preoccupied with a vision from their past—the vision of the moral degeneration of a bureaucracy which is out of touch with the people, the core problem which led to the decline and fall of the Kuomintang." [17] However, this interpretation, by itself, fails to explain why Mao (and the Maoists) should be so much more preoccupied than other elements in China's leadership with the problematic nature of bureaucracy as an instrument for achieving goals—especially revolutionary goals.[18]

To understand Mao's particular ambivalence toward bureaucratic organization, it is also necessary to recognize the relevance of Mao's special experience in Yenan during the revolutionary war—an experience which some observers have seen as responsible for the so-called "Yenan syndrome" or, more derisively, for Mao's attachment to a "primitive political system." During the Yenan days of 1935–45, as John W. Lewis has pointed out, Mao functioned in the role of distant, charismatic leader of the highly decentralized guerilla war.[19] In that role, he emphasized the positive function of the masses[20] and the critical importance of relatively unlimited struggle in maintaining a revolutionary environment; and he was habitually suspicious of elitist bureaucratic organization as the primary medium for waging revolution.

By contrast, Lewis argues, Liu Shao-ch'i operated in those days as chief political commissar (today's "party bureaucrat"), "fashioning a strong Party-army wherein only limited forms of struggle were tolerated." [21] He ritualized these limited forms of struggle in tightly organized local Party units, concentrated on the elitist organization of the Party, and after the establishment of Communist rule in 1949 played a leading role in building the centralizing Party bureaucracy. The result was that, by 1956, China's Yenan-type, flexible, decentralized revolutionary warfare organization had been effectively replaced:

> Guided and dominated by Party structure, that [Maoist] system had made the initial transition to an elite system according priority to the goals of modernization and the requisite recruitment from scientific and technical sectors of the society. The Party apparatus was at its zenith, and the term "thought of Mao" [since resurrected and enshrined in the CR] was dropped from the 1956 Party constitution. Charisma, now routinized, had shifted from Mao to the Party, and with Leninism supplanting "the thought of Mao Tse-tung," the Chairman had subsumed his image under the Party and lent it his authority.[22]

Having basically eliminated, neutralized, and/or delegitimized all hostile competing power elites, the CCP itself became what Professor

Tang Tsou has aptly termed "the establishment *par excellence.*" [23] The Party allied itself with leaders in all segments of Chinese life to form a privileged stratum which kept "the levers of power in various fields in their hands and [lived] fairly comfortably amidst the general poverty of China even during the years of agricultural crisis. . . . The Party organization's sensitivity to the material interests of the various social groups and its ability to work with the privileged groups" enabled this stratum to operate quite effectively in modernizing China, but it also built up repressed dissatisfaction among the Maoists and among some dominated or under-privileged groups.[24]

Thus, the Chinese political system before the CR was dominated by a centralized, hierarchical, incredibly pervasive party-cum-privileged stratum, which has been described—again in the words of Tang Tsou— as "one of the purest forms found in human experience of a type of association in which there is a clear-cut separation between the elite and the masses." [25] In this light, the CR and, to a lesser degree, many of the earlier Maoist-type mass campaigns can be viewed as a critique of, and reaction against, this elitist type of political system.

The Mission of the Party

But with the perspective of the dialectical process between leader and party in mind, Mao's Great Proletarian Cultural Revolution seems to have been less purely anti-organizational in character than has been generally assumed. The CR appears rather to have been aimed at reasserting, on a greater scale and in the face of intense resistance, the earlier balance between leader, masses, and Party organization that prevailed in the 1940's. As such, it may also be said to represent Mao's attempt to reestablish the distinctive quality of the Party organization —which is one key to any organization's survival and continued success.

The distinctive quality of the CCP historically has lain in the content and diffuseness of its goals and in its style. As Professor Schurmann has observed, the Chinese Party, unlike organizations with narrower goals, has made its broad objective "not to produce organizational expertise but to make men into committed leaders who can command [other] men in a variety of concrete problems to be resolved." [26] The Chinese Communist movement has also been committed to achieving modernization, national power, and the ideal Communist society of the future, but increasingly after taking power the Party found that it had little distinctive to offer with regard to the first two of these goals. Writes Schurmann:

> The state administrative bureaucracy planned and operated the economy and seems to have acquitted itself well. The army was doing its best to provide for China's defense. . . . [And] looking at these . . . segments of the trinity of state power, one cannot but have the feeling that the role of the Party was becoming increasingly unclear.[27]

The more the emphasis shifted toward modernization, professionalism, pragmatism, and the use of material incentives rather than spiritual ones, the more the Party found itself deprived of a valid leadership
role. It was left with its ideology, but without organizations for which
the application of that ideology had any real practical value. At the risk
of exaggeration, Schurmann writes that "during the period of liberalization in the early 1960's before the Tenth Plenum of September 1962,
the 17 million Party members had nothing to do except what they had
to do otherwise in their practical roles (for example, as factory direc-
tors)." And he concludes that "to compensate for this, China's leaders
decided to launch a campaign of ideological indoctrination designed to
preserve the Party member's leadership role in the realm of ideology,
even if practically there wasn't much for him to do." [28]

But surely, given a continued concentration on goals related to modernization, such campaigns would simply establish more firmly the
"trained incapacity" of Party members to exercise meaningful leadership. If this is true, then only by reestablishing the primacy of the
Maoist vision of the good society—a society that requires for its realization the transformation of human nature, requiring in turn a continuing cultural revolution—could the Party hope to perform again a
unique and significant leadership role.

The same point can be made with respect to the Party's distinctive
style, a critical element of which is the organizational technique known
as the "mass line." As ideally conceived, this technique is a sophisticated method for encouraging participation by those at the bottom of
the organization (e.g., the peasants), for gathering information, and for
translating high-level policy decisions (made partly on the basis of this
information) into operational decisions on the ground. It is predicated
upon a continuing process of interaction between leaders and led, the
purposes of which are to stimulate initiative below, to reduce the feed-
back problem common to highly authoritarian or so-called "totalitarian" societies, and simultaneously, within the limits of practicability,
to tutor the masses. Ideally, the mass line functions to avoid the twin
extremes of "tailism"—responding primarily to the short-term demands
of the masses—and "commandism"—simply ordering from above, without consideration for the desires of the masses.

With the regularization of Party bureaucratic procedures and the increased emphasis on professional expertise in the early and middle
1950's, however, the elitist element in the Party character tended to
dominate patterns of decision-making, and participation by the masses
came to be looked upon by organization men as regressive. As a consequence, instead of becoming firmly institutionalized as part of routine
decision-making, mass-line techniques tended to be more and more embodied in periodic waves of mass campaigns which the organization
men in turn viewed increasingly as antagonistic to Party regularity.

Such campaigns became *ad hoc* mechanisms for temporarily deregularizing procedures and shaking up the bureaucracy. But in view of the hostility which the campaigns generated within the bureaucracy, the mass line tended to be employed erratically and without the organizational discipline and balance required for its successful functioning.

Leader Above Party

In the CR, Mao seems to have attempted to revive the distinctive attributes of the Party described above. It can be seen that in some sense this required an assault on the Party as then constituted, as a preparatory step toward reinstilling in it a sense of its sacred mission and special competence. The Party, if it is to maintain its institutional integrity, cannot be concerned primarily with modernization, for it has shown no distinctive competence in this realm. Rather, the Party has to concern itself primarily with the quality of life in China as measured, for example, by the standards of the Maoist ideal society. Such a concern may prompt the Party to act at times as a counter-balance to the modernization process. If the likelihood of the Party's success in moving counter to such forces can be regarded as less than certain, the long-run consequence of an abdication in this regard would be to assure the Party's own irrelevance.

In recognizing and acting upon these facts of organizational life, Mao, in his assault on the Party, ironically was acting as the great Party leader. As Philip Selznick points out in his analysis of leadership, it is the function of "leadership in administration" to "define the mission of the enterprise" and to build "special values and distinctive competence into the organization." [29] He goes on to say:

> It is in the realm of policy—including the areas where policy formation and organization-building meet—that the distinctive quality of institutional leadership is found. Ultimately, *this is the quality of statesmanship which deals with current issues, not for themselves alone, but according to their long-run implications for the role and meaning of the group.* Group leadership is far more than the capacity to mobilize personal support; it is more than the maintenance of equilibrium through the routine solution of everyday problems; it is the function of the leader-statesman . . . to define the ends of group existence, to design an enterprise distinctively adapted to these ends, and to see that that design becomes a living reality.[30]

Using Selznick's analytic distinction between "organizations" (technical instruments which are expendable, are designed to achieve relatively definite goals, and can therefore be judged on "engineering premises") and "institutions" (which are "infused with value" beyond their mere utility as a means and are therefore more resistant to change even if they are inefficient),[31] and as Franz Schurmann has pointed out, one can say that Mao has tried to de-institutionalize the Party so that it can be judged by Maoist standards as an expendable instrument. Realistically, one also can say that Mao, aware that the process of institutionalization is a recurring one, has attempted to set leader above Party, to elevate the Thought of Mao Tse-tung to the level of the highest moral standard and to establish the precedent of discovering vanguard elements outside the Party in order to counter the natural tendencies within the Party toward institutionalization.[32]

The cult of personality, which was used in the early 1950's to legitimize roles and institutions through association with a beloved and respected leader (thus, Chinese children's songs praise *Chairman* Mao), has in the 1960's been raised to new heights and used to place leader above institutions. The cult was thus forged into a weapon for assaulting the Party and government.[33] Similarly, the Thought of Mao—which the 1956 Party constitution relegated to second place by substituting the statement that "the CCP takes Marxism-Leninism as its guide to action" for the sentence in the 1945 Party constitution that the CCP "guides its entire work" by the Thought of Mao Tse-tung—has increasingly been treated in the 1960's as a quasi-sacred, magical body of norms.

Mao's extreme reliance in recent years on his own personal authority and ideology reflects the seriousness of his predicament. As Tang Tsou points out, Mao has been "confronted with the very difficult problem of justifying his revolution and legitimizing his attack on the Party organization," whose authority had hitherto been accepted as axiomatic.[34] Moreover, the pragmatic policies initiated by the Party in the early 1960's have been highly successful. Mao therefore felt it necessary to use all his non-organizational weapons in order both to attack the still sacred aura of Party authority and to "override pragmatic standards." [35] Mao's thought was elevated to a new peak higher than that occupied by the thought of Marx, Engels and Lenin, and therefore higher than the Party or any ideology upon which the Party might base a claim to legitimacy in opposition to Mao. This, notes Tsou, served a definite political purpose by setting "a new standard of legitimacy and correctness with which the actions and opinions of many top leaders were to be judged." [36]

At the same time, Mao's strategy deprived his opponents of the capacity to attack him openly, forcing them in effect "to hide under the Maoist cover [and to] 'fight the Red Flag by waving the Red Flag'." [37] In other words, even when opposing Mao, the opposition found itself obliged to rely publicly for its legitimacy upon Mao's thought, thereby reinforcing his primacy. Thus, Professor Tsou rightly observes, the Party organization had "to defend itself under the major premises and rules of the game laid down by Mao. All . . . organizations pledged allegiance to Mao and his thought. All . . . said that they supported the Cultural Revolution. . . ." [38] In short, the Party organization was disarmed by Mao's capacity as supreme leader to manipulate political ideology.

Countervailing Institutions

The proposition that Mao sought through the CR to establish counter-institutions that would assure the realization of his vision of the Chinese revolution finds support in the new CCP constitution adopted by the Ninth Party Congress on April 14, 1969. In startling contrast to the 1956 Party constitution, which lauded Marxism-Leninism without even mentioning the Thought of Mao in its preamble (general program section), the new constitution proclaims:

> The Communist Party of China takes Marxism, Leninism, and the Thought of Mao Tse-tung as the theoretical basis guiding its thinking. The thought of Mao Tse-tung *is* Marxism-Leninism of the era in which . . . socialism is advancing to worldwide victory.[39]

The document goes on to credit Mao with integrating "the universal truth of Marxism-Leninism with the concrete practice of revolution" and bringing Marxism-Leninism "to a higher and completely new stage." Thus, Mao's thought is once more enshrined in the Party constitution.

By contrast, the references to the Party in the new constitution are less grand than those in the preceding constitution, which called the CCP "the vanguard of the Chinese working class [and] the highest form of its class organization." The new constitution simply states that "the Communist Party of China is the political party of the proletariat." The text, it is true, later refers to the Party in more eulogistic terms, but only in conjunction with Mao's leadership: "The Communist Party of China with Comrade Mao Tse-tung as its leader is a great, glorious, and correct Party and is the core of leadership of the Chinese people." Thus, the Party as a separate entity is downgraded.

In line with the explicit emphasis on Mao's thought and leadership, the new constitution also praises Lin Piao as a most loyal and resolute defender of Mao's "revolutionary line" and, in a departure from past precedent, specifically designates him as Mao's "successor." The constitution thus takes the authority to determine the succession to the post of Party chairman out of the hands of the Party Central Committee, where it would normally reside, and assures Mao of a successor acceptable to him. Moreover, Articles 5 and 9, by comparison with the 1956 constitution place heavier stress on the leadership role of the Party chairman and vice-chairman relative to the rest of the Party organization. In particular, Article 5 provides that if a Party member disagrees with the decisions or directives of a Party organization, he "has the right to *bypass the immediate leadership* and report directly to higher levels up to and including the Central Committee and the Chairman of the Central Committee" (emphasis added). Thus the Maoist leadership is upgraded at the expense of the Party hierarchy.

Finally, the constitution fully endorses the "Great Proletarian Cultural Revolution" and exhorts Party members and Party organizations to "consult with the masses" (Article 3) and to "constantly listen to the opinions of the masses both inside *and outside* the Party and accept their supervision" (Article 5; emphasis added).[40]

Thus, taken as a whole, the new constitution appears to formalize Mao's effort to set up countervailing institutions above and below the Party. Mao's thought, Mao's leadership—or, more generally, Maoist leadership—and the role of the masses are all upgraded, while the monopoly role of the Party is downgraded.

Mao, Marx and Rousseau

Mao's experience in Yenan and since, his image of himself as leader, and his conceptions of the nature of the Party and the masses all contribute towards an understanding of his goals in the CR. Beyond this, Mao's goals since the mid-1950's may in some sense best be comprehended in terms of an increasingly observable rejection of Marxism-Leninism, accompanied by an increasing affirmation of Rousseauean concerns and methods.[41]

Although Mao earlier seems to have believed with Marx, that economic development and moral progress were indissolubly and positively linked—that industrialization would produce the "Communist man"—there is little evidence that Mao today continues to embrace this convenient rationalization for withholding concern for moral progress while focusing on material progress. Like Rousseau, and buttressed by world history since Marx, in particular by the experience of having observed the processes and consequences of the institutionalization of the Chinese revolution, Mao appears to have concluded that "the arts and sciences (technico-economic progress) as they . . . developed . . . [after the Great Leap] . . . actually . . . [ran] counter to moral progress and contributed to all the corruptions of society" [42] and of the revolution.

And the parallels to Rousseau do not stop there. Mao's vision of the ideal society is very similar to that of Rousseau. Mao's good society is a kind of Christian utopia, collectivist, austere, egalitarian, and without the need for coercive institutions because it is composed of virtuous men who have internalized such values as self-sacrifice in the common good, and who directly and actively participate as a solidary mass in determining the course of politics. And like Rousseau, Mao focuses on the demand for a new society, the importance of education, and the role of the great charismatic leader who understands the needs of the masses, epitomizes the national character, and at the same time embodies their highest moral concerns. It is the leader who "liberates" the masses from their narrow particularity as individuals so that they can realize their human potential.

But there is a vital difference between Mao and Rousseau which is central to an understanding of Mao's role in the Cultural Revolution. Rousseau was a radical theorist without power. His primary goal, historically conditioned, was to eliminate the sort of immobile particularism associated with feudalism, thereby freeing man to understand the broader potentiality of his nature. Rousseau's mechanism for this miraculous transformation is the "great legislator," who arrives Messiah-like, fuses the people into a moral unity, extirpates traditional institutions which obstruct that fusion, and establishes laws and institutions to perpetuate the good society. Rousseau's whole scheme has frequently and correctly been described as an evasion of the central political problem of how the desired transformation of society is to be effected— an evasion accomplished by the invocation of a *deus ex machina*, the great legislator.

But Mao *is* the great legislator, a *radical in power*—perhaps the first in history who has substantially retained his radical purity after being in power for over a generation.[43] As such he must deal with political problems, the foremost of which is that there will be no Messiah to produce the ultimate ideal state. The cultural revolution required to "liberate" man must be accomplished through, not in evasion of, politics. The great leader must act in history. The problems of institutions cannot be avoided—neither the present problem of how to transform old institutions and men, nor the continuing problem of how to ensure the future integrity of those transformed.

In going beyond Rousseau, Mao has also gone beyond Marxism-Leninism and Stalinism in his effort to resolve institutional problems. He has sought in the CR to transform the most powerful institution in China, the Communist Party. As Benjamin Schwartz brilliantly argues, Mao has declared that the sacred moral values previously associated exclusively with the Party are most purely found in himself and his thought, and that these qualities "may be shared by groups, institutions, and individuals which lie *outside* of the Party. Indeed, the Party as such, when considered apart from . . . [the leader and his thought], may wholly degenerate. . . ."[44] It is the leader, his ideology, and the masses whom he can directly inspire, that offer hope of becoming a counterforce to over-institutionalization and the problems of organizational goal displacement.

Polarization of the Elite

But how and why did Mao determine to follow this strategy? In the 1950's, despite important differences of opinion within the Chinese leadership group over the priorities to be given to various revolutionary goals, there was a shared belief that these goals were compatible—a belief, in short, that by working for China's modernization and strengthening, one was simultaneously working for a Maoist-Communist China. Here again, the role of ideology, this time as a cohesive force, can hardly be overestimated. For Marxism-Leninism, the commonly accepted ideology of the leadership elite, combined a technological approach to history with a moral one. By promising simultaneous fulfillment of technological and moral goals through history, Marxism-Leninism strengthened the Chinese leadership consensus. Particularly in the early stages after 1949, the obvious tensions between professionalism ("expert") and Maoist politics ("red") did not seem unmanageable. Even the Great Leap of 1958 appears to have been conceived and implemented, in large part, in the assumption that the different revolutionary goals were not fundamentally incompatible: it was, to some degree, an attempt to harness the power of "redness" in the service of modernization, an attempt to accelerate economic development through mass mobilization and ideological exhortation, with politics in control.

But the failure of the Great Leap in the immediate economic and organizational sense (there were severe food shortages and breakdowns in organizational control) and the recriminations that followed that failure in 1959–61, including Marshal P'eng Te-huai's attack on Mao's leadership at the August 1959 Lushan Plenum, tended to polarize China's political elite into two groupings. One diffuse grouping, headed —we can say in retrospect—by Liu Shao-ch'i, P'eng Chen, Teng Hsiao-p'ing and others, concentrated their attention primarily on organization-building, regularity and modernization. These men, the "organization men," were in operational control of China after 1959 and built up vested interests in the Party and state organizations. In general, it was their view that economic development directed by the Party and government bureaucracies would ultimately produce the desired Communist society. The other grouping, headed by Mao, was more radical and increasingly lost faith in bureaucratic procedures and in the Marxist notion that economic development would lead to the good society. As the two groups tended to polarize, the struggle between them became more and more a struggle for power—for the power to determine the course of China's development.

In the early 1960's, with the organization men in control of Party, government, and economy and pursuing pragmatic policies, Mao moved rapidly to maximize his influence in the People's Liberation Army (PLA) through a series of internal campaigns to reindoctrinate the army with Maoist goals and techniques. Mao's decision to make the PLA the opening wedge in what he probably envisaged even then as a long-range and vitally needed campaign was natural. In many ways the PLA was the easiest of the three basic organizational hierarchies of China—army, Party, and government—to politicize in Maoist modes of thought and action. In the context of the break with the Soviet Union and China's increasing desire to find a "Chinese path" of socialist development, and given the fact that of the three hierarchies the PLA had the least need to "produce" from day to day, Mao seemed best able to establish his model in the army. Despite some opposition from professionally oriented officers, Mao succeeded in the early 1960's in fashioning the PLA into his most reliable organizational support.

In the years just prior to the launching of the Cultural Revolution, the prestige and power of the PLA's top and second-echelon officers increased rapidly under the tutelage of Mao and Lin Piao, at the expense primarily of the Party and secondarily of the government. The PLA became the embodiment of Maoist virtue, thereby subtly undermining the Party's prestige. PLA leaders assumed important political roles in the government and economy. And as the battle between Mao and the leaders of the Peking Party organization became more intense in late 1965, the PLA's official organ *Chieh-fang-chün Pao* (Liberation Army Daily) became for a time the most authoritative voice among the mass media, superseding even the Party's own *Jen-min Jih-pao* (People's Daily).

On the other hand, too much should not be made of Maoist control of the army. While the PLA has probably been the most loyal organizational support of the Maoists, the events of the CR have made clear that its support has been substantially limited. If Mao hoped in the early 1960's to fashion the PLA into a truly revolutionary force, the prospects for success seemed dim by 1966. The key question has always been: *PLA support to do what?* The upgrading of the PLA to the role of Mao's staunchest ally appears to have been feasible precisely because Maoist demands for its support remained relatively restricted. Until late January of 1967, the PLA was significant primarily as a proclaimed model and as a reserve force which all sides were probably pleased to see remain on the sidelines—in part because of uncertainty as to what action it might take. In short, its role in support of Mao did not directly involve the use of its coercive powers. Nor was Mao's most vocal supporter, Defense Minister Lin Piao, called upon to test on any national scale the solidity and unity of this support.

Red Guards and the PLA

As the CR evolved out of elite polarization and certain mass dissatisfactions, Mao came to rely basically on two groups—the Red Guards (and revolutionary rebels) and the PLA. In retrospect, it can be said that these two groups functioned—ironically enough—in relatively specialized ways: the Maoist Red Guard and revolutionary rebel movement constituted the force for seizing power from below, while the PLA substantially embodied the tendency to impose order from above.[45]

As the CR intensified in 1966–67, reaching its peak perhaps in Augut 1967,[46] it went through alternative cycles of attack and retrenchment—i.e., of revolution from below and control from above. The attack phases were not fully controllable by the Maoist faction, not only because their intensity and duration depended in large part on the degree of resistance encountered, but also because, by the very nature of the CR, the capacity to exercise internal operational control over highly decentralized Red Guard activities was limited. Moreover, even where that capacity may have existed, its exercise often would not have been legitimated by the primary goals of the CR itself. Within the parameters prescribed by the exigencies of the power balance in China and the need to avoid excessive disruption of agricultural and industrial production and distribution, the Maoist Central Cultural Revolution Group found it difficult both organizationally and on ideological grounds to impose internal control from above on a revolution they were trying to stimulate from below. As for external controls, the usual instruments of such control—the Party and the government—were themselves the prime targets of attack by the Maoist revolutionaries, leaving only the PLA as a potential restraining force.

In the first phase of the CR, from its inception up to January 1967, the PLA played a relatively minor role. In fact, most of the events of this phase took place outside and independently of any well-structured national organization. The shift from institutionalized procedures to mass meetings in Peking between revolutionary youth and the supreme leader was more than simply symbolic. The shift was central to the meaning of the CR as an assault on hierarchically structured control mechanisms. In this centrality lie both the peculiar strengths and weaknesses of the CR.

When the CR shifted in 1966 from attacks on relatively defenseless members of the bourgeoisie, shopkeepers, and tourists to an assault on leading Party personnel at all levels throughout China, it encountered expectable resistance. Red Guard units were disorganized and inexperienced. Organizational power, experience in political infighting, and vested interests were all on the side of the entrenched Party apparatus. Even Mao's attempt to legitimize the onslaught and to delegitimize resistance to it could not compensate for these realities. Moreover, in the nature of the situation, the proper targets for attack frequently were unclear. The directives from the Central Cultural Revolution Group in Peking—lacking as they did the organizational apparatus required to translate their vaguely stated and even contradictory goals into practical action—were subject at least to honest misinterpretation. As a result, the Red Guard units—moved by enthusiasm and/or self-interest —often acted erratically, indiscriminately, and too intensely. Once again, Mao could not have the best of both worlds: he could not, on the one hand, encourage spontaneity and broad-gauged attacks from below on bureaucratic organizations and traditional institutions in the hope that this would teach youth the meaning of revolution by encouraging them to wage revolution, and, on the other hand, expect to be able to exercise definitive control even over his own forces in the struggle. As Mao's ideology was severed from organization, ideology manipulated by the leader inspired attacks that led to confusion and chaos.

Mao's Dilemma

In January 1967, the turmoil caused both by the Maoist drive to "seize power from below" through the Red Guard (student) and revolutionary rebel (adult worker) movements and by the subsequent inability of the radical Maoist factions to unify and stabilize the situation made it necessary to call upon the PLA to intervene in support of the left and restore order. But as the military, during February, stepped into the virtual organizational vacuum that had been created throughout the country, it became clear that PLA loyalty to Mao did not mean comprehensive and unified support for his radical goals. In fact, as might have been expected of a military organization trained to keep order—or, for that matter, of almost any large, hierarchical, national organization—the PLA intervened, in terms of practical effect, more on the side of order than of the revolutionary Left. And the more it expanded its governing activities, the greater its stake became in maintaining production and order.

Thus, despite his extensive earlier efforts to radicalize the PLA, Mao found himself confronted, in the final analysis, by a contradiction inherent in the thrust of the Cultural Revolution. The spearhead of the CR was the youth movement and its "assault" from below on the establishment. But when that assault led to excessive disruption or faced defeat, it became necessary, temporarily at least, to impose order from above through the only organization that remained relatively effective —the PLA. Insofar as the latter retained its integrity as a hierarchically organized and still relatively centralized and disciplined organization, it was capable of imposing order on a national scale in response to Maoist demands from Peking, but as such it was likely to favor order rather than revolution, and its very use interfered with the goal of revolution from below. On the other hand, insofar as the hierarchical military structure tended to become decentralized and disunited—as actually happened during the summer of 1967—the PLA inevitably became less responsive to Maoist demands and more likely to be controlled by regional or provincial military leaders who had their own local interests and organizations to protect and were generally antagonistic towards the disruptive activities of the revolutionary youth.

Mao, in short, was faced by a paradox. He needed an organization to wage permanent revolution, but found that organizations tend, at some point in the process of institutionalization, to become counter-revolutionary. There appears to be no single organizational form appropriate to permanent revolution. Hence, the tenuous "division of labor" in the CR between the Red Guards and the PLA; but in that division, final power lay with the PLA.

The CR in Perspective

The major exploits of Mao's life, and the Cultural Revolution in particular, are events which outside observers (and perhaps many Chinese as well) have had great difficulty in appreciating. The sheer intensity of emotions that has marked these events, combined with the not infrequent use of coercive and violent methods and the masses of people involved, has tended to arouse anxieties and antagonisms in much of the world outside China. Generally speaking, revolutions tend to appear less costly and awesome the farther they recede into the past, becoming abstractions in the process; revolutions in the present tend to repel or disturb us.[47] How much more is this the case when the sort of revolution at issue seems incomprehensible, even in terms of our past understanding of revolutions? We were not prepared by that understanding to appreciate Mao's Cultural Revolution. In terms of classical revolutions, the CR seems "artificial," or even superfluous, and therefore obviously excessive and romantic.

Yet many observers sense that something of historic significance has happened in China. Even if we do not pretend to understand its implications we sense that a great leader has fused explosive idealism and intense power in uneasy union and, in the process, has released tremendous energies. In a meaningful sense, the CR has been a struggle waged by the Maoists both to reopen in the most comprehensive manner the issue of China's goals and to determine the issue in favor of their own objectives. The central question for Maoists, in the author's view, is the nature of the society (quality of life) that should be the "end" of the Chinese Communist Revolution. Mao reopened the issue because it became increasingly clear to him that the dominant means employed to institutionalize the Chinese Revolution, while conducive to achieving certain of the Revolution's values, simultaneously appeared to preclude the realization of other values more deeply held by him and others. To a much greater degree than in the Great Leap, the core issue in the CR has been structured dramatically in terms of a choice of priorities—a choice, in short, between "modernization" and the Maoist vision of the good society.

Viewed in this light, the CR should not be dismissed simply as an aberration, as just another succession crisis characteristic of "totalitarian systems," or even as a kind of transition crisis peculiar to a certain stage of a society's development—it appears to be much more than a developmental watershed. In the final analysis, the CR seems to epitomize the tension between reality and ideals (in this case, Maoist ideals). It involves conflicts between societal values, social change, group and individual attitudes and interests, and social organizations and institutions. As such, it may have meaning for the world.

China's Cultural Revolution, in this sense, is part of a worldwide pattern of movement-type challenges to established authority and to related bureaucratic structures, challenges based fundamentally on the stated ideals of the very social systems whose authority structures are under assault. This worldwide pattern transcends stages of development and particular cultures, and it increasingly articulates a worldwide consciousness and sharing of certain values, particularly among the young. While one may point out that the challenge in China differed from analogous movements elsewhere (e.g., in France, Mexico, and the United States) in that it was initiated from above and developed in the context of a power struggle within the elite, the fact remains that the Chinese movement also forged a life of its own: it gained believers, developed with considerable spontaneity, proved exceedingly difficult to control, and sought to realize—too often by methods difficult for most Western minds to accept—a vision of a more humane existence.

China's Cultural Revolution is also part of a worldwide historical tradition having its own vision of how men should relate to one another and to their society—namely, the tradition supported by theorists and practitioners of anarchism and permanent revolution. As Michel Oksenberg observes:

> Mao's policy may . . . be seen as an effort to secure the commitment particularly of the younger generation to the building of a more just society, a commitment that arises from participation in the revolutionary act of defying authority. Mao would rather delay China's industrialization than have its industrialization serve the purposes of an entrenched bureaucratic elite. In this respect, Mao continues to be true to his revolutionary heritage. At the same time, Mao shares with many the belief that bureaucracy and industrialization do not necessarily lead to an improved quality of life. To the extent that Mao's desire is to insure that industrialization serves the interests of his society, he is dealing with the central . . . problem of our age. Seen in this light, Mao cannot be discussed in terms of "success" or "failure." To call his system "primitive" is to do him injustice, for in many ways we are reduced to value judgments. And we can be sure that the faith in voluntarism, egalitarianism and permanent revolution which captured a long line of revolutionaries before Mao, and which [has] . . . gripped Mao in his life, will continue to attract political figures who come after him.[48]

In the opinion of this author, the problem of permanent revolution is not, as is often argued, only of interest to political theorists and intellectual historians. Nor is the concept of permanent revolution merely a romantic ideal of abnormal personalities ("romantic revolutionaries"). Rather, to an increasing extent throughout the world and

—ironically—in advanced industrial societies particularly, permanent revolution is a fact. The motor for permanent revolution in advanced industrial societies is technology. But the problems presented are more universal: how to create flexible institutions which are responsive to popular interests, encourage direct mass participation, and are capable of controlling development on the basis of values meaningfully determined by the people.

The challenge of creating participatory institutions to deal with these problems is, in the author's view, at the core of the Chinese Cultural Revolution. Only time will tell what Mao has been able to achieve in facing this challenge and what those achievements may mean in the concrete for China and for the world.

1. W. A. C. Adie, "China's 'Second Liberation' in Perspective," *Bulletin of the Atomic Scientists* (Chicago), February 1969, p. 14.

2. See, e.g., Benjamin Schwartz, "The Reign of Virtue: Some Broad Perspectives on Leader and Party in the Cultural Revolution," *The China Quarterly* (London), July–September 1968, pp. 1–17; Franz Schurmann, "What's Happening in China?," *The New York Review of Books*, Oct. 20, 1966, pp. 18–25; and Richard Baum, "Ideology Redivivus," [reprinted as selection 6 in the present volume —ED.]. Baum's excellent analysis, which in part argues a "functional nexus between revisionism and modernization," suggests at least that Mao's concern over the deterioration of revolutionary values and spirit in the CCP is well founded. Much of my argument is in line with Baum's analysis, but Baum, like most American social scientists today, appears to assume the "rationality" of modernization and the "revivalist" irrationality of Mao's Cultural Revolution.

3. Regarding the last, see Charles Neuhauser, "The Impact of the Cultural Revolution on the Chinese Communist Party Machine," *Asian Survey*, June 1968, pp. 465–88. The present author disagrees with Neuhauser's view that "the Party as such has not been under attack . . . in the . . . Cultural Revolution"—that it is not the Party as such and its "central legitimizing role as the 'vanguard of the proletariat' and the font of political authority in China," but rather the "Party machine, the organizational command structure," which has come under Maoist attack. While I accept the validity of Neuhauser's analytic distinction between "Party" and "Party machine," I argue in this paper that Mao has attacked the Party as such, not to destroy it, but to transform it. It is precisely the Party's exclusive legitimizing role that has been brought into question.

4. One notable exception is William Hinton, who appears to have become a straightforward Maoist. He writes in his most recent article: "The world has never witnessed anything to approach, not to mention equal, this mass mobilization . . . as hundreds of millions entered the arena of political action" ("Hinton Re-examines 'Fanshen'," *Progressive Labor*, February 1969, p. 107).

5. "The Attack of the Cultural Revolution on Ideology and Organization," in Ping-ti Ho and Tang Tsou, eds., *China in Crisis* (Chicago: University of Chicago Press, 1968), Vol. I, Book 2, p. 551.

6. "Decision of the Central Committee of the Chinese Communist Party Concerning the Great Proletarian Cultural Revolution" [reprinted as selection 9 of the present volume—ED.].

7. Leo Huberman and Paul Sweezy, "The Cultural Revolution in China," *Monthly Review* (New York), January 1967, as reprinted by the Radical Education Project, p. 11.

8. The use of the death imagery is suggested by Robert J. Lifton's *Revolutionary Immortality* [see selection 8 of the present volume—ED.].

9. Huberman and Sweezy, *loc. cit.*, p. 11.

10. Insofar as the CR appears to be a revolution against modernization, it is no wonder that many American social scientists have tended to deride it. In the United States today, modernization has come to be worshipped as a kind of new Hegelianism combining the "is" and the "ought" in history. Despite reservations, American social scientists generally tend to treat it as both inevitable and good. Even so perceptive an observer as Robert Lifton concludes that Mao, in trying to confront some of the problems connected with modernization, is out of touch with reality and guilty of "psychism" (Lifton, *op. cit.*). Also see Baum, *loc. cit.*

11. Huberman and Sweezy, *op. cit.*, p. 13 (Italics deleted).

12. *Ibid.*

13. *Ibid.*, pp. 13–14.

14. *Ibid.*, pp. 15–16. See also Carl Riskin, "The Chinese Economy in 1967," in *The Cultural Revolution: 1967 in Review* (Ann Arbor: University of Michigan, 1968), p. 60.

15. Ray Wylie ("Revolution Within a Revolution," *Bulletin of the Atomic Scientists,* February 1969, p. 32), sees the role of the masses in the CR as setting a possible pattern for the future: "The Maoist press has declared that there will probably be more Cultural Revolutions in the future. That is, the people have in Mao Tse-tung's thought the theoretical basis—and in the present Cultural Revolution the historical precedent—by which to justify an attack on any future regime that loses its revolutionary elan and begins to drift toward despotism. . . . Above all, it is an endeavour . . . to impart to them the ideal of a 'new China' and the idea that it is 'right to rebel' if a future regime betrays the ideal." In this perspective, Mao Tse-tung becomes Chinese communism's own John Locke.

16. The perspective of Mao as radical initiator and Liu as consolidator was suggested to the author by Professor Tang Tsou's "The Cultural Revolution and the Chinese Political System," *The China Quarterly* (London), April–June, 1969, pp. 63–91. [An abridged version of this article appears as selection 14, above—ED.].

17. "The Structure of Conflict: China in 1967," in *The Cultural Revolution: 1967 in Review, op. cit.*, p. 102. Vogel's analysis is deeply informed and frequently brilliant, but it tends to ignore the significance of Mao's maximal goals, mentioning Mao's "major objectives" almost in passing, and treating the CR simply as a great and sophisticated Maoist-type purge. Power is the name of the game, and the relevance of ultimate values, if assumed, is obscured.

18. Chalmers Johnson ("China: The Cultural Revolution in Structural Perspective," *Asian Survey*, January 1968, pp. 3–4) touches on problems of bureaucratic ossification and goal displacement in China. His description of the inefficiencies of bureaucracies, said to be particularly serious in Communist countries, drives another nail into the coffin in which theories of totalitarianism are destined to be buried.

19. John W. Lewis, "Leader, Commissar, and Bureaucrat: The Chinese Political System in the Last Days of the Revolution," in Ho and Tsou, *op. cit.* The following discussion of the roles of Mao and Liu in Yenan is based on Lewis' stimulating piece, but in stressing the different experiences of the two men, I do not mean to imply that other factors may not be equally important in explaining their divergent orientations towards revolution.

20. For a discussion of Mao's "populism" and "his 'mystical faith' . . . in the rural masses," see Lifton, *loc. cit.*

21. Lewis, *loc. cit.*, p. 453.

22. *Ibid.*, pp. 464–65.

23. Tsou, *loc. cit.*

24. *Ibid.*

25. *Ibid.* This emphasis on the relatively elitist nature of the Chinese political system in the mid-1950's should not, however, obscure the complex reality of politics within that system. For an excellent and provocative article which begins to sketch out the contours of reciprocity in Chinese politics in the mid-1960's, see Michel Oksenberg, "Occupational Groups in Chinese Society and the Cultural Revolution," in *The Cultural Revolution: 1967 in Review, op. cit.*, pp. 1–44.

26. Schurmann, "The Attack of the Cultural Revolution . . . ," *loc. cit.*, p. 538.

27. *Ibid.*, p. 546. See also the same author's "China's 'New Economic Policy'—Transition or Beginning," *The China Quarterly*, January–March, 1964, pp. 65–91, especially after p. 83.

28. Schurmann, "The Attack of the Cultural Revolution . . . ," *loc. cit.*, p. 543. Schurmann's vision of the party in the early 1960's ties in nicely with the theory later set forth by Baum (see footnote 2). On the other hand, Oksenberg (in Ho and Tsou, *op. cit.*, pp. 494–96) diverges from Schurmann and Baum in wondering whether the attitudes and values of the Liu Shao-ch'i/Teng Hsiao-p'ing grouping might not be *less* conducive to modernization than those of the Red Guards. Several economists have also begun to raise such questions: e.g., Riskin, *loc. cit.*, pp. 60–64; and Jack Gray, "The Economics of Maoism" [reprinted as selection 7 in the present volume—ED.].

29. Philip Selznick, *Leadership in Administration* (Evanston, Ill.: Row, Peterson, 1957), pp. 26–27.

30. *Ibid.*, p. 37 (italics added). Mao, as leader, can be seen as the receptacle of ultimate values. Dick Wilson refers to Mao as China's "conscience" in his "Where China Stands Now: An Introduction," *Bulletin of the Atomic Scientists*, February 1969, p. 5.

31. Elsewhere in this paper, the terms "organization" and "institution" are not used in the technical sense in which Selznick uses them. Selznick treats these terms as ideal types. In the concrete, the relationship between the organizational and institutional components in a particular unit is complex and a matter of process.

32. In the author's view, Mao is aware that his own personal authority as chairman cannot be bestowed with great effectiveness on another and has therefore sought to establish counter-institutions to protect his value concerns after his death (see below).

33. The author's hypothesis that Mao has consciously used his personal authority, earlier institutionalized in the cult of personality, for grand political purposes is in contrast to the view that Mao is a supervain megalomaniac. While one may disagree with Mao's goals and methods, neither are, in my view, pathological. The "growing personalization of the Mao cult" (noted by Stuart Schram in his *Mao Tse-tung* [Baltimore: Penguin, 1967, revised paperback—ED.], p. 340) has been part of Mao's effort to play an active leadership role in the CR. By deliberately repersonalizing the cult of personality and recreating it as charisma—for example, by his numerous appearances at huge mass rallies—Mao has heightened his own capacity to evoke great emotion and to manipulate that emotion.

34. Tsou, *loc. cit.*

35. *Ibid.*

36. *Ibid.*

37. See Vogel, *loc. cit.*, p. 106.

38. Tsou, *loc. cit.*

39. This and other passages are quoted from the text as reported in English by *New China News Agency*, April 28, 1969; emphasis added.

40. Just what "supervision" by "the masses" will mean in practice is unclear. The revolutionary committees which have been set up throughout China at all levels may well represent, in part, an attempt to institutionalize the role of "the masses," but the nature and permanency of these committees and their relationship to other institutions are problematical. Whatever is meant by "supervision," the vision of an active role for "the masses" will be an empty one if there is no institutional facility through which they can make their power felt.

41. Marx's philosophy, especially his early work, obviously owes much to Rousseau. In this sense, Mao may be said to be rejecting elements of Marxism while selectively reaffirming the concerns of the early Marx. The following discussion of Mao and Rousseau draws to a considerably extent upon the work of Benjamin I. Schwartz, especially his brilliant "The Reign of Virtue . . ." (*loc. cit.*, footnote 2) and his earlier "Modernization and the Maoist Vision—Some Reflections on Chinese Communist Goals" (*The China Quarterly*, Jan.–March, 1965).

42. Schwartz, "The Reign of Virtue . . . ," *loc. cit.*, p. 9.

43. It appears that as 20th-century Americans we may be peculiarly unable to appreciate Mao as a radical in power and as a great man. We tend to view politics as "the art of the possible"—an implicitly conservative formulation. Radicals at home and abroad tend to frighten and annoy us. Moreover, while in the 19th century we had our voluntarist heroes—e.g., self-made men and captains of industry—today we increasingly have come to disbelieve in the power of man's will in the face of overwhelming technological forces. Bereft of white, middle-class heroes at home, we may even resent great men abroad.

44. Schwartz, "The Reign of Virtue . . . ," *loc. cit.*, p. 13.

45. The Red Guard and Rebel groups were by no means all responsive to Mao's desires. According to John Gittings ("The Prospects of the Cultural Revolution in 1969," *Bulletin of the Atomic Scientists*, February 1969, p. 24), "the real rebels were the 'have nots' of China—the unemployed students, contract laborers, unskilled workers, and others who looked on rebellion as the way to remedy their lot." But even many of these "rebels" were more concerned with the material improvement of their lot than with the Maoist values: see Evelyn Anderson, "Shanghai: The Masses Unleashed," *Problems of Communism*, January–February 1968, pp. 12–21. In addition, other conservative groups were set up by "local establishment figures" in self-defense: see Allen S. Whiting, "Mao's Troubled Ark," *Life*, February 21, 1969, pp. 62 f. Naturally, all groups, whatever their motives, called themselves "Maoists."

46. It is arguable whether the violence and dislocation of the CR reached their peak in August 1967 or at certain times in 1968, but August 1967 still appears to have been the major turning point. After that, as Ezra Vogel notes (*loc. cit.*, p. 118), "there was a serious attempt to rebuild local political structures," and the subsequent struggles "should be viewed in the context of rebuilding the organizations." Gittings also observes ("The Prospects . . . ," *loc. cit.*, pp. 24–27) that struggles in 1968 generally involved a jockeying for power in "the whole process of political consolidation and restoration of order." It became necessary at times for the radicals to demonstrate their strength in order to keep from being frozen out in the division and restructuring of power.

47. Of course, the frequently hidden costs of maintaining the *status quo* can also be awesome.

48. Oksenberg, in Ho and Tsou, *op. cit.*, pp. 493–94.

CONCLUSION

Louise B. Bennett

Many have written about the Cultural Revolution; few have stepped back to examine the assumptions on which much of this scholarship rests. Yet, what one chooses to study about the Cultural Revolution or how one interprets it is necessarily determined by the assumptions one initially makes. In concluding this volume, we should therefore like to briefly examine a number of the assumptions shared by scholars studying the CR.

Maoism versus Modernization

The most common assumption relates to what may be called the "modernization syndrome"—the complex of elements associated with Western political and economic development since the Middle Ages. As defined by scholars, it involves:

> the sustained attention to the most appropriate, "rational," and efficient methods for increasing man's ability to control nature and society for a variety of ends . . . , the notion of a highly developed division of labor of "functional specificity" with the corollary that men should have a degree of autonomy and authority within their various spheres of competence . . . , a stress on norms of universality rather than ascription, thus involving social mobility—the opening up of careers to talent. . . .[1]

In many cases modernization also includes a growing rejection of personalistic values and ideology (see selection 6).

Most social scientists today seem to assume both the rationality and the inevitability of modernization. For them it is associated with rising standards of living, technological progress, economic mobility, and efficiency. It is also seen as an inevitable historical trend—the development of a universal technology-oriented culture which, while originating in Europe, is slowly spreading throughout the world.

In analyses of the Cultural Revolution, this assumption has led to certain conclusions. Most generally, Mao and his policies during the CR are dismissed as irrational and utopian, while the programs associated with Liu Shao-ch'i and the Party organization are thought to have been more realistic and pragmatic (see selections 3 and 5). The Maoist goal of creating the "all-round man" is regarded as anachronistic, and reforms in education that shorten school terms and expand political training are viewed as a dilution of standards which China can ill afford. Maoist stress on ideology and ideological rectification is similarly viewed as an attempt to resist pressures for modernization and social change and the development of a more expedient, instrumental, and apolitical ethic (see selection 6). Finally, Mao's use of charisma and the elevation of his thought to legitimize political goals and programs are regarded as suspect because they smack of a personalistic cult, and even of megalomania (see selection 2).

But not only are these Maoist goals and programs allegedly irrational, they are also doomed to failure. They must fail, it is argued, because they are antihistorical and do not follow the model of development which Western countries have "successfully" tested (see selection 16).

Possessive Individualism versus Altruistic Socialism

Closely related to this belief about modernization is an assumption about human nature. Individualistic competitiveness, the acquisitive instinct, and material incentives are all considered to be basic to human motivation. Ideologies or programs which substitute collective goals or nonmaterial incentives for these are regarded as utopian and hence unlikely to succeed.

In the Chinese case, Maoist ideology and programs are therefore subject to criticism. Most of the reforms of the Great Leap Forward— the abolition of private plots and rural trade fairs and the introduction of communes and nonmaterial incentives—are rejected not because of faulty implementation or planning, but because they are basically antithetical to human nature as known in Western societies (see selections 10 and 15).

Revolution versus Evolution

Many liberal social scientists also assume that incremental reform and moderation are preferable to and more effective in achieving basic social change than extreme measures.[2] That violent social and economic injustice may be perpetrated under the *status quo* and extreme measures may be the only way to deal with resistance on the part of entrenched interests who benefit from existing conditions is rarely mentioned.

Very recently, a number of economists have begun to question some of the assumptions outlined above. As noted by Jack Grey (see selection 7) and others, many Maoist ideas are perhaps not so irrational for a country like China.

The modernizing goal of developing "specialized experts" may not meet China's needs for a flexible and generally intelligent working force which may be able to shift from job to job as conditions require.[3] Attempting to overcome apathy, ignorance, and the provincial concerns of peasants by educating people through production and by stressing ideological rectification may not be unreasonable. One of the basic needs of developing countries is mass politicization and mobilization. Decentralization and collectivization, according to the Chinese and not the Soviet model, may meet the need to break down barriers between farm and factory, to stop the drain of talent to the cities and of resources to the communes. Finally, the idea of "unbalanced" economic development and development by the "big push" has long been held as a respectable theory by developmental economists.[4] The Chinese pattern of "Great Leaps" may not, after all, be so nonsensical.

In addition, however, the exclusive concerns with modernization and technical progress are no longer quite so appealing even to citizens of "developed" nations who now face the evils of pollution, bureaucratization, suburban sprawl, and gaping social inequities.

Masses versus Elites

Another assumption of some China experts who deal with the Cultural Revolution is that China is a totalitarian regime directed or manipulated from above by certain top leaders (see selection 11). Thus the possibility for uncontrolled or spontaneous action is dismissed, and with it the explanation for the mass movements during the CR.

Related to the assumption of the totalitarian and manipulating nature of the Chinese Communist regime is the common preoccupation of Western social scientists with studying top-level leadership.[5] In much of the literature on the Cultural Revolution, for example, discussion is mainly focused on such questions as political intrigue, power struggles, and the ups and downs of certain key figures. In the remainder of this essay, therefore, we will briefly turn our attention to two interesting nonelite-oriented aspects of the CR which have been overlooked in most discussions.

The Revolt of the Masses

One of the most significant, but largely ignored, developments of the Cultural Revolution was the outpouring of mass emotion which occurred among workers and students. During the winter and summer of 1967, strikes and even clashes among various urban groups broke out. Shanghai was crippled by harbor and railroad walk-outs that disrupted transport, communication, food distribution, and even bank operations. Many of these actions seemed to have resulted from certain economic grievances.[6]

The complaints were varied. Some related to general working conditions and hours, wage scales, and fringe benefits. Others involved more specific situations: the apprenticeship programs and the worker-peasant system, whereby factories (1) received cheap temporary or contractual rural labor in return for more highly paid permanent workers who were sent down to the farms and (2) passed on payment of expensive welfare benefits and food expenses to the communes. Still other problems resulted from the influx of peasants and workers from the countryside and the frontier areas into the cities. All of these groups formed their own organizations and organized protests to press for their own demands. Further tension arose when some workers, hurt by the disruption, formed groups to oppose and disband the other organizations.

In addition to the outburst from workers' groups, there was an even stronger outpouring from young students.[7] Many seem to have reacted idealistically to Maoist appeals in 1966 to "pay attention to state affairs and carry out the Great Proletarian Cultural Revolution to the end" and to "criticize the reactionary bourgeois academic authorities and the ideology of the bourgeoisie." Others, perhaps, saw the closing of the universities as a good chance to get away from school.

Many students, however, especially the children of poor workers and peasants, guided by self-interest, supported Maoist educational reforms that called for the abolition of entrance examinations, grade marks, and tuition fees and for the revision of curriculum in order to make it more relevant to the needs of society. In previous years, these people had been weeded out of the schools and forced to return to the countryside. Many of them were now eager to return to the cities.

Other groups, who had benefited from the established educational system, did not react as enthusiastically to the Cultural Revolution. For many, it meant the discrediting of established family position and an end to special educational privilege.

As the disruption of the universities and the urban areas continued on into 1967, many students, initially caught up in the fervor of the revolution, may have stepped to the sidelines as they found their own positions being attacked by opposing groups. In fact, during this time, there were many stories in the Chinese press about "wanderers"—unemployed and uninvolved youths.[8]

With the call for the resumption of classes in the spring of 1967, many willingly returned to school. More, however, either seemed to enjoy the freedom outside the classroom or felt that it was still too early to stop making revolution. New leftist organizations, condemned by Maoists for promoting the "black wind of anarchism," continued to spring up, and even turned to "arms grabbing" during that summer.

The mood of revolutionary euphoria was soon dampened by the clampdown of the army and the attack on "leftists" by leading figures in the Central Cultural Revolution Group. The students' feeling of betrayal was further heightened by the successive *hsia fang* campaigns to send unruly radicals down to the countryside and, later in the spring of 1968, to the military-operated "May 7" schools to be "tested and tempered in storm and stress"—i.e., reformed.

Undoubtedly, however this feeling of betrayal was also mixed with less altruistic feelings—disdain for manual labor and frustration at the prospect of giving up "modern" careers for a life on the commune. As one young student was quoted as saying: "Would we have bothered to go through ten years of school, if we had known earlier that we have to get smeared in mud?" [9]

In sum, many of the outbursts during the Cultural Revolution came as a result of conflicting pressures and interests generated by the cross-currents of revolution and modernization. For the most part, especially after 1967, they were uncontrolled and undirected—essentially spontaneous in nature. To understand these pressures and cross-currents only leads to increased doubts about the inevitability and rationality of modernization.

Decentralization

Another important aspect of the Cultural Revolution, largely unmentioned in the literature, was the program of decentralization. While never extensively publicized until the fall of 1968, this idea has for a long time been one of the key elements in Maoist thought. What was initially adopted for reasons of expediency and necessity during the guerrilla days of the 1930s, when it was impossible to establish a centralized command and administration, gradually became a fundamental tenet of Maoist philosophy, closely associated with the cultural revolutionary goals of building a proletarian culture.

The officially cited directive for this campaign is Mao's order of May 7, 1966, attached to his statement on the PLA.[10] According to this document, Mao called on students, workers, and peasants to follow the example of the army. While they were to concern themselves primarily with their assigned fields of education, industry, and agriculture they were also to study and participate in other work. By following Mao's directive, the editorial explained:

> it will be possible to promote the step-by-step narrowing of the gap between workers and peasants, town and countryside and mental and manual labor; to enable intellectuals to become at the same time manual workers and manual workers at the same time intellectuals; and to train hundreds of millions of new communist people who have a high degree of political consciousness and are developed in an all-round way.[11]

In the fall of 1968, this directive began to be implemented on a wide scale. Reforms covered a broad range of fields: education, agriculture, industry and commerce, medicine, and population dispersal. Essentially, they involved the shifting of large-scale responsibilities from the cities to the local three-in-one committees and the growing importance of collectivization.

In education, on the elementary levels, this campaign meant the entrusting of primary schools to the production brigades. Funding for these schools and for teacher salaries was no longer to be shouldered by the central government. Instructors were to be more closely linked to productive labor, receiving payment according to work points in the production brigades and participation in part-time farm work.[12]

On both the primary and middle school levels, educational reforms were introduced which tied curriculum more closely to commune technical needs and which abolished discrimination against poor peasants and workers. Entrance exams, tuition fees, and grade marks were all abandoned. In many cases, special arrangements were made which allowed students from the communes to attend middle school for several years, with the proviso that afterwards they would return to their commune.[13]

In the universities, links to nearby factories and communes were developed, to the extent of locating industry on university campuses or of moving administration down to the countryside. These reforms served both to discipline radical students and teachers and to link schools more closely to production. At the same time, curriculum reforms were designed to break down the "artificial" distinctions between research, teaching, and production and to apply course work more directly to social needs. In many cases this meant shortening school terms, lowering graduation requirements, popularizing course content, and using workers and peasants as instructors.[14]

In the field of agriculture, many of the reforms of the Great Leap Forward were reintroduced. Local units were amalgamated, and efforts made to encourage the transfer of excess private plots, tractors, and other big farm machinery to the communes. The slogan of "learn from Tachai" was revived, and in some cases work points were awarded according to political standards.[15]

At the same time, small factories to process agricultural goods, produce agricultural machinery, and service local needs for fertilizer and electric power were set up on communes, and production brigades assumed responsibility for the simple operations of retail shops and of supply and marketing stations.[16]

In the field of health and medicine, drives were also conducted to decentralize medical service and to handle local needs. Health workers and mobile units were transferred to local levels. Beginning in December, 1968, a campaign to establish medical service co-ops was undertaken. These co-ops, to which commune members paid a small annual sum plus a small fee for each treatment, provided mobile medical service for the commune and worked especially to practice preventive medicine and carry on public health work. They also stressed the use of traditional Chinese medicine and helped to train local health workers —"barefoot doctors"—to deal with simple, but basic medical needs.[17]

Finally, a massive effort was made to shift urban population to the countryside. Both from the big cities and the rural towns, almost twenty-five million people were "sent down." [18] In some cases, the transfer was done for punitive reasons—to discipline recalcitrant or "ultra-leftist" intellectuals or cadres. In others, the aim was to remove the unemployed from the urban areas. For a large number, the goal seems to have been the "integration" of students, workers, and peasants and the dispersal of needed skills to the countryside.

The reasons for this program were many. The most frequently and most publicly cited one was ideological: the elimination of "contradictions" between urban and rural sectors and between mental and manual labor. Through this elimination, a new "all-round" communist man might develop.

Behind this ideological goal were at least three more pragmatic considerations. In many articles, budgetary factors were cited. By decentralizing, the central government would be relieved of many financial pressures and burdens. This claim, however, seems to have been contended by those who feared that local units might not be able to meet costs fully. Some doubt seemed to exist as to whether the expenses of adequate salaries for educational and medical personnel and of supplies, such as drugs, could be met.[20] In most cases, the central government did in fact agree to provide subsidies for the first several years and to guarantee markets for commune factories. Whether these programs will eventually prove to be fully self-sufficient is a question still to be answered.

There is also the military and strategic factor: by decentralizing industry, dispersing urban population, and mobilizing an alert and well-trained human force in the countryside, military preparedness may be strengthened and China may become a harder target to attack.[21]

A third consideration is that of economic development. By redistributing population, decentralizing industry, and modernizing the rural areas, barriers between city and countryside which plague so many developing countries may be reduced, and overall economic growth and regional and sectoral balance may be achieved. Such considerations have been stressed not only by Maoist theoreticians but also by developmental economists throughout the world.[22]

In sum, the Maoist program of decentralization may not, after all, be so irrational for a developing country like China. This is not to say that Maoist policies are necessarily correct or that Chinese "modernization" is assured. For one thing, modernization is probably only the lesser of two major Maoist goals—the other being the development of a socialist society in China. Given the evidence of the Cultural Revolution, it appears that these two goals may, in fact, conflict.

These questions, however, are as yet unresolved. It is our present duty to try to understand what is occurring in the Chinese People's Republic. To do so, we must start by examining our own assumptions and perspectives.

1. See Benjamin Schwartz, "Modernization and the Maoist Vision," *The China Quarterly*, no. 21 (January–March, 1965), 3–19.

2. See Edward Friedman, "Cultural Limits of the Cultural Revolution," *Asian Survey* 9, no. 3 (March, 1969), 200. Also, A. Doak Barnett, *Communist China in Perspective* (New York: Frederick A. Praeger, Inc., 1962), p. 41.

3. See J. W. Gurley, "The New Man in the New China," *The Center Magazine* 3, no. 3 (May–June, 1970): 33.

4. See P. N. Rosenstein-Rodan, *Notes on the Theory of the "Big Push"* (Cambridge: Center for International Studies, 1957); Hans Singer, "The Concept of Balanced Economic Growth and Economic Development: Theory and Facts," University of Texas Conference on Economic Development, 1958, pp. 4, 6; Albert Hirschman, *The Strategy of Economic Development* (New Haven: Yale University Press, 1958).

5. See James Peck, "The Roots of Rhetoric: The Professional Ideology of America's China Watchers," *Bulletin of Concerned Asian Scholars*, 2, no. 1 (October, 1969): 65.

6. See Evelyn Anderson, "Shanghai, The Masses Unleashed," *Problems of Communism*, 17, no. 1 (January–February, 1968): 12–21; and "Sources of Labor Discontent in China: The Worker-Peasant System," *Current Scene* 6, no. 5 (March 15, 1968): 1–28.

7. See Klaus Mehnert, *Peking and the New Left: At Home and Abroad* (Berkeley: University of California, Center for Chinese Studies, 1969), and Edward Friedman, *op. cit.*

8. "Mao's Revolutionary Successors: Part II," *Current Scene* 5, no. 16 (October 2, 1967); and F. T. Mits, "The Wanderers," *Current Scene* 5, no. 13 (August 15, 1967): 1–7.

9. *Radio Kweichow*, October 22, 1968, in Klaus Mehnert, *op. cit.*, p. 42.

10. This directive has never been publicized, though excerpts from it are thought to be printed in a *People's Daily* editorial of August 1, 1966.

11. *Peking Review* 9, no. 32 (August 5, 1966): 7.

12. "Forum on Entrusting Production Brigades to Run Primary Schools," *Current Background*, no. 869 (January 15, 1969).

13. "Peking's Program to Move Human and Material Resources to the Countryside," *Current Scene* 7, no. 18 (September 15, 1969): 11.

14. "How 'Socialist Universities' Should Be Run," *Current Background*, no. 881 (May 26, 1969); "More on How 'Socialist Universities' Should Be Run," *Current Background*, no. 890 (September 18, 1969); "Peking's Program to Move Human and Material Resources to the Countryside," *op. cit.*

15. Colina MacDougall, "The Cultural Revolution in the Communes: Back to 1958?" *Current Scene*, 7, no. 7 (April 11, 1969): 1–11.

16. *Ibid.* Also, "Is It a Good Thing for Poor and Lower-Middle Peasants to Run Rural Commerce?" *Current Background*, no. 875 (March 28, 1969).

17. "Rural Cooperative Medical Service," *Current Background*, no. 872 (February 28, 1969).

18. "Peking's Program to Move Human and Material Resources to the Countryside," *op. cit.*, 14.

19. *Ibid.*

20. *Ibid.*, 9–10, 17; "Educational Reform in Rural China," *Current Scene* 7, no. 3 (February 8, 1969): 4; "Public Health Developments—Continued Focus on the Farm," *Current Scene* 7, no. 24 (December 15, 1969): 2–8.

21. "Peking's Program to Move Human and Material Resources to the Countryside," *op. cit.,* 10.

22. W. W. Rostow, address to the American Chamber of Commerce in Mexico City, U. S. Dept. of State Press Release 431, August 19, 1963, cited in Eugene Staley and Richard Morse, *Modern Small Industry for Developing Countries* (New York: McGraw-Hill Book Company, 1965), p. 302; and Professor Harbison in Malassis, *Economic Development and the Programming of Rural Education* (UNESCO, 1966), cited in Edward Friedman, *op. cit.,* p. 194.

Chronology of Events (1957–1970)

1957   February   Mao Tse-tung delivers speech "On the Correct Handling of Contradictions among the People." Hundred Flowers Campaign reaches zenith as intellectuals encouraged to air grievances.

        June   Hundred Flowers Campaign terminated. Anti-Rightist rectification drive launched.

        October   Great Leap Forward initiated.

1958   August   Rural people's communes inaugurated on nationwide scale.

        December   Central Committee announces slowdown of commune movement. Economic crisis begins. Mao resigns as chief of state, retreats to "second line" of decision-making.

1959   April   Liu Shao-ch'i named to succeed Mao as chief of state.

        August   Central Committee Plenum held at Lushan. Mao's Great Leap policies attacked by Defense Minister P'eng Teh-huai. P'eng purged as Rightist, replaced by Lin Piao.

1960   August   Soviet technicians leave China. Economic assistance terminated. Sino-Soviet polemics begin.

1961   January   Wu Han's historical drama *Hai Jui Dismissed from Office* published.

        March   Central Committee announces further liberalization measures in industry, agriculture.

        October   Veiled criticisms of Mao appear in Peking journal articles written by Wu Han, Teng T'o, and Liao Mo-sha.

1962   September   Tenth Central Committee Plenum convened. Mao warns of danger of "capitalist restoration" in China, stresses continued existence of "class struggle" between proletariat and bourgeoisie. Socialist Education Movement initiated.

1963   July   Sino-Soviet summit meeting in Moscow ends in disagreement.

1964   February   "Emulate the PLA" campaign initiated nationwide. PLA held up as "model of revolutionization" for whole country to follow. Lin Piao's influence rises.

        September   Liu Shao-ch'i issues new instructions on Socialist Education Movement, initiates severe purge among basic-level Party cadres.

        October   Khrushchev falls from power. China tests first atomic bomb.

1965 January   Central Committee holds working conference. Mao issues further instructions on Socialist Education Movement, states that main purpose of movement is "to rectify Party powerholders who take the capitalist road."

February   Large-scale campaign to "study and apply the thought of Mao Tse-tung" initiated under PLA sponsorship.

March   U.S. begins large-scale bombing of North Vietnam. China fears war, steps up defense preparations.

September   Lin Piao publishes important essay, "Long Live the Victory of People's War."

Central Committee holds working conference. Mao appoints five-man group, headed by Peking Mayor P'eng Chen, to investigate "bourgeois influences" in cultural field.

November   Shanghai *Wen Hui Pao* publishes critique of Wu Han play *Hai Jui Dismissed from Office,* charges play is veiled defense of ousted Defense Minister P'eng Teh-huai. Critique marks initiation of major rectification campaign in China's literary circles. PLA Chief of Staff Lo Jui-ch'ing disappears, presumed purged.

1966 February   P'eng Chen's "Group of Five" issues outline report on progress of literary rectification drive.

April   Attack against Peking academic and literary figures intensifies. Leading intellectuals Wu Han, Teng T'o, and Liao Mo-sha criticized as "bourgeois authorities."

May   Peking municipal Party Committee "reorganized" following disclosure of Committee members' attempt to blunt thrust of rectification drive.

P'eng Chen's "February Outline Report" criticized as "monstrous poisonous weed." P'eng Chen becomes first major Party purge victim in newly expanded Cultural Revolution.

First "big character poster" appears at Peking University, initiating campaign of mass "big blooming and contending" among students.

June   Public phase of Cultural Revolution begins with series of editorials in *People's Daily.* Goal of Cultural Revolution stated to be "to sweep away all anti-Party, anti-socialist demons and monsters."

Work teams dispatched by Liu Shao-ch'i and Teng Hsiao-p'ing to guide conduct of Cultural Revolution in schools and universities. Mao absent from Peking.

July   Mao returns to Peking, swims Yangtze river to demonstrate good health.

Chou Yang purged as Minister of Culture.

August   Eleventh Central Committee Plenum convened by Mao. Work teams criticized for suppressing "revolutionary students." Sixteen Point decision on goals and methods of Cultural Revolution promulgated. Liu Shao-ch'i demoted within Party Politburo. Party propaganda director Lu Ting-yi purged.

Red Guards make formal debut in Peking. Mao exhorts revolutionary students to "bombard the headquarters" of "Party powerholders who take the capitalist road."

Red Guards dispersed throughout China to "link up" and "exchange revolutionary experiences."

September   Red Guards exhorted to maintain discipline and conduct "struggle by reasoning instead of by force." Students prohibited from entering factories and farms to "exchange experiences."

October   Lin Piao issues five-point directive on political work in PLA, stresses importance of obedience to Chairman Mao's "proletarian line."

Liu Shao-ch'i makes "self-criticism" at Party meeting, admits committing errors in June and July in connection with work team incidents.

November   Central Committee directs "revolutionary workers and peasants" to launch Cultural Revolution in factories and farms.

1967 January   "January Revolution" erupts in Shanghai. Red Guards and "revolutionary rebels" exhorted to seize power from "bourgeois powerholders" in the Party. Party committees throughout China paralyzed under rebel attack.

Mao calls upon PLA to "support the Left" in power seizure conflicts.

China's first "revolutionary committee" inaugurated in Heilungkiang province, comprising "three-way alliance" among veteran cadres, rebel leaders, and PLA representatives.

February   Red Guards and revolutionary rebels beset by factional difficulties, anarchist tendencies.

"February adverse current" of "sham power seizures" initiated by Party powerholders to preempt power seizures by revolutionary Left.

March   PLA instructed to "support agriculture" and insure maintenance of labor discipline in rural areas during spring farming season.

April   Liu Shao-ch'i officially denounced as "China's Khrushchev" and "the number one Party powerholder taking the capitalist road."

Red Guards and revolutionary rebels exhorted to "love and cherish" veteran cadres who confess their errors and liberate their thinking.

PLA instructed to avoid using force in controlling rebel

factionalism. Military leaders in many provinces criticized for suppressing the revolutionary Left.

May   Rectification drive launched in PLA. Regional military leaders recant their errors.

June   China explodes first hydrogen device.

July   "Wuhan incident" is first major instance of PLA disobedience to Mao's orders. Red Guards and revolutionary rebels exhorted by Mme. Mao (Chiang Ch'ing) to "drag out the handful of capitalist roaders in the army."

August   Foreign Ministry seized by rebels. British Chancery sacked and burned. Foreign Minister Ch'en Yi criticized.

September   Chiang Ch'ing rescinds order to "attack the handful" in PLA. Period of moderation ensues as Maoists seek to impose control on ultra-Leftists.

Mao tours China, issues "latest instructions" urging rebel factions to reconcile internal differences. Factionalism officially denounced as "counter-revolutionary."

October   *People's Daily* stresses need for rebels to unite with and rely on "revolutionary leading cadres." Drive to establish provincial and municipal revolutionary committees accelerated.

November   Party Secretary-General Teng Hsiao-p'ing officially denounced as "another top Party power holder taking the capitalist road."

1968 January   Maoists continue to denounce anarchist, factional tendencies of "extreme Left." Campaign to "support the army" launched.

PLA instructed to "support the Left but not any particular faction."

March   Extreme Left regains initiative. PLA Chief of Staff Yang Ch'eng-wu purged for opposing Chiang Ch'ing. Premier Chou En-lai declares that "at present our principal attack is directed at die-hard conservatives on the right."

Adverse current of "reversing verdicts" on purge victims reported to be gaining strength.

April   "Factionalism of the proletariat" lauded in *People's Daily*. Only "bourgeois factionalism" is to be opposed. This encourages extreme Left to step up attack on power holders and rival factions.

June   Violence on upswing throughout China. Red Guards raid PLA arsenals, turn captured weapons on rival factions.

July   Mao Tse-tung bitterly criticizes Red Guards in Peking for lack of discipline and use of violent tactics.

August   PLA-led "worker-peasant thought of Mao Tse-tung propaganda teams" dispatched to schools, factories, and farms throughout country to suppress violence, restore order.

Mao indicates support for activities of propaganda teams by presenting "treasured gift of mangoes" to team leaders.

Provincial-level revolutionary committees established in Yunnan, Fukien, Kwangsi, Tibet, and Sinkiang, marking completion of nationwide movement begun in January, 1967.

September   Radical students denounced in *People's Daily* as "petit-bourgeois intellectuals." Under aegis of Mao's slogan "purify the class ranks," recalcitrant Red Guards eliminated from positions of responsibility and sent to rural areas to be "reeducated" by peasants.

October   Twelfth Central Committee Plenum convened. Liu Shao-ch'i expelled from the Party. Radical phase of Cultural Revolution ends, campaign to rebuild Party begins.

Decentralization drive launched in industrial, commercial, educational, and public health sectors.

1969 March   Armed conflict between China and Russia breaks out on Ussuri river. Both sides hasten war preparations.

April   Ninth Party Congress meets. New Party Constitution adopted, enshrining thought of Mao Tse-tung as "Marxism-Leninism in the modern arge." Lin Piao formally designated as Mao's successor as Party Chairman. New Central Committee elected, marked by increased PLA representation. Cultural Revolution declared by Lin Piao to be opening round in a new "permanent revolution" in China.

May   Drive to rebuild Party apparatus in the provinces stepped up. Military leaders instrumental in drawing up name lists and screening candidates for Party posts.

July   U.S. government announces relaxation of restrictions on trade and travel to China.

September   Soviet Premier Kosygin meets with Chou En-lai in Peking.

October   Sino-Soviet border negotiations underway.

December   Border talks stalled. Both sides escalate propaganda war.

1970 January   Peking agrees to resume long-suspended Ambassadorial Talks with U. S. at Warsaw.

Chinese mass media stress themes of Party rebuilding, strengthening unity between army and people, and consolidating economy. Coming of a new "leap forward" in economic development hailed in Party press.

September   Central Committee Plenum convened. Emphasis continues to be on Party building, unity and consolidation.

October   Canada and Italy extend formal diplomatic recognition to China.

Selected Bibliography

I. Cultural Revolution—General

A. Books and Monographs

Asia Research Centre. *The Great Cultural Revolution in China.* Toyko: Charles E. Tuttle Co., 1968.

Bulletin of the Atomic Scientists. *China After the Cultural Revolution.* New York: Random House, Inc., 1969.

CCP Documents of the Great Proletarian Cultural Revolution. Hong Kong: Union Research Institute, 1968.

The Cultural Revolution: 1967 in Review. Ann Arbor: The University of Michigan, Center for Chinese Studies, 1968.

Dorrill, W. F. *Power, Policy, and Ideology in the Making of China's "Cultural Revolution."* Santa Monica: The RAND Corporation, 1968.

Fan, K. H., ed. *The Chinese Cultural Revolution: Selected Documents.* New York: Grove Press, Inc., 1968.

Gray, Jack, and Patrick Cavendish. *Chinese Communism in Crisis: Maoism and the Cultural Revolution.* London: Pall Mall Press, 1968.

Hunter, Neale, and Colin MacKerras. *China Observed.* New York: Frederick A. Praeger Co., 1968.

Robinson, Joan. *The Cultural Revolution in China.* London: Penguin Books, 1969.

Robinson, Thomas, Richard Baum, et al. *The Cultural Revolution in China.* Berkeley and Los Angeles: University of California Press, 1971.

Tsou, Tang, and Ping-ti Ho, eds. *China in Crisis.* 3 Vols. Chicago: University of Chicago Press, 1968.

Trumbull, Robert, ed. *This is Communist China.* New York: David McKay Co., Inc., 1968.

B. Articles

Adie, W. A. C. "China's 'Second Liberation' in Perspective." *Bulletin of the Atomic Scientists,* XXV, no. 2 (February, 1969), 12–22.

Bennett, Gordon. "China's Continuing Revolution: Will It Be Permanent?" *Asian Survey,* X, no. 1 (January, 1970), 2–17.

Chang, Parris H. "Mao's Great Purge: A Political Balance Sheet." *Problems of Communism,* no. 2 (March–April, 1969), 1–22.

———. "The Second Decade of Maoist Rule." *Problems of Communism,* no. 6 (November–December, 1969), 1–11.

Fitzgerald, C. P. "Reflections on the Cultural Revolution in China." *Pacific Affairs*, XLI, no. 1 (Spring, 1968), 51–59.

Gelman, Harry. "The New Revolution: Mao and the Permanent Purge." *Problems of Communism*, no. 6 (November–December, 1966), 2–14.

Gittings, John. "The Prospects of the Cultural Revolution in 1969." *Bulletin of the Atomic Scientists*, XXV, no. 2 (February, 1969), 23–28.

Huberman, Leo, and Paul Sweezy. "The Cultural Revolution in China." *Monthly Review*, XVIII, no. 8 (January, 1967), 1–17.

Johnson, Chalmers. "The Cultural Revolution in Structural Perspective." *Asian Survey*, VIII, no. 1 (January, 1968), 1–15.

Neuhauser, Charles. "The Impact of the Cultural Revolution on the Chinese Communist Party Machine." *Asian Survey*, VIII, no. 6 (June, 1968), 3–36.

Oksenberg, Michel. "China: Forcing the Revolution to a New Stage." *Asian Survey*, VII, no. 1 (January, 1967), 1–15.

Schurmann, Franz. "What is Happening in China?" *The New York Review of Books*, VI, no. 6 (October 20, 1966), 18–25.

Schwartz, Benjamin I. "Upheaval in China." *Commentary*, XLIII, no. 2 (February, 1967), 55–62.

———. "The Reign of Virtue: Some Broad Perspectives on Leader and Party in the Cultural Revolution." *The China Quarterly*, no. 35 (July–September, 1967), 1–17.

Vogel, Ezra F. "The Structure of Conflict: China in 1967." In *The Cultural Revolution: 1967 in Review*. Ann Arbor: University of Michigan, Center for Chinese Studies, 1968. Pp. 97–125.

Wheelwright, E. L. "The Cultural Revolution in China." *Monthly Review*, XIX, no. 1 (May, 1967), 17–33.

II. *Red Guards and Educational Policy*

Bastid, Marianne. "Economic Necessity–Political Ideals in Educational Reform during the Cultural Revolution." *The China Quarterly*, no. 42 (April–June, 1970), 16–45.

Granqvist, Hans. *The Red Guard*. London: Pall Mall Press, 1967.

Hunter, Neale. *Shanghai Journal: An Eyewitness Account of the Cultural Revolution*. New York: Frederick A. Praeger Co., 1969.

Israel, John. "The Red Guards in Historical Perspective." *The China Quarterly*, no. 30 (April–June, 1967), 1–32.

Mehnert, Klaus. *Peking and the New Left: At Home and Abroad*. Berkeley: University of California, Center for Chinese Studies, 1969.

Nee, Victor. *The Cultural Revolution at Peking University*. New York: Monthly Review Press, 1969.

III. *The Economy*

Anderson, Evelyn. "Shanghai: The Masses Unleashed." *Problems of Communism*, no. 1 (January–February, 1968), 12–21.

Diao, Richard K. "The Impact of the Cultural Revolution on China's Economic Elite." *The China Quarterly*, no. 42 (April–June, 1970), 65–87.

Riskin, Carl. "The Chinese Economy in 1967." In *The Cultural Revolution: 1967 in Review*. Ann Arbor: University of Michigan, Center for Chinese Studies, 1968.

IV. *Rural Affairs*

Baum, Richard. *The Cultural Revolution in the Countryside: Anatomy of a Limited Rebellion*. Santa Monica: The RAND Corporation, 1970.

————. "Revolution and Reaction in the Chinese Countryside: The Socialist Education Movement in Cultural Revolutionary Perspective." *The China Quarterly*, no. 38 (April–June, 1969), 92–119.

————, and Frederick C. Teiwes. "Liu Shao-ch'i and the Cadre Question." *Asian Survey*, VIII, no. 4 (April, 1968), 323–45.

MacDougall, Colina. "The Cultural Revolution in the Communes." *Current Scene*, VII, no. 7 (April 11, 1969), 1–11.

"Peking's Program to Move Human and Material Resources to the Countryside." *Current Scene*, VII, no. 18 (September 15, 1969), 1–17.

V. *Military Affairs*

Domes, Jurgen. "The Cultural Revolution and the Army." *Asian Survey*, VIII, no. 5 (May, 1968), 349–63.

Gittings, John. "The Chinese Army's Role in the Cultural Revolution." *Pacific Affairs*, XXXIX, no. 3–4 (Fall–Winter, 1966–67), 269–89.

VI. *Foreign Policy*

Gurtov, Melvin. "The Foreign Ministry and Foreign Affairs in China's Cultural Revolution." *The China Quarterly*, no. 40 (October–December, 1969), 65–102.

Scalapino, Robert A. "The Cultural Revolution and Chinese Foreign Policy." In *The Cultural Revolution: 1967 in Review*. Ann Arbor: University of Michigan, Center for Chinese Studies, 1968. Pp. 72–91.

VII. *Miscellaneous*

Chang, Parris H. "The Revolutionary Committee in China: Two Case Studies." *Current Scene*, VI, no. 9 (June 1, 1968), 1–22.

Dreyer, June. "China's Minority Nationalities in the Cultural Revolution." *The China Quarterly*, no. 35 (July–September, 1968), 96–109.

Falkenheim, Victor. "The Cultural Revolution in Kwangsi, Yunnan, and Fukien." *Asian Survey*, IX, no. 8 (August, 1969), 580–97.

Friedman, Edward. "Cultural Limits of the Cultural Revolution." *Asian Survey*, IX, no. 3 (March, 1969), 188–201.

Harding, Harry. *Maoist Theories of Policy-Making and Organization: Lessons from the Cultural Revolution.* Santa Monica: The RAND Corporation, 1969.

Klein, Donald W. "The State Council and the Cultural Revolution." *The China Quarterly,* no. 35 (July–September, 1968), 78–95.

Miller, Arthur, and Chung Hua-min. *Madame Mao: A Profile of Chiang Ch'ing.* Hong Kong: Union Research Institute, 1968.

Oksenberg, Michel. "Occupational Groups in Chinese Society and the Cultural Revolution." In *The Cultural Revolution: 1967 in Review.* Ann Arbor: University of Michigan, Center for Chinese Studies, 1968. Pp. 1–39.

Robinson, Thomas W. *Chou En-lai's Role in China's Cultural Revolution.* Santa Monica: The RAND Corporation, 1970.

Uhalley, Stephen. "The Cultural Revolution and the Attack on the 'Three Family Village.'" *The China Quarterly,* no. 27 (July–September, 1966), 149–61.

Contributors

RICHARD BAUM is Assistant Professor of Political Science at the University of California, Los Angeles. He is the author of numerous monographic works and articles on Chinese Communist politics.

LOUISE B. BENNETT is a staff member of the American Friends Service Committee. She is the editor of the AFSC's *Understanding China Newsletter*.

PHILIP BRIDGHAM is a research analyst for the CIA. He was formerly Foreign Affairs Officer in the Office of the Assistant Secretary of Defense.

JACK GRAY is Senior Lecturer in Chinese Studies at the University of Glasgow. He is co-author of *Chinese Communism in Crisis* and editor of *Modern China's Search for a Political Form*.

ROBERT JAY LIFTON is Professor of Psychiatry at Yale University. He is the author of *Thought Reform and the Psychology of Totalism* and *Death in Life: Survivors of Hiroshima*.

LIN PIAO is Defense Minister of the People's Republic of China and heir-apparent to Chinese Communist Party Chairman Mao Tse-tung.

FRANZ MICHAEL is Chairman of the Research Colloquium on Modern China, Institute for Sino-Soviet Studies, George Washington University. He is the author of *The Origin of Manchu Rule in China*.

CHARLES NEUHAUSER is a research analyst for the CIA. He has written extensively on Chinese Communist Party affairs.

RICHARD M. PFEFFER is Assistant Professor of Political Science at Johns Hopkins University. He is editor of *No More Vietnams? The War and the Future of American Foreign Policy*.

RALPH L. POWELL is a professor at the School of International Service, American University. He is the author of *The Rise of Chinese Military Power, 1895–1912* and *Politico-Military Relations in Communist China*.

GERALD TANNENBAUM is an American student of Chinese Communist affairs. He has lived and traveled extensively in China.

TANG TSOU is Professor of Political Science at the University of Chicago. He is co-editor of *China in Crisis: China's Heritage and the Communist Political System* and the author of *America's Failure in China*.

DATE DUE

2/22			
MAY 3 1 1973			
OCT 1 5 1975			